EUROPEAN
REMINISCENCES

Da Capo Press Music Reprint Series

GENERAL EDITOR
FREDERICK FREEDMAN
VASSAR COLLEGE

EUROPEAN REMINISCENCES

Musical and Otherwise

Being the Recollections of the Vacation Tours
of a Musician in Various Countries

By Louis C. Elson

DA CAPO PRESS · NEW YORK · 1972

Library of Congress Cataloging in Publication Data

Elson, Louis Charles, 1848-1920.
    European reminiscences, musical and otherwise.
    (Da Capo Press music reprint series)
    Reprint of the 1896 ed.
    1. Europe — Description and travel — 1800-1918.
2. Musicians — Correspondence, reminiscences, etc.
I. Title.
ML423.E492 1972   914'.03'287   72-125046
ISBN 0-306-70011-5

This Da Capo Press edition of *European Reminiscences* is an una-
bridged republication of the 1896 edition published in Philadelphia.

Published by Da Capo Press, Inc.
A Subsidiary of Plenum Publishing Corporation
227 West 17th Street, New York, New York 10011

Manufactured in the United States of America

EUROPEAN
REMINISCENCES

LOUIS C. ELSON.

EUROPEAN REMINISCENCES,

MUSICAL AND OTHERWISE.

Being the Recollections of the Vacation Tours of a
Musician in various Countries.

———

By LOUIS C. ELSON.

———

PHILADELPHIA:
THEO. PRESSER.

PREFACE.

This book is the informal record of several vacations of a musician abroad. During some years the author was correspondent of the New York Tribune, the Boston Advertiser, the Boston Transcript, and other journals, and the following pages are largely collated from his foreign letters sent to the American press. Naturally the chief interest is a musical one, but it was the delight of the writer to study the kaleidoscopic phases of European life in many different aspects, and the result was at times to take him very far from the musical field. He trusts that these discursions will not detract from the interest of a book which is only intended to represent the playful side of a musician's life. This also will excuse the autobiographical ego which is used in these pages so freely by

THE AUTHOR.

TABLE OF CONTENTS.

CHAPTER I.

CHAPTER II.

CHAPTER III.

CHAPTER IV.

CHAPTER V.

CHAPTER VI.

CHAPTER VII.

CHAPTER VIII.

CHAPTER IX.

CHAPTER X.

CHAPTER XI.

CHAPTER XII.

CHAPTER XIII.

CHAPTER XIV.

CHAPTER XV.

CHAPTER XVI.

CHAPTER XVII.

CHAPTER XVIII.

EUROPEAN REMINISCENCES.

CHAPTER I.

THE VOYAGE. OUTWARD BOUND.

MUSICAL AND GASTRONOMICAL DOINGS ON SHIPBOARD.

BEETHOVEN once composed a comic song! It was called "Urian's Reise um die Welt," and began:

> Whene'er a man abroad doth go
> Great problems he'll unravel,
> I took my pack and was not slow
> To go about my travel.

I shall follow the example of Beethoven's Urian and caper about Europe in a playful manner, studying people rather than palaces, and abjuring in advance all statistics and guide-book information.

There are two especially thrilling points in the sea voyage —the moment of leaving land and the moment of sighting it. Between these, as between the covers of a railroad sandwich, there is much that is trying to the soul, and much that cannot be described. Why is it that no poet has yet given adequate expression to the woe unutterable which characterizes *mal de mer?* The first day out everything was calm, and the ocean smooth as a mirror. In fact, I may say that our movement was in seven flats—sea flat.

Poets have used up a good deal of " divine inflatus " on the subject of " Night at Sea." I desire earnestly to enter my protest against their deceiving any more people. A night at sea, under the bewitching influence of a fog horn between

A and B flat, makes one remark with M. Clarence, "Oh! I have passed a miserable night." Then, also, one reads about the "silent watches of the night," which, on an ocean steamer, are not as silent even as a Waterbury watch. Every half hour the bells wake one up until one is haunted like Matthias in Irving's play. Even the dog-watch, (so called because it is curtailed), is not a silent one.

The next day came a fog, and with it grief. The upper deck was soon occupied by the members of a large excursion party, who improvised a hospital ward of reasonable dimensions. The day came to a fog-horn conclusion. After observing the patients a while, I decided that, although they were not lively, they were very active. A tenor singer on board instantly threw up his engagements. It must not be supposed that these persons were sick for want of preventives. For the benefit of my readers, and humanity generally, I record the remedies for the malady: First, champagne. Second, eat all you can. Third, eat very lightly. Fourth, take phosphates and lemons. Fifth, avoid everything sour. Sixth, Ginger. Seventh, Bromide of Sodium. Eight, Peppermint. Ninth, Strychnine, in light doses. Tenth, Seltzer Aperient. Against such an array it would appear to be impossible for the sickness to make any headway, but I suppose it gets its work in during the intervals between the taking of these remedies. One party on board the ship confided to me a real remedy. He advised me to drink Bass's ale in continuous and allopathic doses. This, it seems to me, changes the name of the disturbance, but does not essentially alter the symptoms. But then this man belonged to the "unregenerate party." Let me hasten to explain. The ship had among its passengers an incredible number of reverends—as many as Mark Twain met with in his "Innocents Abroad." In fact, were it not for the above described illness and its kindly remedies, we might have had one continuous service all the way across.

A crusade was soon organized and the goats driven away from the sheep. These rampant animals took refuge in the smoking room, where they gathered around tables and played a game whose name is derived from one of the innocent instruments used to stir the fire. In this case the game stirred up the fire. The sheep sent a petition, that card playing be stopped, to the captain. The goats concocted an anonymous and satirical proclamation, wherein many were held up in ridicule to an unsympathetic world. They spared none. Even I (who am a sheep) was lampooned with the rest. The sheep appealed to the captain to protect the fold, but that hardened official replied in substance, "A plague on both your houses," only he improved the force of Shakspeare's language by judiciously interspersed adjectives. The captain loved not the fold, and there was a degree of justice in his dislike. Many of the passengers had pinned their faith upon him with a confidence which would have flattered the oracle at Delphi. They frequented the vicinity of the bridge to consult him as to the various details of the sea and of the voyage. They regarded him as a sort of oceanic time table. "How long will the fog last?" "Will this wind continue all the way over?" "When will we see an iceberg?" were some of the riddles which I heard propounded at the oracular shrine. But on his part there was none of the Delphian dignity. He would gaze at his questioners with awe-struck and open-eyed wonder, and then recovering from his astonishment, would inquire whether he was taken for a (profane) weather prophet.

There is never quite the homogeneity on a large ship that one finds on a small one. People gather into small groups and even cliques instead of being an entirely united community. Even "the solitary plank between us and eternity," of which the preacher speaks in his Sunday sermon, does not weld them together. But in one thing there is not only sociability but communism, and that is in the matter of steamer chairs. Label your chair if you want to, let letters as large as the scare-lines of the Daily Thunderbolt proclaim that it is personal property, yet some fair female in a state of eruption, or of exhausted somnolency, will curl up in it, and you (being a modern chevalier Bayard) will walk the deck until she gets through. The only way to keep outsiders out of your steamer chair is to set fire to it. There is a certain caste on an ocean steamer; it is not founded on wealth, nor brains, nor character, but on voyages; the man who has made a dozen is a veritable Brahmin—the one who is on his first trip is a meek and lowly Pariah. He is patronized, he is bullied, and his opinions, if he dares to express any, are pooh-poohed.

The days on board of an ocean steamer pass with varying success. I must dissent from the poets in so far; after the first few days out, "familarity doth breed contempt," or at least disappointment, with the summer sea, and then the days hang heavily. Shovel-board and ring toss fill in an occasional chink, but in this voyage the main relaxation was in religious services. From twenty prayers which I heard, I gathered that the clergymen all approved of the manner in which the Atlantic ocean was made. The passengers practically indorsed the empty fifths and non-harmonic cross relations of the "Gospel Hymns" which they conscientiously sang in season and out of season, but which were occasionally varied by the Miserere from "Trovatore," sung by a young lady with a rather vague and hesitant knowledge of the matter. It suited admirably to the condition of the limp parties of the "hospital ward," as the reclining place of the internally-disturbed ones on the upper deck came to be called, but was not adapted to those enjoying reasonable health. But as it was given at regular intervals during the day, quantity made up for quality. Meanwhile the unregenerate played "Napoleon," regard-

less of any moral law. They kept it up night and day as assi-
duously as the hymnists did their hymns. In short, they
had a long "Nap," but little sleep. But on Saturday night
they joined in the sailor's toast and remembered "sweethearts and wives at home," and that was a bit of sentiment which balanced many sins, for they seemed to mean it.

But a dreadful fate befell us from another quarter. On
discovering that the ship had no secular musical works
aboard, I settled down in calm content. Suddenly a fiend, a
Nihilist or a mistaken philanthropist, revealed the fact that
he had a musical album in his trunk. It was one of those
economical collections that give you two or three hundred
of the most worn-out tunes for fifty cents. And after that
we had the "Danube River" for breakfast, "I Cannot Sing
the Old Songs" for lunch, "In the Gloaming" for dinner,
and "Once Again" for supper. There was a perfect eruption of Molloy, Sullivan, and Pinsuti, The awful fact was
developed that we had more singers than clergymen among
us. We were between Scylla and Charybdis, which is the
polite way of saying that we had got out of the frying pan
into the fire.

Music on board ship is more or less of a nuisance, but
we had a few good artists aboard who made the inevitable
concert bearable. However, I had left my critical pen
(with all the vitrol carefully wiped off) in camphor for
the summer, and shall not analyze even my own musical
performances. Of course "Rocked in the Cradle of the
Deep" was given, and equally of course the irreverent
smoking-roomers spoke of it as "Locked in the stable with
the sheep."

The regular singing during the concerts was by no
means so bad, and the *finale* was especially charming, for
we all took hands and sang "Auld Lang Syne" in true
Scotch style.

And now (as this was Saturday) came the preparations

for Sunday. Arrangements for divine service were easily made, for there was to be a church assembly in Belfast, and we had, as already intimated, some fifteen clergymen on board, and a goodly sprinkling of deacons. But the "best laid plans of mice and men" went to pieces. These clergymen fell to offering sacrifices to Neptune with a zeal that proved that they were not good Baptists. One sturdy minister, however, was left, like Elijah, "one solitary prophet of the Lord," and he gave a sermon which was emphatic and interesting. I was especially obliged to him that he did not bring out the "solitary plank" in his discourse. This is as often present in a sermon at sea as the "solitary horseman" in the novels of G. P. R. James. It sends a thrill of horror into the breasts of the unregenerate to tell them that there is but a solitary plank between them and eternity, and they are only reassured by going below and finding that the plank is some two feet thick and well braced, whereupon they at once fall back into their evil ways. I have always thought that the scriptural text, "Cast ye up!" would furnish excellent material for a sea sermon, yet I have never heard it used.

A large part of the time at sea is spent at table. After one has ceased being a "contributor to the Atlantic," one feels as if he were built hollow all the way through, and the work of filling the vacuum begins.

There was, however, one disturbing element at our table in the shape of a steward (or waiter), who had evidently just been captured on an Irish bog and pressed into service. When we first met, he leaned cordially on my shoulder and confidentially asked for my order. Disentangling myself from his embrace, I gave him the details of my projected meal, but immediately found that his friendly interest was somewhat hampered by a lack of knowledge. He brought me many articles of food, but never by any chance what I had called for. Now began a series of object lessons which would have done credit to any kindergarten. I taught him that cucumbers were green, and tomatoes were red, and that in this respect they resembled the port and starboard lights of the vessel. I caused him to refrain from falling upon my neck when receiving my order. I taught him that a meal could sometimes pass without eating potatoes, which he continually and confidently brought me. I could *not* teach him, however, that the hardness of a hard-boiled egg should extend below the shell, and I once sent him for "boiled fowl," when his voice was pathetic as, suspecting me of playing a joke upon him, he replied, "We have no bald fowl, sorr." I suppose he thought that I, as an American, wanted a bald-headed eagle. But he was willing to learn, and under the influence of sundry coins of the realm he became constantly, if less affectionately, attentive. He was possibly a near relative of the scriptural steward "with one talent;" *his* one talent was breathing down my neck and then forgetting my order.

The tip end of the voyage brought the charitable concert, in which the day and night gangs of our musical laborers joined forces and produced a tonal feast large enough to give the passengers musical dyspepsia. Then came " land ho!" distant views at first, then a land breeze which brought the peat odor so characteristic of Irish cabins and Irish whiskey. I want to add a trifle to the Shakespearian discoveries of Donnelly. The Bard of Avon was an Irishman! He has described both the Irish breezes and the Hibernian potheen in the exquisite but hitherto misunderstood line, " 'Tis true 'tis peaty, peaty 'tis, 'tis true."

The usual bother with customs follows, but as the eminent Liverpudlian, who gazes at my wearing apparel and my soiled linen, finds neither alcohol, nor cigars, nor dynamite (I have no small vices) he decides to admit me to the land where the letter "H" is so badly treated, and where I myself receive the Satanic title of "Hell. C. Hellson."

CHAPTER II.

A CHANNEL PASSAGE—COLOGNE—GUIDES—THE CHURCH OF
ST. URSULA—AN INTERVIEW WITH DR. FERDINAND HILLER
—A MUSICAL FESTIVAL.

Naturally one goes with the stream of continental travel,
from London to Rotterdam and on to Germany. The way
from London to Cologne is long and decidedly uncomfortable.
The channel is as unreliable as a spoiled beauty, one day all
smiles and dimples, the next in an ungovernable temper and
fury.

May all the last syllables of half the cities in Holland be
showered upon the boat that took me across! I have been
in Turkish baths at 210°, and I have been in St. Louis during the heated term, but never have I been in an atmosphere like that which filled the cabin of the steamer of the
Great Eastern Railway.

The channel boats are an abominable, eternal, and un-
mitigated nuisance; they would not be tolerated in America
for five minutes. Four first-class passengers are packed in
what is ironically called a "state-room;" there is certainly
no state about it, and precious little room. Four basins
are prominently put under the four passengers' noses,
whether they want them or not. The atmosphere of the
cabin is so dense and peculiar that I wonder that somebody
doesn't cut it up and sell it in Germany as Limburger
cheese. In the morning we get up, one at a time, and
scratch, for it would be impossible to scratch a duet or a
trio in the confined space, and circumstances over which we

have no control seem to make scratching necessary. Thank heaven it has been a calm night and Ossa has not been heaped upon Pelion in the way of misery.

The weather in Rotterdam reminds me of home. If ever a meteorological bureau is started in Holland it will run its reports about as follows:—

Cold and clear, followed by warm and rainy, interspersed with thundershowers, followed by light frosts, after which the weather will become changeable.

What a tantalizer the Dutch tongue is! One moment sounding like English, another like German, yet always eluding you if you speak either.

I had my triennial search for a bath (I trust it will be understood that this does not refer to bathing in its totality, but the Holland branch of it only), and after hunting all over the city for Guricx's barber shop, where I was told I could get one, found only a poor joke instead of a bath. I broke up a little German to make it sound like Dutch, and said, "I want a bath," whereupon the facetious barber responded in good German, "Very well, you may take one, but I haven't got any!" The idea of having that ancient joke sprung upon me in a strange land, far away from home, was too much, and that evening I shook the dust of Rotterdam from my feet and started for Cologne.

I soon saw the vast dome of Cologne rising from the plain, long before any other building was visible, and in half an hour was crossing the Rhine to get under its mighty shadow. Heine has pictured the city too well for any amateur tourist to say much about it.

"Im Rhein, im heiligen Strome
Da spiegelt sich in den Well'n,
Mit seinem grossen Dome
Das grosse heilige Cöln."

But Cologne has become somewhat monotonous to me, because it seems to have only one resident—Jean Maria Farina. I went to the cathedral; under its eaves were four distinct Jean Maria Farinas; I went along a back street, there was another J. M. Farina who had evidently strayed away from the rest of the family and got lost; I went to the church of St. Ursula and passed another farinaceous settlement on the way. I think that the only solution of the mystery is that the original Mrs. Maria Farina must have had twins with a regularity very painful to her husband, who brought them all up in the perfumery business. I dreamed that night that Cologne was a great Farina pudding, and was being stirred up with the dome as a pudding stick. I have mentioned the fact that I went to the church of St. Ursula and the eleven thousand virgin martyrs. That noble institution interests me. Long ago St. Ursula came to Germany with eleven thousand young ladies. The Teutonic warrior calmly saw the price of chewing gum and confectionery go up three hundred per cent.; he saw his morning paper disappear to make bustles, and yet he made no sign—possibly because sign-painting was not yet invented. But when these eleven thousand and one ladies demanded the ballot, and outvoted him at every ward election, he saw that the time for action had come; he wrote a few articles to the Atlantic of that epoch—"What shall we do with our girls?" and "The superfluous woman,"—and then killed the whole lot and started the "church of the Holy Boneyard" with them. The bones are all there and can be exhibited to any skeptic. I saw them, and also the wine bowl used at the marriage at Cana, and a few other relics of antique conviviality.

The pleasantest event of my earliest Cologne experience was my visit to that Nestor of German music and literature, Dr. Ferdinand Hiller, just eight months before his death. It was fortunate that I came to Cologne a few days earlier than I had expected, for Dr. Hiller had given up the post of musical director of the city of Cologne, which he had held so honorably for so long a time, and was about leaving the city to take up his residence in Bonn. He gave me a most cordial greeting and seemed to take an especial interest in informing himself about our progress in America. Dr. Hiller was then an old man, but advancing years had left no trace upon the brightness of his conversation or the keenness of his intellect. His personal appearance was still impressive, although he had become very stout, and his gait was slow, if not feeble. His broad face was, however, full of animation when he became interested in any subject, and his words then flowed rapidly and he exhibited fire and enthusiasm much at variance with his usual quiet mood. He began the conversation (after greetings had been exchanged) in English, but I observed, spite of his apparent ease in this language, that when he became forcible he slipped back into German. His first inquiries were for his friends in America. Mr. Dresel, Mr. Lang, Mr. Floersheim and Dr. Damrosch were especially remembered, and greetings sent to them in German fashion. Dr. Hiller knew our Boston symphonic programmes quite thoroughly, but was not acquainted with the works of any of our American composers. I was unfeignedly sorry that the works of Paine, Whiting, Chadwick, Buck, Parker and others should not be known in Europe, for undoubtedly some of the musicians there think that we still occupy ourselves in producing negro melodies and " mother " songs. Dr. Hiller was pleased to learn that his little tone picture—"The Sentinel"—had won much success at the Symphony Concerts. " It is only a trifle," said he, "but it seems to succeed, as far as it goes." But he would not speak much of himself or his own work, although he grew eloquent when I spoke of his old friend Auerbach. He had but recently written an article in a Cologne journal about the great novelist; "Not anything extensive, but a friend can always write best about a friend," he said.

Speaking of American music, he remarked: "I fear that you are sometimes too gigantic, in musical festivals for example. It is a natural fault in a young nation which likes to do things at wholesale." He earnestly inquired about the standing of opera among us ("The human voice always remains the greatest instrument," said he) and, deprecating the star system, hoped that we would not give German opera unless every part, great and small, were adequately filled. Speaking of the epochs of composition, he thought that, spite of the universal striving for a master's crown, which is apparent to-day, we would make but a poor showing beside the golden period when Haydn, Mozart, Beethoven, Schubert, and Weber followed in such quick succession, which he compared to the Raphael epoch in painting. "But," he added, "to-day is the epoch of execution. The great works have never received such performances as they do now, and this is true not only of orchestral but of almost all musical works." Happening to speak of England, he interrupted me to say that the English were more than mere art patrons; they appreciated what was really worthy, and he cited examples from Handel to Mendelssohn; "but," he concluded, "their drawing-room music is often very bad," and he shuddered, possibly at the recollection of some English drawing-room tenor. I ventured to quote the partisan spirit which was shown in England against Schumann, in the cause of Mendelssohn. "Ah, yes," he replied, "but almost the same could be said of Germany at that time. Schumann was a plant of slow growth the world over." Again reverting to the dearth of really great composers, he said: "Whom have we in the symphonic field to-day? Possibly Brahms only. Of course time will sift all composers justly. Only the really worthy works remain after a generation has passed away. Unfortunately sometimes very little remains."

In speaking of American literature—and Dr. Hiller was as
great in literary as in musical analysis—he expressed great
admiration for some of the works of Bret Harte. "We
have no such characters in Germany, but they are so vividly
drawn that they must have real prototypes somewhere."
This is all, (save matters of a private or social character),
that I can recall of an interview with one of the greatest of
the musicians of the pure school of Germany. All through
the conversation I was struck by the conservative bent of
the mind of Dr. Hiller. He scarcely mentioned the modern
radical composers, but when he did he did not altogether
condemn, but seemed to think their claims "not proven,"
and that their influence was pushing aside a worthier and
healthier school—Mozart's, for example. As I rose to bid
farewell, the doctor reiterated his greetings to American
friends, and as I expressed a wish that we might yet see him
amongst us, he smiled and sighed, and said, "Ah, no! it is
too late now." And so I left one who has "fought the
good fight" for music, and whose influence has been a shin-
ing light to those who desire to see the musician become
less of a specialist and more a man of broad culture.

And now followed a musical feast upon which I stumbled
almost unawares. I had found an American resident in
Cologne, who insisted upon taking me around the city. As
we were seated at table preparatory to this circular enterprise, an editor of the "Kölnische Nachrichten" took a seat
near us in the restaurant. We were speedily introduced and
soon joined by an editor of the "Kölnische Zeitung," with
whom I had journeyed to Bayreuth a year before. At once
the *Amerikaner* was made the honored guest, and when I
mentioned that I desired to gather musical education unto
myself, they shouted, "You have come just right! We
will go to the Maennerchor and Schubertbund!" I was
ready to go to the stake in such good company, so I yielded
a willing consent. The occasion turned out to be a special

one. The Schubertbund—a male chorus of Vienna—had
come hundreds of miles to pay a visit to a rival society away
up here in Cologne. Your true German Maennerchor likes
to have heartiness, mirth and *gemüthlichkeit* mixed in with
its singing, and I knew beforehand what I might expect;
for had I not been at "salamanders" and other festivities at
our own Orpheus Club in Boston? Arrived at the hall I
found about a thousand people present seated at long tables,
and ready to begin the ceremonies of welcome. These began by the Kölner Maennergesangverein (some one hundred
and fifty members) stepping upon the stage and singing four
songs of welcome to their guests. Such solid, manly singing can seldom be heard. The Apollo Club of Boston may
sing with more perfect finish, but not with such a noble enthusiasm or genuine heartiness. Now the Cologne society
left the stage and the Austrians took it. They sang four
songs also, but with thinner, more sugary voices. The
company present was a distinguished one; all the litterateurs,
physicians, lawyers and great merchants of Cologne were
there, and the speeches were of a brilliant character, although
a mutual admiration element was naturally in the fore-
ground. Some good points were made, however, as when
the president put the old conundrum "Was ist des Deutschen
Vaterland?" and answered it—

> "So weit die Deutsche Zunge klingt
> Und Gott im Himmel Lieder singt,"

which brought the Austrians into the fold. Then, of course
the Danube and the Rhine were made to intertwine, and the
toasts were followed with plenty of vocal " Hochs," and
finally musical slips were passed around, and we all united in
singing a song of welcome.

But every one who knows the spirit of the German
Maennerchor (where singing is a means, rather than an end)

will understand that the real fun began after the speeches and formalities were concluded. Then came impromptu poems (*knittelversen*), burlesque orations, stage representations, and other enlivening proceedings. A bass whose voice seemed to come from a sub-cellar, and whose compass seemed in the neighborhood of twenty octaves, sang the mournful ballad "Im tiefen Keller," without which no German would be heartily jolly. At 1 A. M. I thought I would go to my hotel, although the hilarity showed no signs of diminishing. I heard the next day that at 3 A. M. some wilted Austrians were trying to open the great door of Cologne Cathedral with their latch keys, under the impression that they lodged there; but only a decorous and reasonable *Katzenjammer* visited the sedate American guest.

CHAPTER III.

"I was borne to Bingen,
    Sweet Bingen on the Rhine,"

By a steamboat which stopped at about every excuse for a
wharf along the entire river.   Probably this is the best way
to study the beauties of the historic stream, and it is better,
too, to take a boat on the upward journey, as it goes slower
than the downward bound ones.   The express boats are less
desirable for the traveler who desires to see as much as possible of the scenery, although I have found them comfortable enough for traveling.   Of course the musician will stop
off at Bonn, and go to the house where Beethoven was born;
but here he will find himself in a quandary, for there are
two of them!   The guide would like to persuade you that
Beethoven was twins and born half a mile apart at that!
And also, if possible, get a double fee for having shown you
two birthplaces where you only expected to find one.   The
house near the river is probably the only genuine birthplace,
although both are labeled by the city.

The Rhine scenery only begins to grow beautiful above
Bonn, so the traveler can go thither by railroad if he
chooses, and take the boat there.   Of course I am not about
to inflict a detailed account of this scenery upon the "gentle
reader," lest he should become ferocious, but I may at least
state that on a Sunday or a holiday the Rhine becomes a

CARL REINECKE,
DIRECTOR OF THE ROYAL MUSICAL CONSERVATORY OF LEIPSIC.

perfect river of song; there is a constant visiting and repaying of visits going on among the Maennerchöre, and as the boat draws toward a landing you will hear songs of greeting and songs of welcome, from both wharf and steamer. Germany may not be a land of vocalists, but it is certainly a land of singers, and if "die Meistersinger" have passed away, their mantle has fallen on broad shoulders, and still broader waists, in the male choristers who swarm on every hand; and they sing with a heartiness that would atone for many more vocal sins than they commit. And when they are very jovial they dance too. But do not dance with them, unless you enjoy pleasure mingled with danger, for most of them dance very much like pile drivers, with a ponderous vertical motion, and the inexperienced partner cannot always escape. At St. Goar, if there is a singing society left on board they will frequently favor you with " The Loreley," in honor of that first cousin of the sirens.

Bingen does not show much that is either historical or musical, but it is tranquil beyond belief. It nestles among vineyards, and if the landlord of the hotel likes you he will give you a room overlooking the Rhine, with just space enough between you and the river for a little arbor, where you can take breakfast in the open air.

In the evening I took the ferry to Rüdesheim, and climbed up amid the vineyards to the place where they have erected the colossal statue of Germania, in memory of the Franco-Prussian war. How out of place it seemed! Below lay the peaceful valley, with the sunset gilding the quiet villages; a shower had just passed, and over Johannisberg there lingered a faint rainbow; the sweet earth-smell and the odor of "the green things growing" was all around; the vesper bells sounded softly from Rüdesheim and Bingen—and there, amidst it all, was the grim military memento, and the tablet of the emperor and his generals.

But, after all, one cannot lose the military impression in Germany—soldiers, soldiers, soldiers, everywhere and at all times.

Mainz came after Bingen, and seemed very prosy by contrast, but I stayed one day at a prison-like hotel and meditated. In the morning the waiter brought breakfast to my room and insisted upon setting the table there. It took the most earnest representations to convince him that I had not been condemned to solitary—only to ordinary imprisonment. But then came Frankfort and made amends, for Frankfort is one of the liveliest cities in Germany. It offers much to the antiquarian also. Its old streets and narrow alleys are in most instances exactly as they were 300 or 400 years ago. The houses lean over confidentially to within a few feet of each other as if they were whispering their opinions of the modern life now going on under their eaves, and were comparing it with "the good old times," which I think were very bad old times, times of torture, of rapine and cruelty, and of prejudice. Nevertheless, one can wander about the old city for hour after hour and never grow bored. There is no need of special sightseeing when every street is a sight, and where everything is quaint and peculiar. However, it is incumbent to go across the old bridge (14th century) and taste the apfelwein at Sachsenhausen. This beverage is twin brother to very ancient cider of Maine. When I first tasted it I exclaimed, "Oh, this is hard!" The average tourist may devote a day to this excursion, the morning to apple-wine, the afternoon to colic.

There is the usual bother at the hotel (a thoroughly German one, and not the tourist's great Hotel Schwan), about a bath. Every trip this occurs somewhere, and it is always annoying. It is embarrassing to take a warm bath which will not get warm, and (when you are in dishabille, and complain through the door, which never locks, to the waiter) to have several persons enter and hold a council of war over your head. When the debating society has quite finished, they deign to tell you the results of their deliberations which are, first, the building is being repaired, and the bath has suffered thereby; second, there are fine warm baths on the Main river, a mile away; third, the waiter doesn't understand how to manage the bath; fourth, the plug which he has pulled to let cold water out, lets it in; and lastly, the chambermaid shall bring up hot water in pails until the required temperature is attained. I courteously return thanks to the assembly and intimate that if they will retire I will ablute regardless of temperature, which they do, and I do, although I take the precaution of barricading the keyless door, resolved to resist any further invasion to the death.

At the little hotel I had the typical German food (I may as well confess to enjoying it), and at each meal, while I hoped for the best, I was prepared for the *Wurst.*

Speaking of that leads me to say a word about meats of continental Europe. Beef is generally execrable; mutton, not much better; lamb, generally of Pompeian antiquity; but veal always excellent and pork good. There are separate butchers in each branch, and "beef butcher," "swine butcher," "calf butcher," are the usual signs over their shops.

Have you ever heard of the traveler who declaimed against Pisa as the wettest of cities? "Why," said he, "twenty years ago I left Pisa and it was raining; I come back and it is raining still!" Well, that may suit to Heidelberg. It rains there even in the finest weather, I think, and the same is true of the Black Forest.

I believe the moist weather is considered good for the grapes which are flourishing. They only gather them in after they are touched by the frost. This came about by accident at first. One year the grapes ripened slowly and they were left on the vines until late in autumn. There came a nipping frost, and all the vineyard owners thought the wine was ruined. The Johannisberg grapes were sold in one batch to a speculator. That year the wine was better than ever, and since then the wine makers have profited by the lesson. Of course in Heidelberg one must go straight to the castle. It is the most picturesque ruin in Europe. The kitchen, with its enormous spit and chimney, where they roasted oxen whole, and the great banqueting hall, are impressive enough still. They dined and wined heartily in those days, and then they roasted a few Protestants as an agreeable pastime for dessert, and said " by my halidome " and " away with him to the castle moat," and other things that we only get in the dime novels nowadays. I was greatly interested in one statue of wood, which they kept appropriately in the cellar opposite the big wine barrel. It was the duke's jester, who lived somewhere in the beginning of the last century. His claim to historical perpetuity lies in the fact that he drank eighteen bottles of wine every day. I think he should have made it an even twenty, but I suppose he did not wish to become a hard drinker merely for the sake of two bottles of wine daily.

After the castle the university is the spot that most attracts me. There is a story of a person seeking this institution and asking another the way to it:—

First party: "I beg pardon, but can you tell me where the university is?"

Second Party: "I'm very sorry I can't; I'm a student myself!"

This might be true for two reasons: Firstly, the buildings are small and unimpressive, and secondly, the students are not obliged to attend any lectures whatever. When it

comes to examinations, however, they cannot pull through
in the manner of some American college students that I
know of, and on the whole the results are as thorough as
those achieved by universities with more exacting details of
discipline. I went through the main building with a proctor of radiant nose and beery breath, and through him suc-
ceeded in speaking to a couple of the professors, (who are
addressed as "excellenz,") one of whom invited me into his
recitation room, where I heard a pleasant discourse upon
" Goethe and Schiller." But the students interested me
most. Evidently the baneful practice of duelling has not yet
become obsolete, for some of them had faces that reminded
me of modern magazine articles, they were so "copiously
illustrated with cuts."

I also visited a newspaper office in Heidelberg, and was
amazed at the calmness and tranquility which pervaded the
place. If you want to live in pensive solitude and meditation, become an editor of a German newspaper. They do
not exchange over there, because the papers are of different
prices, and they think it would not be fair all round. They
have no American news whatever, spite of the fact that almost everyone in Germany has relatives among us. The
advertisements are often abbreviated to save expense, and
the result is sometime rather ludicrous. I translate here for
example:—

"CORELIGIONISTS.

A young man, reduced circ., well ed., Luth. church, 25
yrs. o. makes strenuous app. for imm. posit. Ab. and will.
to work. Add. 2104 this off."

The above is literal, and is difficult to decipher as a rebus.
The pathos is, however, largely taken out of it by abbrevi-
ation.

In passing through Baden I noticed that woman's rights
were much respected. They have the right to labor even
harder than the men. I saw many a hideous Maud Muller

in the fields, not only raking hay, but mowing, plowing and doing all the farmers' work. If they would only introduce Mormonism there, a large farmer might have an easy and profitable time, but one wife is scarcely enough working capital, no matter how hard it is worked.

The railroad from Heidelberg down to Freiburg is one of those calmly deliberate institutions that annoy an American. The train goes as slowly as a district messenger boy, and stops as often as a man at work on a job for which he is paid by the day. I was, however, preserved from ennui by the fact that the conductor, or guard, was a new one, and had a phenomenal lack of memory. I was kept busy almost the entire time in showing him my tickets. At the twentieth examination my patience gave out, and I asked him (in English) if he knew that he was a nuisance from Nuisanceville.

"Ja! freilich?" ("Yes, certainly,") said he, rather than confess that he did not understand me.

I had a more crushing revenge at the end of the trip, for after he had quite got through with his punching, clipping and examining, I found that he had punched just one ticket too many in my round trip book, and I introduced him to the superintendent at Freiburg, who delivered an oration which was Spartan in brevity, but sulphurous in quality. No one knows what language can do until he has heard a German official swear. But all petty annoyances subside in the cool, calm atmosphere of Freiburg, the city which stands at the edge of the forest. One can see one evidence of mountain neighborhood in the peculiar drainage of the city

In every street are deep gutters of clear, rapidly-running water. In Freiburg, at least, rolling in the gutter, would not mean uncleanliness. The neat, commercial hotel, "The Roman Emperor," where we stay, adds to our contentment, and its host, Herr Spreter, is a veritable Hans Sachs, burly, hearty, and a vivid contrast to the fawning type of landlord one finds so numerous in Europe. He has his opinions, too, and he told the fisherman of our party (for here I met a quintette of American friends "doing" the forest), that he was a lunatic for desiring trout fried in lard when he could have them boiled in the Black Forest style. This style was peculiar, I must say, for the fish were always brought to the table *alive*, at first, swimming in a bucket of water.

Although this dish was peculiar, the table d'hote was of the conventional pattern. All table d'hotes are. Do you know what this infliction means? It is as if a French cook were pursuing you through Europe! Everywhere the same food, cooked forever in the same manner. The solemnity begins with soup, after which comes a long pause, so long that you fear that the waiters have gone off to catch the fish. Finally they appear with the viand in question, together with a butter sauce and a dish of boiled potatoes. Now follows a long hiatus, ample time being given to digest the fish and get up a new appetite. Slowly and mournfully the waiters approach with bad roast beef and string beans. Again an interregnum, and then comes veal in some shape. The lapse of time which now follows is such that the guests feel old age coming on; at last the waiters come on also, and donate a piece of chicken or capon with salad to each victim. Finally the now decrepit and toothless guests receive some pudding, fruit, etc., and depart. The man who has lived ten years at a European hotel has probably spent six years waiting for courses at a table d'hote, and the above lines apply to every table d'hote in Europe.

A fact worth recording is that when we leave the Freiburg hotel our burly host not only wrings our hands almost off, but gives to each a little present. To me he gave a bottle

of Kirschwasser, strong enough to burn through the stomach
of a bronze statue. I, however, used it on the guides and
drivers along the route, and they do not curl up and die,
but smack their lips and enjoy it, as the Irishman did the
aquafortis.

We leave the land of railroad and stage here, and on
horseback and in a wagonnette, hired by the day, pursue
our explorations into the forest. The very names are awe-
inspiring. Our first point is the "Höllenthal."

> "Down into the valley of Hell
> Rode the six—tourists."

A fanciful name, but well enough deserved, for steep
cliffs, dark glens and weird gorges are in it, and just after
it comes the "Himmelreich," or "Paradise," a smiling and
pleasant valley, in fine contrast. We pass innumerable
crucifixes. On almost every house there is a holy horror
of some sort. It seems to be a sort of celestial fire insurance.

The tiny chapels and churches in the depth of the woods
are, however, a charming feature of the tour. We passed
one little forest church which was so diminutive that if
Phillips Brooks were to preach in it, it would be full, without any congregation whatever. At the little village of
Höllenthal, just in front of the Star Hotel, we organized an
impromptu game of base ball. The nines were very frag-
mentary, but energetic, and the natives got out of the way
with much celerity whenever a hot one came from the bat.
They evidently thought that we were members of some
insane asylum, and treated us with respectful pity.

Finally one of the party knocked the ball into a mountain
stream and another tumbled in after it while trying to fish
it out, and the game came to an untimely end, but we had
the satisfaction of being the first to play the American game
in the Black Forest.

Then followed a walk through the Rabenschlucht—the raven's gorge—the beauty of which I cannot represent even if I were to print this chapter in colored ink. In every direction are beautiful walks and grand views, and a whole summer could not exhaust the interest of these valleys and hills. If the peasants could exist on scenery they would have an easy time of it; as it is they live mostly on potatoes, and are underfed and overworked. We go on to the Titi See, which is a lake in the midst of hills, full of fish. The roads all through this wonderful region are marvelously well made, as smooth as a table, and as clean.

At this point I made a detour alone, to the little hamlet of Untermünsterthal, in the dark recesses of the famous woods. A ruined castle stands at the entrance of the forest, which is black and gloomy enough to countenance all the terrible legends of robbery and violence which cluster around the place.

On the way to the place I pass through the busy little city of Stauffen. Along the road I count fifteen crucifixes and shrines and ten breweries, from which I conclude that the inhabitants are devoted to religion and beer. As I drive along in my lordly coach every one takes off his hat in humble salute, which I acknowledge with a wave of the hand, as I suppose a great lord might do, but my dignity sits rather heavily upon me. I might ride all around Chicago in a hansom, and pay double the fare I am now giving, and not get so much homage. I feel like the rightful lord of the manor, returning to his own amid the joyous shouts of the happy peasantry, in the fifth act of a Bowery melo-drama.

But, alas, the peasantry are not all happy, as I soon find out, for I have undertaken to bear the greetings of an absent son to his parents in the far-off forest, and in the little cottage the mother weeps and weeps to think that her boy has somehow come nearer to her, and yet is so far away. "The short and simple annals of the poor" have been to me the dreariest thing in all Europe since I first landed on that side. Yet there is something to be said in favor of vegetating as some of these villagers do. The pretty cottages, with low, over-hanging roofs, are not uncomfortable, and the barn at the side, the piles of wood near the door, the mountain torrents rushing by, the wind soughing and singing in the trees, and the weird yet alluring depths of the wonderful enchanted forest, make up a picture which must make some impression on the inhabitants, even though they know it not. Their very legends and folk-lore prove it.

On my return I find the party quite ready to proceed to Furtwangen, a distance of fully forty miles through the forest by stage. It is a delight to get away from the iron horse, to leave railroads and civilization altogether, (even if we cannot leave the beer saloon), and come to the quaint little villages nestling among the hills, where the inhabitants know nothing of tourists, not even enough to bleed them. From the valleys our road goes up into the clouds, and at Gütenbach it is as cold as the most cultured Bostonian. Allured by the frigidity, and the apparent proximity of the peak, three of us leave the carriage, strike across lots, and endeavor to reach it on foot.

Put not your trust in mountain distances! Before I get there my collar has gone down the back of my neck, I am breathing like an asthmatic locomotive, and my feet seem to weigh six hundred pounds each.

Furtwangen is a small city (over 3,000 inhabitants), but it is not down in the guide books and it has no city ways. It is also far from any railroad and devoted to clock-making and woodcarving. All the inhabitants study the latter and I visited the school where it is taught and saw the youngsters begin on carving raised diamonds on wooden plates, and the advanced classes end with most intricate and

beautiful works of art in wood. Outside of the city I again
tried mountain climbing; it is disgusting to toil up a couple
of thousand feet and when you imagine that you have
achieved something, to find a peasant complacently mowing
or raking on top. They cultivate the land at unheard-of
heights in this country. I imagine that they plow with
balloons, and roll the harvest over the precipices into the
valley, when it is ripe.

We left the Black Forest at Triberg, and in the most dismal of rainstorms. All these charming mountain districts
become fearfully dull when it storms, for then one can do
nothing but sit in-doors (or ride in a closed carriage), or
play billiards on tables with stony-hearted cushions, or chat
with the *schöne Kellnerin* in the *Wirthschaft*. Even the
latter resources failed, for when the fair maiden grew confidential and told me her name was Gretchen, I told her my
name was Faust, and she didn't believe me, and went away.
It is hopeless to joke with a driver here. In the midst of a
pouring rain, our Jehu, who was taking us to Triberg, pulled
up and asked if we wanted to see the waterfall! I told him
that we could see the water fall very readily from where we
sat; and he responded that that was impossible, for we would
have to walk ten minutes through the woods before it came
in sight.

> The Spanish fleet thou canst not see
> Because—it is not yet in sight.

He wore cotton wool in his ears—all the drivers wear
cotton wool in their ears. I think it is to keep their brains
from evaporating. Naturally, they cannot hear very well.
I told my driver to go into a wayside inn, where we stopped
a while, and take a glass of beer at my expense; he took a
bottle of good wine and charged it to me. But even good
wine does not cost much, and no good traveler ought to
worry over the small extortions of travel. With ordinary

care the entire cheatings of a long trip will not cost much more than a $10 bill will cover.

How lonely one feels abroad when suddenly separated from traveling companions! I have a distinct fit of the blues as I make the journey towards Saxony alone, while the quintette leave the forest solitudes for the activity of Paris. But once in Leipsic I find friends again and, best of all, plenty of musical companionship. The famous old spots are visited in turn, beginning with a thirsty trip to Auerbach's Keller, made immortal by Goethe in his '' Faust.'' To those who have read the work I can asseverate that no great band of students would find room to sing in its quarters, and Mephistopheles would have been scared away by the high prices before he had a chance to sing his song. But it looks very ancient, and the mural paintings look old enough to have been done by Holbein. A pleasant call at the Leipsic conservatory followed, and I met Professor Jadassohn, who is not only a splendid musician and composer, but a witty gentleman as well. His definition of the different species of composers struck me as epigrammatic. He said: '' There are two species of renowned composers in the sea of music. Some of them are fishes, and some have learned how to swim. Mozart was one of the fishes.'' Reinecke, the veteran director of the Gewandhaus concerts and of the Conservatory, also made a remark which will bear transcribing. Speaking of new countries and their growth in music, he said: ''The chief trouble is that they inherit too soon the wealth of the older countries. They receive at once the most highly spiced and richly developed music of the modern masters, instead of growing up to them as we had to do.'' He feared that this would militate against a love of the clearer and simpler masterpieces of art, and that the mind beginning with the modern school would never duly appreciate Mozart or Haydn. He is very liberal, too, this Nestor among conductors, and while deprecating the vulgarities of Verdi, recognized the inspiration of parts of the Requiem and of the quartette in "Rigoletto." This may astonish many of the lesser musicians, who deem it incumbent to kick at Verdi at least once a day. Kapellmeister Reinecke in himself illustrates the modestly great character of the German musicians of rank. He has no tremendous salary; he does not dictate royal terms for every appearance of himself and orchestra; but he is sincerely honored by every one in Leipsic, and in his autograph album are letters of heartiest recognition from Schumann and Berlioz, down to kings and queens. It is, however, no longer a combination of poverty and honor for the musicians in Germany. Mozart's day of suffering is past. An eminent professor at Leipsic told me that the high prices paid in America are having their influence in Germany. The great institutions find that if they wish to keep the musicians from starting for the New World, they must give pecuniary inducements to stay in the Old. I had some charming glimpses of the home life of Kapellmeister Reinecke, as he took me from the Conservatory to his modest quarters in the *Querstrasse*, somewhat nearer the sky than some of our less learned native composers dwell. A number of charming young ladies of assorted sizes greeted my view in the drawing room, and I was presented, one by one, to the daughters of the Kapellmeister. Astounded at the rather numerous gathering, I ventured to ask whether any had escaped, and was informed that some of them had,—into the bonds of wedlock. The sons, too, seemed especially bright, and the wit and badinage around the dinner table was something long to be remembered. Reinecke has not got the American fever to any extent, and a very short sojourn showed me why he is not anxious to change his position for one in the New World. It is true that he has not a salary such as our directors and conductors of first rank obtain, but on every side were tokens of friendship and homage from the greatest men and women of Europe, and when, the next day, he took me to his *Kneipe* near the Conservatory, I noticed that every one in Leipsic took off his hat to the simple and good old man; every one, from nobleman to peasant. It counts for something to be thus honored and beloved, and perhaps a few thousand dollars would not compensate for the loss of such friends. How kindly and paternal Reinecke is, may be clearly shown by relating the origin of the beautiful violin part to the song "Spring Flowers." He had composed this without any violin obbligato whatever, and it was to be sung by a young lady at her debut in a Gewandhaus concert. The evening before the concert the artist came with a decided fit of the "nerves" to Reinecke's home, and in trembling and tears expressed her forebodings for the debut of the morrow. The good-hearted composer sat down to think matters over, and then exclaimed, "I will give you some extra support for the voice so that you cannot fail," and then wrote the violin part, which is so tender and characteristic. Immediate rehearsal followed, and thanks to the violin support and the goodness of Reinecke, the debut was a success. And at the *Kneipe*, too, I saw how much of contentment, passing riches, there was in such an artistic life, for here in the corner of a very modest *Wirthschaft* were gathered some of the greatest art-workers of Leipsic (literature and painting were represented, as well as music), and every day at noon they met and spoke of their work, their hopes, their plans, and their arts; in such an atmosphere the plant of high ideality could not but thrive, and I could only wish that we might some day have such unostentatious and practical gatherings among the artists of America.

CHAPTER IV.

NORTHWARD TO KIEL—THE NORTH SEA AND BALTIC—COPEN-
HAGEN—GADE AND THE DANISH STATE CONSERVATORY—
AN INTERVIEW WITH SVENDSEN—MUSIC AT THE TIVOLI—
A CONVIVIAL ARTIST'S GATHERING—SCHARWENKA, DAHL
AND OTHERS—A DANGEROUS BATH—UNEXPECTED FRIENDS.

From Leipsic I made a speedy allegro through the north.
During the larger part of this trip I had with me a very
lively cornet player from Boston, a member of the symphony orchestra, and a very genial comrade. We had a
sudden addition to our party, while traveling through Germany. It occurred thus: We had just passed the Saxon
frontier, and were settling down to smoke and meditation,
when, to our annoyance, two other travelers came into our
compartment to claim seats. One then inquired of me in
German which was little short of barbaric, if the train went
through to Hamburg. Having answered in German, my
answer was duly translated into English by the questioner to
his companion. "Those fellows wanted to have the entire
train to themselves," said one of the newcomers to the other.
This remark was *not* translated to me. After a silence of some
minutes, for the translations to and fro were rather arduous,
one of the strangers began to get hungry; "ask that duffer
if we are ever to get any lunch," quoth he; it was high time,
evidently, to arrange a *modus vivendi* with the newly arrived

delegation from the United States; therefore I suggested, as a relief from the strain of thus being filtered through German into English and back again, that we talk in the United States tongue at first hand! Tableau of joy and celestial happiness! The rescued wanderers were from the west; they were railroad men; they represented the Chicago, Milwaukee & St. Paul railroad, one as its general emigration agent, the other as its European agent, their names were Powell and Norton, and they were in for any missionary efforts in the wickedest capitals of Europe that we might suggest. They agreed to join our caravan as far as Copenhagen. Another gentleman, who will be readily recognized by his name—Mr. Smith—had also agreed to go the northern route with us; so it will be readily seen that I was a sort of railway "Pied Piper of Hamelin," whose services would be of enormous value to Cook, or any other well conducted tourist office.

Our carriage, after the advent of a whole American railway company, became the scene of a prolonged revelry. The emigrant (by which it will be understood that I mean the gentlemanly emigration agent) spoke English and Welsh. The latter language was a blessing to us, for by it we overcame many a pompous official. If we came to a custom house where the officials spoke English, French, German, Danish, Italian and Spanish, we would send forward the emigrant, who would address them calmly and serenely in a language in which one consonant tumbled over the other. No hotel porter dared withstand this master stroke. But I grieve to say that a disease broke out in the party during the long railway journey to Hamburg. It was not cholera. It was kleptomania. Our trumpeter (cornetist aforesaid) and the emigrant, were suddenly seized with a vehement desire for relics of the trip, and after that at every station a wild rush was made for the refreshment counter. Beer was the ostensible motive, but alas! after leaving each station their pockets disgorged matches, match boxes, a cracked beer mug, a placard, and one even purloined a railway illustrated time table. During that devastating ride through Germany our car became more and more like a bric-a-brac shop. If America ever comes to a war with Germany (which Heaven forbid!) I should suggest to our government to engage our party as raiders. Sherman's march to the sea was nothing to our advance upon Hamburg. As this was the only time in my life that I became a relic hunter, I hope that my depredations, which were amply paid for in extra "tips," may be forgiven.

Arrived at the Hamburger Hof, a hotel which is as grand as a castle, and has a splendid view, we allowed the emigrant to practice Welsh on the porter, while we engaged rooms, and after we had scrubbed off all the German real estate acquired on our journey, and disposed of all our ill-gotten "relics," we sat down to a champagne supper, in which the C., M. & St. P. R. R. formally expressed its joy at making our acquaintance.

When the traveler strikes the continent he leaves behind him two important conveniences—gas and soap. I can understand why the continentals don't use each other's soap, and extend them my sympathy; but why they should build a hotel like a palace, and then put a few tallow dips in a room as large as a concert hall, passes my understanding. It must be that somebody once blew the gas out, and they wouldn't take any further chances.

The next day our goodly company started for Copenhagen. The journey through Altona to Kiel was of a gentler and more subdued character than that to Hamburg, and the thirst for seizing upon movable property had departed from us. At Kiel we found the boat in which we were to brave the raging sea to be a very small ship with a very large

captain. At first the voyage bade fair to be a prosperous
one, and in the glee of a misplaced confidence we formed
ourselves into a male quartette, and, taking seats upon the
paddle-box, began an impromptu concert. In the midst of
our singing we became aware of a series of violent knock-
ings upon the paddle-box. Thinking that possibly some
official of an effete monarchy was desirous of silencing our
warblings, we only sang the louder. It was now "Good-by,
sweetheart," that we were mangling, when, just as we had
musically announced our intention of never leaving, though
we'd said " Good-by, sweetheart, good-by," the knocking
burst into a roar, and the whole paddle-box arose in the air
in a shower of splinters. We concluded to retract our sentiments and leave. We left; I may even say that we left
rapidly. We all thought the scenery on the other side of
the boat was more attractive. The boat came to a stand-
still, and an examination showed that some rivets had become loosened and the wheel had been thrown from its
bearings. We were obliged to lay to for three hours on the
Ostsee in a heavy swell. There was nothing to do in the in-
interim but to begin to fraternize with the passengers. But
as these all began to have an ominously pale look and clinch
their lips strangely, their conversation was not brilliant. I
had watched a young Frenchman of obese tendencies at the
table d'hote go through every dish on the table, and I found
a few moments' relaxation in mentally going through the
bill of fare backwards and checking off the viands as he
gave them up; but after he had passed the soup on the
return journey, even that amusement failed me. I was then
struck with a happy thought and, borrowing a line which was
on board, I philosophically went a-fishing. As the net result
of half an hour was one misguided "torsk" (a diminutive
rock cod), I gave this up, too, and went back to the passengers. This time I was more fortunate, and found a

young lady who had traveled all over South America, and spoke all languages except Welsh, so I had no fears of the irrepressible emigrant interrupting our conversation. I do not intend to inflict all the details of society conversation upon my readers, but I do think it worth while to record one fact that I was informed of, which is that the wild German youth do not have dime novels, but indulge in reading translations of an American author—J. Fenimore Cooper. I fear that our adventurous "small boy" would find Cooper rather slow.

Finally the wheel was repaired, and the boat proceeded to its destination—Korsör. Here we took a railroad for Copenhagen, whose every move was a volcanic eruption and an earthquake; but finally we arrived, and sought hospitable beds in the Hotel d'Angleterre. The Danes must be very ignorant. They spell Copenhagen *Kjobenhavn!* Fancy asking a party of young ladies to join in a game of Kjobenhavn! They are far more honest, however, than the southern Europeans toward the tourist. They take their " tips " regularly, but with perfect frankness, and without any sacrifice of dignity. I experienced this, when, on my arrival, I asked a gorgeous creature with huge side whiskers and a black dress coat, where I could be brushed and cleaned. He beckoned me aside, and, taking me to a side room, dropped on his knees. It was not to confess that he had embezzled the funds of a Danish savings bank, or to say that he was the traitorous ambassador of some Norwegian king; it was simply to black my boots; The operation was an embarrassing one; I felt as if I were receiving a shine from an archbishop, and it was with difficulty that I could bring myself to give him a half krone (fourteen cents) which, however, he took.

In the evening we all went to the Tivoli. This is one of the chief sights of Copenhagen. It is a pleasure ground not unlike the Prater at Vienna, but smaller. Every kind of

amusement is going on within its limits, from whirligigs to
classical concerts. First we went to a military concert here,
where we sat and sipped our beer in sweet content, and without even feeling a desire to steal the beer glass; and here I
had my first encounter with the Danish language. I had
been carefully preparing myself with stock phrases, which
I was ready to throw out easily and gracefully at any Dane
who would stand them. The waiter stood them, but I cannot say that he understood them. He even answered back,
as if it were my business to understand *him*. He finally got
me so snarled up that I didn't understand myself, but by
expressive pantomime we obtained our beer, and the Rubi-
con was passed.

I am not going to describe Thorwaldsen's Museum, where
he lies at rest in his most fitting monument, amidst his own
works. Any artistic reader who desires to know more about
the impressions which thrill one in seeing these must buy
" Baedecker's Guide," and get seven shillings worth of
emotion.

There is a wonderful steeple in Copenhagen. The steps
which lead to the top go around the outside, and when one
gets there a view bursts upon the beholder which em-
braces all Copenhagen and the surrounding country, and
causes him to thrill with, etc., etc. (see guide book again for
further details). I didn't go up. But I did see the great
race of the year at the suburb of Klampenborg. It was sufficiently important to draw horses and jockeys from Germany
and England, and naturally drew out all of Denmark's aristocracy. A ride of an hour, and then a walk through the
most beautiful of woods (the king's deer park), brought us
to the race-course.

The crown prince and family were there, and carriages
innumerable, as at an English Derby. The great stakes
were won by a German horse, quite unexpectedly. I saw

his jockey hold him back until past the quarter pole on the home stretch, and then, with the grandest possible rush, pass by everything and come in, not a full length ahead. At the finish (in sporting parlance) a blanket could have covered them all—if it had been large enough. The crowd burst forth in wild "hurrahs," but when the name was announced they changed these to hisses. Why? Because Denmark cordially detests Germany, and remembers Schleswig-Holstein. After seeing a poorly run hurdle race, I went down to the fair which followed. I saw a Danish Punch and Judy. I did not fully understand the dialogue, but when I saw a gentleman with a crown seized by an imp and dragged off, I knew it was the German Emperor being escorted to a land where ulsters are unknown. I felt then that the Danes did not like Germany. The fair was like all other European peasant gatherings—people dancing in a heart-rending manner in hot sheds; soldiers parading with pretty sweethearts and smoking cigars that can be imagined but never described; booths with orchestras, a bass tuba and a cornet; and a general enjoyment of everything that was unenjoyable, and chatter and noise everywhere.

Back to Copenhagen after this. But never can pen of mine describe the agonies of getting back. The State railroad of Denmark was unequal to the task of transporting fifteen thousand people, and the passengers had sometimes to wait two hours before getting a train, although they ran every fifteen minutes; the people were herded together like cattle, and admitted to the cars in separate droves. Yet all were so patient and uncomplaining that it was a perfect revelation to an American. Not a word or a murmur was heard from even women who stood with children in their arms. Meanwhile, the Chicago, Milwaukee & St. Paul railroad, in the person of its accredited representatives, waxed wroth. " If we dared to do anything like this," said the European (the European agent, as distinct from the Emigrant), "the people would mob us, and they would be right. This comes of centuries of endurance! They'd better import an American railway," and so on to the end of the chapter. It availed nothing. Completely fagged out, we finally reached Copenhagen. On the way, I had a question to ask of the conductor. I began, " Taler er Tisk?" (Do you speak German?) " No," was the snarly answer, "and I don't want to learn." I begin to suspect that the Danes don't like Germany. On the way home I was suddenly aroused from my lethargy. I smelt a smell. It was a strong smell. One that was richer than any of the hundred smells in Cologne, and stronger than any to be found in Naples. It was a Danish cheese store. They have very many cheese stores here, and each smells worse than the other. It brought back to memory Shakespeare's famous description of a Copenhagen cheese factory—" Something is rotten in the State of Denmark." This is the " something " referred to, and the description is quite correct.

Our Copenhagen experience was a brilliant and varied one. Our emigrant (the aforesaid emigration agent of the Chicago, Milwaukee & St. Paul railroad) showered down Welsh and English in terrible combination on the heads of the defenceless Danes, until we had to restrain him. One combat was particularly ferocious. We had been tarrying at the beer mug in a Danish " Oltonnel," when the waiter, in bringing me my change, gave me an *ore* among the silver. An *ore* is a mite of a coin, value one-fourth of a cent. The emigrant was immediately seized with a desire to possess a similar trophy of the cheapness of the country. He made the attempt in English. " Me want one like dat," he shouted, imagining that mangled English would be reasonable Danish, and giving the waiter a silver coin. This intelligent individual took the coin, and presently returned with—five glasses of beer. A second attempt only brought some smaller silver and a two-*ore* piece. The waiter evidently could not understand why any one should desire to keep an *ore* as a relic. Then the Chicago, Milwaukee & St. Paul railroad arose in its might. Taking out a well-filled pocketbook, the emigrant opened it before the *kellner*, and cried—"Put in here! Keepy when go away!" and held up my solitary *ore* in the other hand. The waiter looked on with awestruck wonder. He evidently thought that it was a great American railway about to declare a dividend. I gave Mr. Powell the *ore*, but that did not prevent him from leaving the place in disgust.

During one of my visits to Copenhagen I met Gade, the composer, then head of the Royal Danish Conservatory. He was old and portly, and his appearance would not give a clew to the genius within. Short of stature, round eyes, ruddy face, and bushy, gray hair, with a manner in which joviality and impetuosity were combined, Gade impressed one as a professor of the old school, wrapped up entirely in his work and his art. He took me over the conservatory spite of the evidently pressing duties, and explained to me the system, also inquiring as to the status of teaching in the United States. He was astounded to hear of our vast conservatories, and of the progress we were making in music. Of our composers he knew very little. He wished that he were younger that he might visit America. "Now I must wait for a still longer journey," said he, sighing. The good old man has since gone on that journey, dying December 21, 1890. He has fought the good fight bravely, and fairly outlived those who called him "Mrs. Mendelssohn." He was very busy then with the final examinations of the school year, and showed me some of the papers with evident pride in the standing of his classes in composition. He expressed a wish that he might have some of our talented Americans to teach, "but they all go to Berlin and Munich," he added.

I now went to see Svendsen, the great symphonic composer of the north. I had difficulty at the outset, for the servant told me that he was out, and my Danish was not equal to the task of asking when he would return. I spoke to her in German, French, Italian, and finally in English. The latter seemed to impress her deeply, for she went away, I was left in doubt for a moment as to whether she had taken me for a linguistic book agent, and had gone to unchain the bulldog; but she soon reappeared with a young lady. Again I let fly the various European tongues, but she interrupted my flow of polyglot eloquence by saying, "you can speak English; I am an American." This was Mrs. Svendsen. I was soon in a comfortable armchair in an elegant music room, awaiting the arrival of the Kapellmeister. He soon came, a tall, handsome, genial looking man, with wavy blonde hair, looking not more than thirty years of age, although he is more than ten years older. He gave me a most cordial welcome, and in a few minutes, over fragrant coffee and cigars, we were conversing about America and American musicians. Svendsen has been in the United States on a visit, and remembers New York and Niagara with enthusiasm. He asked after many of his American fellow students, and also after some of his most talented American pupils. In the discussion which followed, regarding woman in music, he expressed the opinion that no very great female composer would ever arise. He thought that woman was receptive but not creative, and that this enabled her at times to outstrip man as a performer, and to become a pianist with greater ease, but militated against her expressing great or original thoughts as a composer. I hope that my fair readers of musical tendencies will not vow vengeance on Svendsen for this sentiment. Svendsen is said to be one of the great orchestral conductors of the world. He showed me two trophies of his work in this direction, both gifts of admirers. One was a gold and ebony baton of exquisite workmanship, a gift from ladies in Christiania, the other a quainter one of ivory, made especially valuable by the autograph of the former owner upon it—"Carl Maria von Weber."

A pleasant half-hour of study of the composer's recent orchestral scores followed, during which he explained to me the intention of many of his effects of instrumentation. I was especially struck with the wealth of fancy displayed in his "Zorahaide," a Spanish tone picture in which he has caught the true Spanish and Moorish spirit, although he has never been in Spain. The subject is taken from Washington Irving.

The day was now far spent, and Svendsen suggested that we should go together in the evening and hear the Brahms (third) Symphony, and promised to make me acquainted with such musical lights as should be at the concert. In the meantime, as I felt that during my travels I had acquired considerable Danish real estate, I thought I would seek a warm bath and scrub it off. I wandered around, but found no Danish words on any sign that could be tortured into meaning warm baths. Finally I went into a small hotel and in desperation asked for the means of becoming a next door neighbor to godliness. They had a bath on the third story, and I proceeded thither in company with the *hausknecht*, who showed me into a rather dingy room which evidently had not been used recently. There was in one corner a boiler somewhat like that of a piledriver, (with a thermometer riveted to it), from which pipes ran to the tub.

The young man kindled a wood fire under the boiler, and told me, in broken German, to let on the water when it got hot enough. I disrobed and waited. I let on one faucet—it was cold. I let on the other—it was frigid. I waited ten minutes and tried again—same result. I now found that if the water wasn't hot the room decidedly *was*, and on approaching the boiler my hair stood on end to find the thermometer registering somewhere in the thousands, and the lower part of the iron work in a dull red glow. The water was still cold. On second thoughts I felt that there was really no necessity to take a bath. I concluded to dress. I was somewhat hastened in my toilet by the thermometer cracking and dropping at my feet, and by sundry ominous reports from the interior of the pile driver aforesaid. Under the circumstances, I thought a shirt and a pair of trousers quite an elaborate toilet for a bathroom reception, and prepared to ring the bell. There was no bell! A glance at the sparks beginning to fly from the piledriver convinced me that I was in sufficiently full dress for even a corridor reception. I took my shoes in my hand, as I had heard that it was the custom in the east not to wear shoes on state occasions. I found a bell, and soon summoned a chambermaid. There was no occasion for any Danish remarks. I showed her my impromptu display of pyrotechnics. The effect was magical. She rushed down stairs to summon the landlord and others to view so interesting a sight. When they arrived a blue flame had begun to show itself at the top of the piledriver, where some solder was melting. A hurried consultation resulted in the withdrawal of the fires, and a wetting down of the woodwork. Meanwhile I stood like Marius among the ruins of Carthage, only my costume was more picturesque than that of Marius. An interesting discussion followed, during which I stated that I wanted neither a cold nor a Turkish bath, and was not accustomed to rooming with red-hot piledrivers. At any rate it was not the fault of my broken Danish *that* time, for investigation showed that the young man had forgotten to put any water in the boiler before lighting the fire, whereupon he was incontinently discharged, and I was invited to take a cold bath free. But I felt that I had done bathing enough for one day, so I sallied forth to the Tivoli to meet Svendsen.

Our seats were fortunately together in the little concert room, and I was delighted to find that not only the, at that time, new Brahms Symphony (No. 3) was to be performed, but also X. Scharwenka was to play his own concerto. The work was given by forty-five performers under Baldwin Dahl, a good conductor. Scharwenka's playing was of the broadest, most massive character. He seemed at times to lose himself in the passions excited by the music, but generally, also, displayed a commendable artistic reserve. I only wish that he had had an American piano to perform upon instead of the rather muddy-toned Danish instrument.

The post-musical proceedings were the really interesting ones. Svendsen, (I do not call him Mr. Svendsen any more than I would call Socrates Mr. Socrates—one of the penalties of greatness), suggested that we proceed to the green-room together. On the way I was struck with the deference paid to the composer. All the orchestral performers bowed to the earth before him, and every man, woman and child seemed to know him. We found Mr. and Mrs. Scharwenka quite willing to supplement the concert with a supper, *al fresco*, and soon were seated around a hospitable piece of mahogany. Xaver Scharwenka was a striking contrast to Svendsen. He was also strikingly handsome, but there seemed something of melancholy in his piercing black eye, and his dark face seldom smiled heartily. His wit, too, which was seemingly inexhaustible, was at times cynical and bitter.

Our company grew apace. First came Baldwin Dahl, with his pretty daughter, a charming specimen of pink-and-white Danish loveliness; then came a pianist from Holland, Van Seil by name; then came Mr. Hamerick, brother of the well known Asgar of Baltimore. I cannot remember all who were present, but our table soon had nearly twenty occupants.

Only the artist can know of these charming hours in Bohemia. The cosmopolitan character of art was strikingly shown in the number of nationalities present. Five languages were spoken at that table. Our first toast, therefore, was "patriotism," and we drank it with all the honors, but when the patriotism had full steam on, it had its drawbacks. One fair Jutlander refused to speak German, could not speak English, and was obliged to compromise with me by speaking French. But I cannot describe the hilarity, the *bon mots* and the *verve* of that little assembly, and when at a certain hour which shall be nameless, we separated, I felt that I had found the musical world of Copenhagen, but that it was not Danish, but belonged, as art should do, to every country and people.

The next day we started for Göthenburg, in Sweden. I need not dwell upon the passage by boat to that city. The chief event of the trip was that the trumpeter, (our cornetist), discovered an American drink on board, which was sold under the mystical name of *Chery Koplers!* "A rose by any other name would smell as sweet," and a sherry cobbler in Sweden was an unexpected event.

Göthenburg is sure to produce a strange impression on the traveler. The fact is that it is a "city of the future." Its rapid growth has induced capitalists to build up a street of palaces, which are all untenanted as yet. This street is as fine in its way as that finest street in the world—the Radial Strasse in Pesth; but, seen in the ghostly twilight of a northern summer night, it produces the effect of being in a city of the dead. This will change very soon, for Göthenburg probably is destined to become the largest city of the north.

The hotel we chose in this city was the "Gota-Kollare," because if any of our party got lost and could not find their way back, the dreadful inquiry, "got the cholera?" would be near enough to it to bring us safely back to our hostelry. I had to study Swedish customs at once, for my bed had no pillows, and an enormous hump, like a camel, in the center. I remonstrated gently, but firmly, with the maid, and told her that to sleep on such a hemisphere would bring on curvature of the spine. She uncovered the hump and showed me the pillows architecturally disposed in the center. That night I found all these pillows, and more, at the head of the bed, the chambermaid having evidently taken the notion that I desired to sleep standing, or very nearly so. My room was not cheerful. It had a tall reservoir of a water pitcher near my head, which looked like a tombstone, and a vast tile stove some ten feet high, which resembled a monument. So I naturally dreamed of sleeping in a Swedish cemetery, and read "sacred to the memory of," etc., on the tile stove.

Speaking of that, reminds me that these summer nights are severe on the northern ghosts. They have to do all their haunting in the short space of an hour, or else walk by daylight, for it is light at 11 P. M., and the new day begins to dawn at 1 A. M., or earlier.

From Göthenburg we came to Christiania. There was but one train a day, but that was the lightning express. Lightning moves slow in Sweden. So does the express. It has one convenience. If you miss the train you can run after it and catch it. But I forgive the journey, for the sake of the good humored guard who spoke English, joked back at all our fun, and smoked our bad cigars as if he liked them.

CHAPTER V.

The midnight sun is a delusion and a snare. After 9 P. M.
it has a washed-out look as if it were growing pale through
keeping such late hours. The railroad system of the north
is another painful disappointment to an American. We
took our solitary, daily express train to Christiania, antici-
pating some degree of rapidity. When we found it to consist of three freight cars to one passenger wagon, we had
our doubts. When it stopped between two stations to
allow a lady to get off who had forgotten something, we
doubted no longer. But at least it was prolific in some re-
spects: it gave six miles of shake to one of travel. At
twelve o'clock it stopped for dinner, for the Norwegian
dines at midday. The dinner was a revelation, and made
some atonement for the difficulties in getting at it. On a
sideboard were spread out sardines, sausages, omelette,
sardelles, eggs, brown biscuit, mackerel, caviare, and her-
ring salad, as well as sweet liqueurs, and burning *aqua vitæ*.
This was not the dinner—only the preface. We were to
eat and drink these things *to get up an appetite*; after that
came the dinner, but I am bound to say that it was not of
the same relative size, otherwise I should not have survived
to tell the tale. It is said that these restaurants consider
hospitality a duty, and make no effort to detain, or even
remind, a traveler who goes off without paying, and every

one is free to eat according to his appetite, helping himself always. It will therefore pay the American tramp to go to Norway.

After this meal I no longer felt so disconsolate at the erratic wanderings of the train, although I still felt aggrieved at the efforts of the engineer to dislocate our spines every time that he started the train. I suppose I must keep to my recorded vow and not describe the scenery; nevertheless, I must let off a little rapture about the approach to Christiania. The fjord is beautiful in the highest degree. Lovely islands of deep green hue, among which yachts and boats twine in and out; heavily wooded banks, which are mirrored in the water, which also has the deepest green color; all these adjuncts go to make up a picture which must make an indelible impression on every traveler. But the fjords to the north make a deeper impression still, for here all is silence; the bustle of Christiania fjord is absent; the gloom and solitude are intensified; the boatman is taciturn, and it ends by the traveler being plunged into a profound melancholy. *All* persons who travel long in Norway, experience a touch of this dreamy sadness, and only recover from their depression of spirits when they reach a city again.

I must speak a word here about the hospitality of the Norwegian. Never have I met so free-handed and open-hearted a race. They vie with one another in making the stranger's lot pleasant. Before I arrived in Christiania, for example, I made the traveling acquaintance of Consul-General Petersen, who, on learning that I had never been in the city before, made me promise that if I felt dull I would at once seek him out and avail myself of both his hospitality and his knowledge of the city; and this is but a sample of the kindness I experienced from the people, from the hands of the prime minister down to the office boy of the *Dagbladet*, the

evening journal of the city. But as I had letters of intro-
duction to residents of the place, I soon availed myself of
the opportunity of visiting friends and enjoying Norwegian
home-life.

My first visit was made to the manager of the great
Aktien-Bryggeri, the great brewery of the north, which
exports its products to every portion of the globe. I
learned here a fact which shows how commercial extremes
meet; Norway is in the closest business relation with Spain.
Many Norwegian youths go to Spain for their commercial
education, and almost all of the Norwegian merchant princes
and sea-captains speak Spanish.

A dinner with the family of the manager aforesaid followed, which impressed me greatly with the sweetness and
gentleness of the manners of the Norwegian upper classes,
who replace the French polish (which exists in the upper
classes of southern Europe) with a naive simplicity which
is far more charming.

I was received at the home of the prime minister of Norway in precisely the same courteous, genial way. It
happened in the following manner: My host who had been
a prominent member of the Conservative party of Norway,
yet understood that an American's sympathies would be
with the Liberals, and suggested that I should send my
card to the celebrated Liberal minister of state—M. Sverdrup. This was just after the peaceful revolution which had
taken the veto power from the king of Norway. "Upon
the hint I spake"—or rather called at the office of the
minister of state, whom I found an old man, with a bright
and piercing eye, and a pleasant although wrinkled face,
surrounded with callers on political matters, and evidently
fatigued with the legacy of unfinished business left him by
his predecessor. He regretted that his time did not allow
of long conversation, but desired me to call again on the

morrow. But that evening as I sat at supper in the Hotel
Victoria, I was surprised by a visit from M. Cornelius Lee,
an editor of the *Dagbladet*, who informed me that he had
heard of my call upon the minister; that it would never do
that the scope of the Norwegian liberal movement should
be misunderstood in America; and telling me that the prime
minister had sent a dispatch requesting my presence at his
house, a few miles out of the city, and that the carriage was
waiting; in a few moments I was rolling along towards the
premier's residence.   Outside the city, with the fjord lying
tranquilly below our feet, and the rich fragrance from the
gardens around us, I awoke to the glorious beauty of Christiania.   But soon the road wound in among cornfields, and
then among rocks and more desolate scenery, and I began
to think that the prime minister might turn out to be a
bandit who had his cave in some hidden fastness, who would
seize the American newspaper correspondent and demand
ransom of his journals, sending my ears, nose, fingers, etc.,
in separate installments, in the Italian style.   My fears
were soon allayed by the carriage making a sudden turn,
going up a short avenue of trees, and then halting before a
beautifully located mansion surrounded by gardens.   My
hopes were somewhat dashed on learning that important
business had again seized the prime minister, who had, however, deputed his son to speak *ex cathedra* with me upon
Norwegian politics.   The home of the great statesman of
the north interested me greatly.   It lay on an eminence
from which one could view all Christiania; its rooms bore
evidence at every step of the taste and life of the distinguished occupant.   On the walls were portraits of the leading diplomats of Europe, all of them gifts, and generally
signed with the autographs of the originals.   A bust of
Sverdrup himself graced one corner.   The study in the
second story was filled with books in many languages, for

the minister is familiar with almost all modern tongues. M. Jacob Sverdrup, the son of the premier, is himself taking an active part in Norwegian politics. Although young, he was *Stadtrath* of Christiania, and has held other important political positions.

Seated together in the library, over some excellent sherry and cigars, he gave me a succinct account of the causes which had led to the recent constitutional changes in Norway. The king's prerogatives have been reduced so that to-day our president has far more power, and, during all the crises which led to this bloodless revolution, the eyes of Norway have been fixed upon the United States as the model which they must follow. In the debates in the Storthing, as also even in the Reichstag of Sweden, the example of the system of our country and of its success has been frequently cited. The danger of our republic may lie in this very fact. An error of foreign policy would give a certain pretext for more despotic governments to attempt forcibly to cripple a nation which gives such a dangerous lesson to oppressed races. M. Sverdrup thought that the ground gained by the liberal party would never be lost. "Progress never recedes," said he, "if it is allied to moderation."

He acknowledged that America had been a school to his father and himself, and showed a surprising familiarity with our politics, literature and men. Lincoln he esteemed especially, and he was persistent in inquiring as to whether the son would bear the mantle of his father, possibly thinking of his own case, and why he had not come forward prominently in the politics of his country. He knew Beecher, Ingersoll, and many concerned in the religious and political movements of our country, and expressed the hope that some day he might visit us and in a series of lectures explain how closely Scandinavia and America should be natural allies. After this conversation a pleasant stroll in the garden followed, and the conversation became non-political. I was glad to learn, however, how much influence the liberal-minded Björnstjerne Björnsen exercises in Norway. The very fact that he so thoroughly understands American institutions adds to the weight of his influence at home. Now followed a parting " Skole," and I took my departure. A vivid thunder storm enlivened the ride, during which the driver covered the entire carriage with a huge rubber blanket, so that I rode on in total darkness, only hearing the roar of the elements, and alighted at the hotel in a perfect deluge.

The next day, although it was not public day, I was invited to see the old Viking ship which had recently been brought to Christiania. I was astonished at the grace and symmetry of its model. No modern boat could excel it in any great degree. The ship is in excellent preservation, and much of the Viking paraphernalia is also preserved. The large soup kettle, the beds, the shields and the cruel spears bring one vividly back to the heroes sung by the poets. To my mind, they were not heroes at all, only courageous and brutal murderers, and one honest, patient, blue-eyed, flaxen-haired Norwegian of the present is worth the whole ancient lot. Seated that evening by the fjord, I mused upon the contrast, and broke uncontrollably into rhyme, as follows:

A SONG OF THE NORTH.

In ashen twilight of the north,
  In murmured rush of distant streams,
My fancies all went flying forth,
  And I lay wrapt in waking dreams.

Now all the waters of the fjord,
  And all the hills of gloomy green,
Were peopled by a warlike horde
  Of sturdy men of fearless mien.

I saw the fatal Viking's fleet
  Sail out from shore, with strident cries;
I saw the slender warships meet,
  I heard the din of battle rise.

And then the past lay with its dead.
  Again the green hills came in view,
But now there stood in warriors' stead
  A smiling group with eyes of blue.

Their only war was with the soil,
  Loving and gentle all their ways,
They lived and died in simple toil,
  And never knew the poet's praise.

With Viking's laud all harps have rung,
  And singers chant them without cease;
But is there not a kinder tongue
  To sing the victories of peace?

And when the final scroll is read,
  A greater one than that of fame,
Which shall stand nearer to the head—
  The peasant's or the Viking's name?

The next day, after the perpetration of the above poem, I left Christiania suddenly. But not in fear of any dire consequences; I went northward, for M. Sverdrup had informed me of a " Halling " which was to take place in a little village some fifteen miles from the city, and it was too good an opportunity to become acquainted with the music of the peasantry, to be lost. I went in a *carriole*, which is a cross between a hansom cab and a hurricane, and got to the barn where the festival was to be held much quicker than if I had been carried thither on a railroad train—at least a Norwegian one. The people received me pleasantly, for the " stranger that is within thy gates " is more than a mere symbol with these kind-hearted souls, but I found that they were becoming shy of giving vent to all their fun in the presence of an unknown party from across seas. My card helped matters somewhat, for they took the name "Elson" for a mere variation of "Olsen," and as my appearance did not disprove any Norwegian ancestry they might attribute to me, I was gradually passed into the higher degrees of their favor, and when I finally sang a Swedish song, all doubts vanished, in spite of my innocence of the language, and the hilarity soon reached a high pitch, aided just a little, I suspect, by the presence of much of the innocent-looking, but decidedly exciting, aqua vita.

The Halling is a peculiar dance, and belongs to the men only, for the object of the dancers is to touch the overhanging rafters with one foot. Such kicking would have been impossible even in a political convention. Wilder and wilder grew the music, the two fiddlers playing with constantly increasing vehemence as the dancers threw their feet higher and higher, and the applause, the stamping, and clapping, and shouting of the lookers-on grew more emphatic every second. It seemed in vain, for some time, however, and one by one the dancers gave it up, but at last one sturdy youth reached the beam, and with such force, too, that the dust fairly flew around, and he was made the hero of the occasion, and we all drank " Skole " (" Good Health ") to him. The music to all this was very wierd; it was in 2-4 rhythm, full of strong accents, and accompanied almost throughout with a drone bass. Such folk-dances are never vulgar, they are too characteristic for that, and Grieg and Svendsen have done well in perpetuating such rhythms in their classical works, where my musical readers may find them without much search. Even the Russian composers, Rubinstein, Tschaikowsky, etc., have introduced a first cousin of the Halling into their symphonic forms, in the wild Kamarinskaia, a male dance of like character.

But one could not listen to such a hurly-burly forever, and a little aqua vita went a long way, so the next morning found me leaving Norway. I again took the same sedate daily express train, and went down into Sweden. As we wound round a valley I was much interested to see what I thought was a funeral procession coming toward us. As we came nearer, however, I saw that it was the daily express train coming up the line. It must be very difficult for a Norwegian train to keep to its time-table, as it is almost impossible to avoid getting ahead of it. But the engineers are very cautious and reliable. They have a terrible legend, however, of a wild engineer who used to run ahead of time and once nearly had a frightful accident. A man fell asleep with his leg on the railroad track, when this engineer and his train came along. The sleeping man felt something pinch his leg, and awakening saw that it was the express train. He then got off the track in time to save himself. Had he slept five minutes longer, the train would have been completely over his leg and broken it. The engineer was blamed greatly, for he was a reckless man, who sometimes ran as fast as ten miles an hour. I think, however, that this legend has no foundation in fact, for I never saw a Norwegian train in a hurry.

CHAPTER VI.

To SWEDEN—STOCKHOLM—SUMMER MUSIC IN THE FAR NORTH
—THE JOURNEY SOUTHWARD—A CANAL VOYAGE—A BOY
ORCHESTRA—A PROUD PORTER.

Trolhattan, in Sweden, is one of the prettiest places along the northern route. Were it not that the loveliest spots along the river are defaced by numerous sawmills, I should call it "grand." But the charm is somewhat destroyed when one finds the impetuously dashing water busily engaged in slicing wood, and finds its grandeur reckoned at so-and-so many horse power. It is but another case

"Where every prospect pleases,
And only [lumber]-man is vile."

The best view of the falls is obtained from a neighboring height, which, however, is private property, and to which an entrance fee is charged. After my experience in Switzerland, where almost every charm of nature is fenced in and retailed at so much per charm, this did not seem a great hardship, although unusual in the north, and I toiled up the hill, where my companion, the trumpeter, at once sought immortality by cutting his initials on a bench which he found there, while I endeavored to make a profit on my investment of half a *krone* by taking two *krones'* worth of gaze. The water comes down in a manner that recalls Southey's description of the "Cataract of Lodore," and one cannot rid one's self of the impression that such a rushing must soon exhaust the supply; but after waiting an hour for the water to get by, I concluded that it would run on for some time yet. For the benefit of the utilitarian, (whom I despise), I will say that these falls have about 225,000 horse power. There are plenty of "Devil's cauldrons," "Devil's holes," and other satanic places around about, and the evil one evidently did much of his domestic baking and boiling about Trollhattan. Walking back through the town, we passed several instances of the endeavors of the inhabitants to entice the English tourist by mangling his mother tongue. One sign read "shaving house," and I can certify that the mangling inside was equal to that without. I found a touch of home in watching a game of "hop-scotch" among the village children, but when these all made me pretty bows and curtsies at the end of the game, the resemblance to the American "small boy" ceased altogether. Our hotel was the Railway Hotel; but let no misguided reader suppose that we were rendered sleepless on account of the bustle of travel. During the day and night we stopped here we saw but one train, and even that came forward in a shy and bashful manner, as if ashamed of disturbing our tranquility. Only when the bill came in were we made aware, by the solid charges, that we were at a railway hotel. The "Charge of the Light Brigade" was not a circumstance to the charges of Hanna Andersen, our blue-eyed hostess.

At Trollhattan we took the canal boat for Stockholm. It is a long journey, as the Göta canal, (including the lakes), is 260 miles long, and if Swedish railroads are slow, Swedish canal boats are slower. The boat on which we embarked was the Wadstena, and I shall never forget what a floating home she became to me, because of the hospitality of Captain Julius Ericsson, who took me under his wing with a jovial kindness that cannot be found anywhere outside of northern

Europe. I also found a hearty comrade in a young German lieutenant, Herr von Bötzow, of Stettin. This gentleman, when at home, is an *Oberlandesgerichtsreferendar*, but he is young, and his title may grow longer in time. I have said that Captain Ericsson did all that he could to make me comfortable, but he could not hold the boat quiet on the larger lakes. The Göta canal is a queer institution. It moves along as quietly as a duck pond in a garden, for a while, and after you have settled down to a solid *dolce far niente*,the boat suddenly emerges into a lake a hundred miles long, and furious in proportion, and sadness, sorrow, and seasickness drive out all thoughts of repose. I shall always remember Lake Wenern, during the passage of which the boat tried to turn double somersaults, with a reasonable degree of success. It was dinner time and I sought the cabin, where I found the stewardess plunged in despair and sugar. The meal had been spread when the boat struck the lake, which struck back and upset the arrangements—and the table. The floor was strewn with a substratum of sugar, upon which were super-posed portions of caviare, bread, butter, cake and other comestibles. It called to mind the interrupted feast of Belshazzar, and various other classical and scriptural pictures of culinary desolation, but it chiefly brought to mind the fact that we should have no dinner until the lake was crossed—a matter of some hours. When dinner did come it was of the solid Swedish type, with half an hour's preparatory exercise upon the viands of the sideboard, as described in a previous chapter. Truly the Scandinavians work upon the French motto— "L'appetit vient en mangeant."

Although I have heard many people abuse the mode of travel on the Göta canal, I must say that it is among the pleasantest of my northern reminiscences; and to a traveler who will divest himself of all American hurry, and who desires to travel right through the heart of the country, I can confidently commend it. Many were the pleasant customs we saw; many the delightful side excursions that we made. At one lock, in the midst of a beautiful flower garden, some Swedish maids came out and bombarded us with dahlias as we passed through. At Vreka we walked a few miles into the country while the boat was receiving freight, and viewed an old church founded in the twelfth century, and not far from this we passed an old ruin which was once the home of the Douglases, who had left Scotland and taken service with the Swedish kings. Of this castle a legend is told which may interest Free Masons. During the session of a lodge of Masons at the castle, a lady was imprudent enough to conceal herself and listen to all their secrets. She was discovered and beheaded. A terrible *denouement*, but I believe it is not the only instance of a lady losing her head when she had an important secret to keep.

We made a very interesting side trip on foot at Södersjöping. The Wadstena had to go through several locks here, and we determined to see the town or perish in the attempt. We also desired to see the Tivoli Garden, in order that we might have our collection of Tivolis complete. Our advent in the public square of the place caused a sensation. I had inquired our way of some of the inhabitants, in the choicest Bostonian Swedish, without eliciting a satisfactory reply, and the concourse about us were evidently taking an interest in the newest thing in languages, and trying to find out what I meant. It was as good as playing rebuses, only the fun was all on one side. It was not on our side. At last a happy thought struck Mr. Smith; giving a tremulous "tarantara" he began playing an imaginary cornet; our trumpeter, with a "boom, boom," started a bass drum; I played an aerial flute. This object lesson was not thrown away upon the attentive audience.   They thought us a brass band in search of an engagement, and took us to the Tivoli.   Lieutenant Bötzow and myself had acquired a decided hunger in our wandering, and ordered a light meal.   This is what they brought us: Radishes, sardines, sausages, cheese, schnapps, oat cakes, potatoes, bread and butter, onions and beefsteak. The expense was one krone—twenty-seven cents.   A pleasant summer concert in the open air, in the long twilight of a northern climate, is one of the dreamiest tastes of paradise that one can attain on this mundane sphere, and a mere Tivoli concert becomes as enjoyable as a symphonic one when the beautiful surroundings are taken into consideration.

After hearing some very fair music, we wended our way back to the " Wadstena," and soon were again steaming towards Stockholm.

I cannot descibe the enchantment of that last night of the trip.   The canal ran through heavily shaded parks and wonderfully romantic groves.   The moon was out in its full glory and was reflected in the water, on which not a ripple could be seen save the broad wave made by our own boat. The passengers had gone to rest; only the captain and I were on the upper deck; everything breathed tranquility and rest. It was Rosenthal's picture of Elaine (where " the dead, steered by the dumb, went upwards with the tide ") transferred to a living canvas; a fitting end to one of the most peaceful of journeys.   The next morning all was changed; we were upon Lake Malaren, and approaching Stockholm.   All was activity and life.   Pleasant country-seats fringed the sides of the various inlets.   Boats of all kinds dashed past, some gayly decorated with banners.   Active preparations for a regatta were being made at one of the suburbs, and racing yachts were gathering in profusion; and when, in the bright, cool Sunday morning air, we heard the church bells of Södertelge ring out a crisp chime, I was ready to believe that I was a special correspondent in Fairyland, and that such a brilliant, contented scene could not belong to earth. Several peddlers of gingerbread came on board the boat, however, and convinced me of the mundane reality of the picture. I had forgotten to state that previously, on the canal, I had been inveigled into the meshes of a lace vender, and had bought wonderful Swedish laces (sealed with a seal, too) at wonderfully high prices. But the gingerbread was still more wonderful. So was the dyspepsia which followed it. But here we were at Stockholm, and it only remained to bid farewell to our kindly captain, who, however, told me that he should look me up in the town after I had got fairly settled.

Arrived at the Hotel Rydberg, I felt that it was a duty which I owed to society to get shaved; and stepping out of the front door, I found what promised to be an elegant tonsorial establishment, two doors to the left. Seated in the barber's chair, with the memory of the encounter at the Trollhattan " Shaving House " still before me, I prepared to submit to the ordeal. A fair maiden of some sixteen summers stepped forward, and to her I expressed the desire that she would send her father, brother, or cousin, to torture me. She stepped forward, she put the towel under my neck. I was a prisoner in the hands of a young and handsome female barber! There was no escape! Disregarding my blushes, she took hold of my nose; she lifted my mustache, she prodded her fingers into my cheeks, she smiled in a heavenly manner all the time. I do not know how long it took, I only know that it cost four cents, and that when I recovered from my astonishment, an hour afterwards, I wanted to go back and get shaved again. I took a bath afterwards, but when I saw there was a motherly-looking lady who brought me the accessories, I barricaded the door, as I felt that I was not quite used to Stockholm customs yet, and didn't know how far they might extend.

Stockholm impressed me as being topographically somewhat like Geneva. Its division by water, and the rows of large hotels on both banks, aid this resemblance greatly; but the great hills and the vast pleasure parks of the city are totally different from the Swiss metropolis. The English and American papers at the hotel were a perfect godsend, for I had seen nothing but Swedish papers for some days, and these always seemed more like an alphabet in a fit of delirium tremens than anything else. I went with Lieut. von Bötzow to see guard-mounting at the palace. The Swedish soldiers did not seem excessively military in appearance, and my companion often snorted out his disdain; but to a German officer all the rest of the world seem but raw recruits. After that we went to the National Museum, one of the finest (especially in the department of antiquities) and certainly the best arranged in Europe. I studied how the prehistoric man prepared his corn, cooked his coffee, and attended his debating society—with a stone club. I feel bound to state that I did not find any traces of the rise of the Italian operatic chorus among the relics of the stone age, although I fully expected to. But I am not going to describe the museum. After going through half a dozen museums one is ready to acknowledge that the ancients knew every modern improvement. I am so surfeited with European museums of antiquities that if any one were to show me the bicycle used by Homer, or Nero's private transmitter in the consolidated Roman telephone company, I should not wince or be astonished. I feel in entire sympathy with the little boy in "Punch" who, when his grandfather promised him a reward if he would tell him what pleased him most in the Crystal Palace World's Fair, instantly replied, "The veal-and-'am pies; give us the sixpence!"

I want to pay a New Englander's tribute to the Swedish weather. For rapidity of change, for highly seasoned contrast, and for catching one unawares, it is the champion weather of the world. When I had been rained upon, dried in the sun, smothered with dust, and again wetted down in the course of a short hour, I began to feel at home, and thought I was enjoying a beautiful spring day in Boston.

One consolation is denied me. I cannot watch the fluctuations of the thermometer, for the Europeans go by the Reaumur system, and when I am baking I find the mercury only at 28°, and when I feel very comfortable I find it at 20° and know that I ought to be shivering.

Stockholm is a wild and giddy town, unfit for theological students and newspaper correspondents. It has cafés enough to give one apiece to every inhabitant, and each café has its own brass band; consequently the effect upon a Sunday is as if one had dropped into a circus unawares. One of the prettiest of the pleasure resorts, and right in the heart of the city too, is the *Strom-parterre*, a neatly-kept little peninsula, which juts out into the green waters of the *Saltsjon*, and affords a beautiful view of the city. Here I heard an orchestra which was unique in its way. It numbered some seventy performers, all of whom were small boys. It was interesting to see three feet of humanity trying to play six feet of bass fiddle, and to find the big drum towering high above its performer. But they made good music and would make the fortune of any manager who should bring them to America. I will not give your readers an inventory of all the cafés that I passed (some of which I did *not* pass) during the first day of my stay in Stockholm. Suffice it to say that at last I found myself in the Djürgarten at Hasselbackers. This dreadful name is not Swedish for "lockup." It is the pleasure park *par excellence* of Stockholm. Seated in the open air, with a beautiful view spread out on every side, the Stockholmer can listen to excellent music, and drink his beer or coffee at the same time. I only wish that any words of mine could impress the geniality, the respectability, the sobriety of the picture upon the American public. Here are entire families sitting contentedly in the pure, fresh air, taking recreation in a manner which all can afford, and which will brighten up the entire week of labor. They have attended to their religious duties in the morning, the afternoon is given to this absolute rest. There is, of course, no trace of intoxication, and none of the hurry and excitement of an American excursion.

Stockholm is absolutely encircled by beautiful suburbs. The approach to most of these is by water, and little steam launches carry passengers in every direction. On the second day of my stay in the capital I made a flying trip to some of these in company with some gentlemen well acquainted with the neighborhood. Captain Ericsson did not forget his promise to look me up, for on my return from the Djürgarten I found a card desiring me to come on board the Wadstena the next morning at 8:30 o'clock. Arriving on board the vessel, I found my noble captain still in the arms of Morpheus; but a little thundering on the door of his stateroom brought him out, and a pleasant Swedish greeting and a matutinal cup of fragrant coffee followed, during which the plan for the day was unfolded to me. It was that we should board a neighboring steamer and go down to Drottingholm, where we would have an opportunity of visiting the palace of King Adolf Frederic, and meeting other friends of Captain Ericsson.

At that early hour, on a windy Monday morning, it was natural that few passengers should be aboard. We had the ship all to ourselves, and the commander, Captain Erwitsson, soon joined our circle. The journey to Drottingholm revealed again the beauties of the environs of Stockholm.

Dainty white villas, nestling in valleys of velvety green, heavily wooded hills that seemed primeval in their solitude, and the foaming green waters, wildly driven in the fresh and healthy breeze; a more revivifying *entourage* it would be impossible to imagine. But this breeze had its effect elsewhere than upon our hearts, and when we arrived a wild cry went up—"Breakfast!"

At the end of half an hour we had recovered our calmness, and started for the palace. First we came (through grand avenues of lofty trees) to a Chinese pavilion. This building is said to have been completed in a single night, by Adolf Frederic, to surprise his queen. It is a very solid building and it is a very solid story. In return I told them the story of George Washington and his little hatchet, and added that if they deceived innocent journalists with such "Aladdin's lamp" stories, R. E. Morse would dwell with them after I had gone. It is not necessary to describe the palace. I have visited most of the palaces of Europe, and not one of the potentates has returned my call, although I generally wrote down my name and address so that they might know where to find me. The king's family was out when I called at Drottingholm palace, but perhaps it was wrong for me to visit on washing-day, and in the morning, too! Pleasanter than the palace was a cosey sit-down in the garden, where we were joined by two Norwegian friends and took coffee. You will observe that we punctuated our trip with many of these pauses, but the Scandinavian eats and drinks anywhere, and the climate enables him to stand a strain that would carry off a New York alderman. We all went back together and, once on board of the Wadstena again, we gathered all the neighboring sea captains, and in glasses of a truly national drink—Swedish punch—we drank our parting "skole."

Swedish punch is strong enough to deserve an article all by itself. It has a sweet and gentle taste.

> "Take care! Beware!
> Trust it not, it is fooling thee."

I left the party betimes, first bidding a cordial farewell to captain Ericsson, than whom I have never met a more hearty companion and kindly gentleman.

The next day I started on a long and tedious journey to Malmö in southern Sweden. Again came all the horrors of railway travel at the pace of a stagecoach, but here at least they were mitigated by excellent railway carriages. The scenery was generally flat and uninteresting, and time hung heavy on my hands. Soon, however, an intelligent fellow traveler entered my compartment and opened conversation with me in German. The news of the rescue of a party of arctic explorers had made some sensation in the north, and our chat soon turned to this subject. To my surprise the gentleman spoke as one having authority in such matters. "You Americans," said he, "have more bravery than any other of the explorers, yet your expeditions do not always bring out the best results. There is often more daring than calm, scientific research in them. But you have given some information about the northern botany, and I hope the Greely expedition will give more." With that omniscience which belongs to a journalist, I told him that the northern botany must be very insignificant indeed. He smiled and—contradicted me. He gave me dozens of ten-syllabled names of plants that grew around the arctic circle, until I began to think that the north pole must be a sort of May pole gayly festooned with flowers. Then I suggested that we exchange cards to facilitate conversation. It was Professor Berggren, botanist of the two great Nordenskjöld expeditions. After that I gave him no further hints about arctic flora or fauna. But at all events, fate had sent me a pleasant *compagnon du voyage* on what promised to be a most tedious journey, for Mr. Smith and my trumpeter had gone on before and were waiting for me in Hamburg. I did not stay in Malmö more than half an hour, and therefore will not write a full description of the manners and customs of the inhabitants. I took the boat at once to Copenhagen and was soon again in my old quarters in the Hotel d'Angleterre. In Copenhagen I found the thermometer down to a chilling point, Svendsen in bed with a severe cold, and M. Ovide Musin shivering through Mendelssohn's violin concerto at the Tivoli. To add to my discomforts I had a delicious bit of an illustration of the beauties of the tipping system, at the hotel. During my first day here I found the servants most obsequious. They gave me the title of "von" Elson, and I felt that I might yet rise to an earldom, if I behaved myself and the small coins held out. *Vanitas vanitatem, omnia vanitas!* In an evil moment I had left the hotel in a hurry, in the early morning, and thus had tipped only the night porter and his subordinates. The day porter and his squad had been wounded by me in their tenderest point—the pocket. Thenceforward I led a dual existence. Dr. Jekyll and Mr. Hyde were twins in comparison with the difference of my estate by day and night. If I came in at night I had a reception of high degree; the night porter bowed to the earth, and his minions addressed me in humble tones by noble titles. But, alas! when day came all was changed. The proud day porter belonged to a "stiff-necked generation" apparently and would not unbend even so far as to nod to me. His followers looked at me with scorn and reproach in their glances, as if to say, "This is the man whom we took for a nobleman, and who has turned out to be a pickpocket and has robbed us of our tips." Coleridge speaks with tremendous power of "the curse of a dead man's eye." If he had seen the glances of my waiters and porter, he would have changed his simile. At last I determined to make good my omission, if only to see the effect upon the porter's joints. I gave him a krone. Thenceforward all was well. He became like the "proud young porter," in the ballad of "Lord Bateman," and almost "fell on bended knee." All my old titles were restored to me and new ones added, but they were only Dead Sea fruit. How could I believe that the hireling thought me a count, when but the day before he had held me of no account?

The above is "founded on fact," as the novelists say, and very much so. It shows the bane of the system of tipping, and also to the servility to which it leads. In Germany the latter is even more pronounced, and I more than once had to pity the poor wretches who have positions beneath these flunkeys. I saw one waiter cuff a refined looking lad who was late in bringing a dish, through no fault of his own. I saw this insolence and brutality on one side, and absolute humility on the other, extending through almost every part, and in almost every rank, of the empire, and I felt glad that I was an American, and that at home the dignity and equality of man was recognized. Better far an occasional insolence from one of the uneducated classes than such a general stamping out of self respect. And I felt the more sorry when I thought that each of these abused underlings would abuse somebody else when his turn came.

I left Copenhagen, and my now affable porter, behind and went to Kiel. There was little else to do but to read the Hamburg paper which I found there. A Hamburg newspaper is a whole library in itself. It has about seventeen supplements, and as many of them run back for a week or so, they equalize matters by dating the evening edition to-morrow morning. By the time this was finished I was ready to take the train for Hamburg, and from Hamburg I started on my pilgrimage to the mecca of the musician of the 19th century, (or at least this end of it), Bayreuth, and the performances of "Parsifal."

WAGNER'S OPERA HOUSE,

BAYREUTH.

CHAPTER VII.

BAYREUTH—A SLEEPY GERMAN TOWN BEFORE THE FESTIVAL
—A VISIT TO MADAM WAGNER—THE FIRST PERFORMANCES
OF THE FESTIVAL—PARSIFAL—DIE MEISTERSINGER—AN
EVENING AT ANGERMANN'S—MIDNIGHT REVELRIES—A
MEETING WITH THE PRINCE OF HESSE—A RECEPTION AT
MADAM WAGNER'S.

There is a story of a conductor on a certain slow railroad
demanding a ticket from an old man. "Why," said the
ancient, "I gave it to you when I got on at Ashtown Junc-
tion!" "Not much," responded the conductor, "there
was only a little boy got aboard the train there." "I know it,"
said the old man with a sigh, "I was that little boy!" I used
to doubt the probability of that story but after my ride to
Bayreuth on the "post-zug" I doubt no more. It must
have happened on the Royal Bavarian Railway. The inhabitants call the train "der Bummelzug," which may be
freely translated as "the railway-bummer."

Nevertheless, I am not going to quarrel with anything
that happens to me in travel after the great and elevating
experience of the Bayreuth festival.

The frame of the picture was not less interesting than the
wonderful festival itself. Fancy a small German city
changed in a night from a sleepy community into a gather-
ing-place of the highest nobility and the greatest musicians
of the world. The approach from Hamburg was animated

enough. French, Germans, English, Spanish, Italians, and
even Turks and Russians were on the train, all having one
object and one sympathetic bond. The tickets for the first
performance of "Parsifal" had been sold out weeks before
and fancy prices, even up to 100 marks, were offered for
seats. It must be confessed, however, that this enthusiasm
expended itself more spontaneously (in 1888 and 1889) on
" die Meistersinger " than on " Parsifal."   The latter work
is certainly a great one, but it is of that uncomfortable order
of greatness which demands considerable intelligence and
study on the part of the auditor. Hearing it for the fourth
time, I only begin to comprehend the vastness of its ideas
and the depth of its expression. How, then, can one expect the pilgrims who come for the first time to the Wagnerian shrine, to glow with a really honest fervor?   To study
Bayreuth in festival time is to study nearly all of the greatest
musical celebrities of Europe.

July 20th the town was still in its normal condition, dull,
sleepy and apathetic ; but early on the next morning
matters began to change with the rapidity of a fairy transformation scene. Train after train came in, crowded in
every compartment, and bearing the motliest assemblage
that ever a caricaturist could dream of. Fat, florid, and
bespectacled men jostled against lean, long-haired specimens
of the genus music professor, and the way in which greetings and kisses were interchanged was appalling to the
American eye.

At eight in the evening fresh impetus was given to the
growing excitement by the arrival of the special train from
Vienna, bearing a vast crowd of South German artists and
musicians. Locomotive decked with flowers, and flags hanging over some of the carriages, it slowly pushed into the
immense crowd gathered at the station to welcome it. As
it came the band on the platform began "Gott erhalte Franz,

den Kaiser,'' and to the strains of the Austrian National hymn, and amid wild and prolonged cheering, the travelers stepped into the crowded streets. Many Americans were at the station.

Correspondents from all over the world were there, and anxiety about lodgings grew apace. It was an odd spectacle to find princes lodging above grocers' shops and princesses coming to dwell with well-to-do sausage makers. The little city was full of hackmen, and I wondered how they got a living in ordinary times. The mystery was soon explained. Jumping into one of the carriages I loftily said, "To Villa Wahnfried!" The driver looked at me in a dazed condition (no, it wasn't bad German!) and helplessly asked, "Where is it?" I thought it strange that a Bayreuth hackman should not know Wagner's villa, but waived the question and said: "First to Herr Apotheke Meyer's, 435 Friedrichs-strasse," whereupon my charioteer incontinently weakened, confessed that he knew nothing about the town, but had come with many others of the same sort, from Nuremberg to make an honest penny during the festival. It was the blind leading the blind! We wandered together through many streets, my Jehu drawing up at almost every pedestrian who looked native, for further instructions. It was an undignified and plebeian sort of a carriage ramble, and I declined to seek Villa Wahnfried after we had found my domicile in the Friedrichs-strasse.

It was a great delight to live with a quiet German family during the rush of the festival, and to be able to withdraw occasionally from the bustle of publicity into the cool and neat rooms which we occupied. I use "we" no longer in the editorial sense, for three companions joined me in Bayreuth, Messrs. Geo. E. Whiting and Carl Faelten, and Miss Fanny Paine, were these musically inclined ones, and welcome arrivals they were to the somewhat isolated traveler.

But they were not the only ones.   Mr. Gericke soon put
in an appearance in the city, then Franz Kneisel and Svecenski; then came Clayton Johns, Arthur Foote, and Eliot
Hubbard, then Otto Floersheim, of New York, then Misses
Everest and Knox, of Philadelphia, until an entire American
colony was formed.   You may imagine that a jolly Kneipe
was soon arranged at Angermann's, the artists' restaurant of
the city.   How the frenzy of anticipation grew!   Everybody
was fraternizing with everybody else the next morning; beer
was being poured down with a vigor that spoke volumes
for the irrigating powers of Wagnerians.   Informal receptions were going on everywhere.   I heard my name called
just opposite the Golden Anchor Hotel.   On looking up,
there was Materna in the second story of a fruit dealer's
house, holding a sort of sidewalk levee from her window.
"I won't see any of you to-day," she called out, "not till I
have finished my part of 'Parsifal';" but none the less half
a dozen friends kept up their conversation with her at long
range.   Many were disappointed regarding tickets to "Parsifal."   When a young man heard that I had an extra one
which I would sell him at regular rates, he embraced me,
(bother that continental fashion), and almost wept for joy.
He wanted to repeat the same performance in the theatre,
but I would allow no encores.

I put in part of the morning in a call on Mme. Cosima
Wagner.   I scarcely dared hope that at such a busy time
she would receive me, and the stately butler bore out this
impression by saying: "The gracious lady may perhaps see
you next Tuesday evening, but not now;" but took in my letter and a greeting from Mr. Emil Mahr, our Boston violinist,
and almost immediately came out with an invitation for me
to enter.   Through a fine entrance hall, in which stood a
magnificent piano and organ, we went into a room half
drawing-room, half boudoir, in which sat a slim and graceful,

FRAU AMALIE MATERNA,
AS KUNDRY IN "PARSIFAL," BAYREUTH, 1888.

but not beautiful, lady, writing. She arose and greeted me with cordiality, and in a few moments by kindly question and unaffected conversation put me at ease.

I have said that she was not beautiful, but there was something more than real beauty in the noble face and expressive eyes, that kindled with loftier light when she spoke of the works of her great husband. She inquired whether the Wagnerian music was taking root in America, and expressed a dread lest it should become merely a fashion. "It must be explained, it must not be misunderstood, or half understood," she said, "and then it will grow." She spoke of America as a great field for such work, and hoped that it might be cultivated properly. She was delighted when I told her of what had been done there by lecture and essay. She inquired after American friends, and particularly Mr. B. J. Lang, and was interested in Mr. Damrosch's Wagnerian labors among us. She said that Mr. Anton Seidl, of New York, was a worker whose labors would bear fruit for the cause, and his letters to her gave her ground to hope for a spread of the appreciation of her husband's music. In all the interview, while never becoming excited, she impressed me as a woman who is terribly in earnest, and who lives, like the great Clara Schumann, to glorify her husband's memory and fame. She was not entirely satisfied with the number of rehearsals which had preceded the festival. "We have been at work steadily for three weeks," said she. "It ought to have been six, but the singers could not leave their theatrical engagements. It is true that many of them have sung 'Parsifal' before, but 'Parsifal' is an opera that needs to be studied over anew every time it is performed. 'Die Meistersinger' is easier, but that also cannot have too much rehearsal."

She then asked if there were many Americans in the city. "Every year they say a great many are coming, but when

one counts them up they scarcely number a score." I
hastened to assure the gracious lady that I knew personally
of some fifty who were coming, and that I had no doubt
the number would reach two hundred or more, at which she
expressed hearty gratification, as also at the fact that the
nobility were coming in great numbers. "One wants the
people, but it is gratifying to have an audience of exceptional rank on such an exceptional occasion." She hoped
that my stay would be prolonged over her reception evening
on the following Tuesday, and gave me a cordial invitation
to call again before leaving the city.

Our conversation was in German, but I understand that
the daughter of Liszt has all the linguistic abilities which
her father so richly possessed. The resemblance of Madame
Wagner to her father, Liszt, was more marked than ever
as she grew animated. Our interview soon drew to a close,
as both of us had to prepare for the festival. A short visit
to the grave of the great master followed. It is a broad
slab of stone, simply set in a wide mound, which is covered
with ivy and is at the rear of the house—the Villa Wahnfried. I recalled a visit to that grave, when Madame Wagner
had not yet taken up the noble mission which now causes
her to live and to take interest in life. It was in 1883. The
sudden death of her beloved husband had almost destroyed
her reason. She had cut off her beautiful long tresses (because Wagner had admired them) and placed them in his
coffin; Liszt had come to Bayreuth, but she refused to see
him; only the boy, Siegfried, because he was the favorite of
his father, was suffered to approach her; and every day, in
rain or sunshine, she would sit two hours or more beside
that lonely grave. She allowed none other near it, and it
was only by the connivance of an underling that I was finally
able to visit the resting place of the greatest composer of
his epoch. Now all this has changed, and the imperial

band, by command of the Kaiser, played a dirge there during the festival.

And now for the opera! Through the town, past the railway station and up the hill beyond, we drove, and there in its wealth of picturesque surrounding stood the large but simple building. When I use the adjective "large," it must be understood to apply to the stage rather than the auditorium. The latter is not large, but every comfort is there for the public, and every facility for scenic effect. The orchestra is out of sight. The auditorium is very plain, so as not to distract the attention of the audience from the stage. The pitch of the seats is at such a steep angle that not even the highest hat worn by a fashionable lady could obstruct the view. All is shrouded in utter darkness in the front part of the house during the performance, every ray of light being concentrated on the stage. Applause during any part of the opera is not tolerated, not even at the end of acts, but rhapsodical frenzy may be indulged in, ad libitum, at the end of the opera.

Between the acts the entire audience files out of the theater and seeks refreshments in the beautiful grounds and lovely walks of the great park in which the theater stands. Those who are not ethereal enough to live on mountain scenery can find beer, wine, and food (if they can capture a waiter) in the great restaurant belonging to the place. These are necessary precautions, for the operas begin at 4 P. M. and last until 10 or 10:30, while the waits between the acts range from thirty to sixty minutes. What a crush outside the theater! Princes, counts, dukes, musicians, professors, peasants, police, waiters, carriages, celebrities of all kinds, and great composers are as plenty as blackberries in August. If the building were to be blown up during the performance, there would be very little music made in the world for the next ten years, and half the conservatories of music would have to put up their shutters.

And what a set of artists are to perform! Even the
chorus singers to-day are great artists, the very smallest
roles being taken by soloists of eminence from all over
Europe. Every performer in the orchestra is a great solo
artist. Never in the wide world was there such a gathering and never, except at Bayreuth, can it be again.

The lights are down, and amid an almost painful silence
the prelude begins. Comparisons are odious, but at least I
(the professional fault finder) may compare Bayreuth with
Bayreuth; the "Parsifal" of one festival with that of the
other festivals. In this comparison, I find Conductor Mottl
a little inclined to drawl matters; a little given to mistake lack of spirit, and slowness, for majesty. But there
are no actual faults to be found when one considers that
"Parsifal" is the most difficult opera ever written, and that
Bayreuth is probably the only city where it can be produced
at all.

Just a shade of nervousness is apparent in the opening
notes, betrayed by a slightly flat intonation, which is afterward caught by Kundry also, possibly from the holy hermit
Gurnemanz. But this passes away very soon, and Materna
becomes what she has been in the previous festivals—an
ideal Kundry. When Van Dyck enters as Parsifal, all are
for a moment anxious, for Winkelmann has always sustained this role, and grandly, while Van Dyck is known to
sing well enough in Dutch and French, but can he fully
succeed in a German role? At the first sentence, "Gewiss!
im Fluge treff ich was fliegt," I felt a cold shiver, for it was
given with the sharp articulation of the Berlin tradesman.
A Berlinese Parsifal (a character akin to the Saviour) would
be a holy terror. Fortunately it is only the first plunge,
and Parsifal becomes really marvelous in the hands of the
great singer and actor.

Can I describe the scenic effects in cold type? No; that

would be as difficult as to explain Raphael's "Fornarina" to a blind man, or the fifth symphony to a deaf one. The great panoramas of the walks to the castle in the first and third acts, the wonderful processions of the knights and pages, the disappearance of Klingsor's Castle, the changing of the tropical garden to a desert—all these and more can only be understood and marvelled at by those who have seen them.

The care with which the Wagnerian traditions were preserved may be illustrated by the fact that the bearer of the holy grail was the same woman who was chosen by Wagner years ago for the office because he noticed one day in Bayreuth that she had a stately walk. This may also serve to show Wagner's care in all details of stage management.

Yet it is but a step from the sublime to the ridiculous, and the single stride and pause of the march of the knights seems a trifle like theatrical pomposity, while the lifting up of the grail and its suddenly giving forth a red glow, is a rather prosaic effect in these days of electric lighting, and suggests frivolous rather than deep thoughts. Yet ridicule dare not find a place here, for as one hears the motive of pity, broken and anguished, at the end of the first act, expressive of Parsifal's compassion and inability to express himself, one forgets a few slightly bombastic effects in the true greatness of the whole.

The wonder is, too, that the man who could compose so lofty a first or third act could also write so enticing, passionate, and sensuous a scene as the second act. It is a contrast almost unparalleled in the domain of music. Van Dyck was to my mind very great in this latter part, and his wild cry of "Amfortas!" as Kundry almost succeeds in her temptation was thrilling in the extreme. Certainly Materna and Van Dyck shared the honors. Strange to say, there were few to share. I had never seen so little enthu-

siasm as at the end of the "Parsifal" performance in
Bayreuth in 1888. In later years poorer performances won
much greater applause. The next day "Die Meistersinger"
made amends by causing an absolute furor. I attribute the
lack of enthusiasm to two causes: first, the performance,
great as it was, was not quite as great as those of the preceding three festivals, and the musicians who had built their
hopes higher than ever felt just a shade disappointed;
second, those who saw the glory of the work and the performance for the first time, were unaware of the rigid rule
not to applaud "Parsifal" until the end of the entire piece,
and after they had endeavored to applaud at the end of the
first and second acts, and been twice sternly repressed with
hisses, they did not dare to venture on any further display
of enthusiasm.

At the end of the performance all the artists rushed to
Angermann's. Angermann's, now, alas! no more, was the
tavern where all the Wagnerians used to meet after the performances in the old days. Beer went up nearly 50 per cent.
(from 13 to 20 pfennige per glass) and went down yet more
rapidly, while a babel of voices in half a dozen different
languages were yelling their comments on the first performance of the festival, and they kept on commenting, I hear,
until the witching hour of 6 A. M. Consequently many
musicians were seen the next day with that calm, subdued,
resigned expression which indicates either *Katzenjammer* or
piety. I dont believe it was piety!

The second day found us climbing up the hill to the
theatre again to hear "Die Meistersinger." To me "The
Mastersingers of Nuremberg" seems the very best of Wagner's works, and the greatest opera ever written. It does
not bring the auditor in contact with gods and goddesses,
but presents to him a story full of human interest. Its auto-

biographical style (for Walther is Wagner) but adds to this, and the fierce and grand satire of it all is worthy of Aristophanes.

The opera gives abundant opportunity for stage display (it is the most faithful and perfect picture of life in the 16th century), and as the Bayreuth theatre is famous for this kind of thing and as Richter was to direct the music, expectation was on tiptoe.

The house was entirely sold out. From the first scene already one felt that the masterwork was to receive a master performance. Let me, in order that I may uninterruptedly sing praises, at once state the only faults that took place in the six hour's representation. The dispute of meistersingers at the end of the first act was out of tune, sinking almost a semitone below the orchestral pitch; the riot-finale of the second act had the same fault (not a great fault in this scene, however); the prize song of Walther was out of tune with the accompaniment (Richter was right and the singer, Gudehus, was wrong); Pogner's address was rather lifeless; and, finally, the curtain did not go up promptly after the prelude of the last act, and one heard Richter's bass voice shouting from the pit in which the orchestra is concealed (sometimes satirically called "the Olympian heights"), "Auf! Auf!" a thing which does not often occur in the Bayreuth theatre.

There! the fault-finding part of Othello's occupation's gone! The keenest microscope could not detect another shortcoming worthy of mention. It was a performance worth traveling across the ocean to see and hear; it was the most perfect rendering of the loftiest work; it was something which my readers must take on faith, for no pen can describe it. Frau Sucher was Eva, while Gudehus, although no longer in his first youth, made a brilliant Walther von Stolzing. Hans Sachs was performed by Reichmann and

with all the hearty German humor that the part demanded.
Hofmüller was David, and a fine one, but Beckmesser!
glorious Beckmesser! in whose person Wagner typified his
own enemies!   Friedrichs made a triumph in this part with
which all Bayreuth rang that night and the next day.

Spite of the impossibility of the task, I want to impart
some little idea of the wonders of the performance to those
who skip along with my European staccato.   The scene of
the second act is a narrow street in Nuremburg; one of
those mediæval *gassen*, in which the houses lean over and
hob-nob with each other in a friendly manner, as if they
were telling each other stories of the past.   In New York
this scene was given in a street almost as wide as Broadway,
but in Bayreuth the proper proportions were observed.
The riot was superb in its effect in the narrow thorough-
fare; the whole street seemed filled with a struggling, howl-
ing mob.

Meanwhile in each of the houses one could see people
getting up, window after window was opened, and in various stages of dishabille, people looked down on the scene
below.   The watchman did not attempt to sing his part, but
gave it in the unpolished manner in which Nuremberg
watchmen sang the hours.   His horn was not set in pitch
with the orchestra, but was purposely in a key of its own,
so as not to give a musical, but a realistic effect.   These
latter are slight points, but they serve to show the attention
given to every minor detail.

No historian could have made the great scene of the last
act more truly representative of its epoch.   The marching
of the Guilds, the dance of the apprentices, with its wonderfully constructed rhythm of seven-barred phrases, the
entrance of the singers, the costumes of the vast crowd,
(every one in the great chorus being a solo singer or concert
vocalist of eminence), and to crown all, the magnificent

"WAHNFRIED,"

WAGNER'S RESIDENCE AT BAYREUTH.

painting of Nuremberg in the background, made a scene which none of the spectators will ever forget. Orchestral details were as carefully observed. Natural trumpets were used in the fanfares; the quaint effect of the muted trumpets at the march of the toymakers' guild, was well brought out, and the shrill-toned harp with steel wires was used to accompany Beckmesser's ludicrous solos.

The climax of the last act was simply overwhelming. I cannot chronicle every perfection of the performance, but it may convey some idea of its success when I state that absolute frenzy took possession of the audience at its close. For ten minutes hurrah upon hurrah, waving of handkerchiefs and general tumult proved that the marvelous performance and the grandeur of the work had struck home. Then everybody went to Angermann's—the artistic rendezvous for beer and plebeian food,—and no wonder; for six hours there had been little but music poured into them. There were, to be sure, two restaurants in the theatre grounds, but they were calculated to serve about fifty guests; when, therefore, fifteen hundred appeared, the mourners were somewhat crowded. You have often read of the pleasures of the chase; there was plenty of excitement, but very little pleasure, in chasing those Bayreuth waiters. I have often applauded Mr. Franz Kneisel's performances in Boston, but never did I appreciate his artistic worth as thoroughly as when, after the second act, he plunged into the thick of the melee and emerged, like Venus from the sea, bearing five sandwiches and four glasses of beer! Decidedly he is a genius! To see orchestral directors take up the role of waiters, (many of them were obliged to do so or famish), was exhilarating. "They also serve who only stand and wait."

And so, at the end of it all, we had all of us gravitated to Angermann's and sat in the little vaulted room (in the midst of an atmosphere that could have been cut with a knife) on boards, beer barrels, anything that afforded a roosting-place, somewhat crowded but supremely happy. Let not any strait-laced New Englander imagine that we were descending the social scale. At the particular plank which served me for a table, there sat a gray-haired, florid-faced individuality named Edward Lassen, a certain fat and hearty beer connoisseur named Hans Richter, also a near-sighted, genial ruler named Alexander, Prince of Hesse, and half a dozen other celebrities and highnesses. The intoxicating strains of Wagner's music had been exchanged for intoxicating drains of Bayreuth beer, but the company was still the same. Mr. Gericke, Mr. Kneisel, Mr. Svecenski, Arthur Foote, Clayton Johns and a lot of Bostonians soon joined our party, and all went merry as a marriage bell.

Now, even if I make Mme. Cosima Wagner's reception wait, I must manage to convey a slight idea of how the post-musical exercises went on at this bohemian hostelry. At about 12 o'clock a shout went up, and lo! there was Materna coming to repose on her laurels. She had won a triumph as Kundry. By an odd coincidence, the name of the hostess at Angermann's was also Kundry, and Kundry No. 2 met Kundry No. 1 at the door with a foaming beaker of beer, which was drank to the health of the company. Then another "Hoch!" went up, and behold Beckmesser, the successful, receiving congratulations from all around. The charm of it all was that there was no pretence at formality, no effort to carry around any top-heavy dignity. I have spoken of the Prince of Hesse; let me take him as an example. I did not know that he was a prince until I had chatted with him about half an hour; when I found it out it was too late to try on any stately behavior. I resisted the temptation to tell him that I was the Duke of Oshkosh or the Marquis of Kalamazoo, but kept my character as a humble American citizen. As for his highness, any rich western speculator would have put on more airs.

Alas! there are no handbooks of etiquette on "How to converse with a prince," and even the Baedecker phrasebook omits this necessary chapter. I feared to ask if the prince business was good at this season, and he did not once say "By my halidome!" as the princes do in novels. On the contrary, he began talking very quietly and most learnedly on music, in which he seemed to be one of the best-informed gentlemen I had ever met. A more intelligent Wagnerian it would be impossible to find. He was a very near-sighted potentate, and I suppose, as I also am nearly as blind as a bat, that the bond of myopia drew us together somewhat.

How little of stuffy dignity and pomp there was in the upper circles of the Bayreuth gathering! It was only the bourgeoisie who tried to inflate themselves and carry as much of a title as the law and the alphabet would allow. The wife of an assistant sub-notary would not abate one jot or tittle of her grandeur, whatever dukes or princes might do. If I were to write out the titles of some of these as given in the "Fremdenblatt," I should cause the printer to die of brain-fever.

In the morning Mr. Kneisel and I set out to visit Herr Richter. His number in the Richard Wagner Strasse was 277 1-8. I did not know into how many fractions a house could be divided, but after finding 277 1-2, 1-4, 1-5, 1-6 and 1-7, I felt that the city must have been founded by some great mathematician who wanted to enforce an arithmetical problem on everybody searching for a residence. Herr Richter was out when we called, but I made sure that I should find him at Madame Wagner's reception in the evening, and therefore did not search for him in the park where he had gone for a promenade, according to the statement of the servant who answered the bell; but as the gathering at Angermann's had lasted until 6 A. M., perhaps 11 o'clock was too early for a musical call, and the promenade a social fiction.

At noon I again met the Prince of Hesse, and although not formally presented (such is the democracy of art), we entered into a comparison of notes about the festival. Prince Alexander is one of the best informed Wagnerians even in this stronghold. He told me that the great march of the meistersingers had been discovered to be almost identical with a march of the fifteenth century, and that the most rigid study of "Die Meistersinger" only led him to wonder more and more at the fidelity with which every detail of mediæval life had been followed. He inquired after Mr. Walter Damrosch and the success of his Wagner lectures, and showed great interest in the spread of the cause in America, just as Madame Wagner had done two days before.

The great reception was given on Tuesday night, and I can assure you there was effort enough made for invitations. I was fortunate enough to have been graciously invited by Mme. Wagner in person. Again came the comical affair with the alien coachman; after hiring him I had to show him the way to the great villa, but as the coach looked well and the butler had seen me before, he came down the steps with all dignity and handed me out, while the guards and police round about gave me a military salute. For a moment I felt again that I ought to put at least "Earl of Kalamazoo" on my card, but again fought down the temptation. I will not describe the general appearance of the villa, which, I believe, is generally known even in America, but I may say that the music room is one of the finest imaginable, and in it there stand an American piano and an American organ, the make of which I dare not mention, lest the suspicion of puffery attach to my chapters.

To the right of this was the dining room, in which a copious collation was spread; to the left the drawing room boudoir, spoken of already, in which were displayed a half dozen silver laurel wreaths, presented to the dead master. In front was the entrance to a magnificent library, in which Mme. Wagner was receiving her guests. If I were a Jenkins I could describe to you all the toilettes there displayed; but, alas, I do not know a gore from a tuck, a flounce from a train, or a Worth costume from a worthless one. Mme. Wagner herself was in black, with a black lace headdress (against which her gray hair stood out in fine contrast), looking very noble with her slim, lithe form, and her aristocratic yet genial manner.

She greeted me cordially and accorded me the honor of a few moment's especial conversation, which, considering the manifold duties pressing upon the hostess on such an occasion, I made as short as permissible.

She expressed pleasure that some American Wagnerians were present, regret that Mr. B. J. Lang, and her especial friend, Mrs. Lang, was not to be in Bayreuth this season, and the convential invitations for me to return, to feel unconstrained in Villa Wahnfried, etc. Spite of the invitation, at the first it was difficult to feel unconstrained, for although the rooms were crowded, none of my friends or acquaintances had yet arrived, and I put my foot in it with characteristic awkwardness at the very beginning. A solemn-faced gentleman had taken pity on the friendless one, and began an animated conversation with me. As the subjects began to give out I took refuge in the one which was being universally discussed—viz., the success of Herr Friedrichs as Beckmesser in the opera of the day before. The animation seemed to ooze out of the conversation at this point, and as I thought everything had been pumped dry, I bade adieu to the party, and gave him my card. He said sadly, " I have no card with me. My name is Kürrner! I am to play ' Beckmesser ' on Thursday!!" I had praised Beckmesser to the one man in that entire assemblage who did not want to hear about it!

But one by one friends and acquaintances began to appear. Most delightful of all, there was a little American corner in that drawing room, which contained Mrs. J. L. Gardner, Arthur Foote, Clayton Johns, Eliot Hubbard, and a few others who were strangers to me. Here we talked our native tongue and compared notes a little while. Then in came Materna, resplendent in jewelry and smiles, and saluted me with cordial greeting, "Grüss Gott, lieber Freund," and began chatting of America, which she longs to see again. Then there came Van Dyck, the glorious Parsifal of two days before, who was introduced to me by Materna, and who to my astonishment scarcely spoke German at all, but began conversation with me in French. He too, so he told me, had had some overtures from American managers, but dreaded the trip, and feared it would be some time before he came to us. Then came fat and burly Richter and began a long tirade against the sea, saying that he would never come to America until the ocean passage was abolished, he was so afraid of its dangers and its peculiar illness (he resembles Verdi in this), and then he sent best greetings again to his friend Emil Mahr in Boston.

Now matters began to mend; even Herr Kürrner smiled on me and showed that I had not struck a very deep wound, and finally there came the Wagnerian hero—Lamoureux— to whom I had been presented the previous day, and beckoned me into a seat for a quiet chat. He is short, fat, gray, wears spectacles, and seems a type of the genial, good-hearted Frenchman. He speaks no German and only four words of

English. He has fought the good fight for Wagner in Paris, but the gamins and lower classes were too much for him, and his splendid preparations for "Lohengrin" at the Eden Theater came to naught. [Three years later "Lohengrin" was given in its proper home in Paris—the Grand Opera House.] He inquired eagerly about America. "I love to travel," said he, "and I intend sometime to go there. It's very audacious of me, when one thinks of the number of musicians you already possess." I assured him that such as he would still be welcome, and said that I considered him the real hero of the evening, since only he had been persecuted for Wagner's sake. I asked also if he intended to give any more Wagner music this season. "At almost every concert," he responded, and then, seeing my gesture of surprise, he added, " it seems to be only when costumes are added that Wagner becomes exciting to the French. It is droll but true. They even applaud him in concert. *Mais sur le scene, c'est autre chose!* As for me, I make music, not politics, and I do not believe that Wagner should be pushed into the field of politics. Nevertheless, I know that it would have been dangerous for me to have given even one more performance of 'Lohengrin'." I complimented him again on his sturdiness in the cause, and he, not to be outdone, complimented my French, which was of the kind ascribed by Chaucer to the abbess,

> " After the schoole of Stratteford-atte-Bowe
> For French of Paris was to her unknowe!"

I again met the Prince of Hesse, who was as musically instructive as before, and then came a hush in the conversation, and they began to make music. I cannot describe that part of the evening. Herr Scheidemantel sang Schubert's " Sei mir Gegrüsst " in most excellent style, giving each strophe a different expression, and moderating his great baritone perfectly to the room. Then Miss Fritzsch, of the Carlsruhe Opera House sang a Liszt number. Then Herr

Stavenhagen, the best of the younger pianists, played a selection, and then Frau Materna obliterated all that had gone before by singing the finale of "Die Gotterdämmerung" as I have never heard it before. She was inspired by the surroundings, and Herr Mottl himself was at the piano, while Frau Cosima Wagner turned the leaves. It was a fitting crown to that glorious evening, and soon after this the company began to disperse, many of them returning to more plebeian joys at Angermann's.

The above is an account of the season when "Die Meistersinger " was first produced in Bayreuth; it is none the less typical of each of the festivals, which have now departed from their biennial character. Both before and since the events thus recorded, I have found the same democracy of art, the same joyous *camaraderie*, the same excellence of musical work, a permanent memorial of the great master.

RICHARD WAGNER AT HOME,
"WAHNFRIED" 1880.

CHAPTER VIII.

Some features of Bayreuth—the trip to Munich—Franz Lachner—Nuremberg—Rheinberger—Wagner's first opera, "the fairies."

It was Wagner who discovered Bayreuth, and this statement is true in spite of the fact that the city is very pretty in itself, and that it was known in some degree to the literati before the evolution of the Wagnerian opera, as the place where Jean Paul wrote his rather sentimental philosophic treatises. I have already intimated that when there is no Wagnerian festival in progress the city is as out of season as an oyster in August. Yet the pedestrian can find scenery to his heart's content, and possibly might call its chronic lethargy a "heavenly peace." The park of Fantasie is a gem in its way and the Hermitage is a charming pleasure resort. Memories of the aforesaid Jean Paul are in all the surroundings, and a statue of the same personage graces the public square. The Wagner theatre is just out of the town on a hill from which one can view beautiful valleys stretching in every direction, so that as one steps from the building where one has seen the choicest representation of German legend and mythology, one seems to see Germany itself spread out at one's feet, and the entire scene is in harmony with the thoughts that have been awakened. Yet not the *entire* scene; the large restaurant must remain an exception, and it is a rapid descent from the sublime to the ridiculous to come fresh from the struggle of Siegfried with the dragon, and then enter into a vehement struggle to get a sausage; to watch the flight of the Walkyries and then watch the still more rapid flight of the waiters. In former days it was still worse. It is but a few years ago that half of the Wagner-ites were obliged to go beerless and sausageless, and I have a recollection of seeing the grand duke of Saxe-Weimar draw a sandwich from his pocket and eat it in public with a smile of self-gratulation at his foresight. But the living show outside of the theatre between the acts is something that can scarcely be described; all ranks, all nationalities are there, and our world is then proved to be a very small place, for one is sure to find a dozen people whom one last met a few thousand miles away. The din of many languages is in itself a revelation, and one comes to look upon the theater as a modern tower of Babel, or at least to find a hidden meaning in the placard which I found in a carriage in the city—"To the Theater, *or to the lunatic asylum*, 2 marks!" Among the crowd I found one specimen of humanity whom I shall never forget; he wore a plum-colored coat, a blue vest, a frilled shirt, his hair was as long as that of Ibsen, his fingernails were of most imposing growth, and his complexion swarthy. Here, thought I, is an Algerian, or a Turkish pasha come to worship at the Wagnerian shrine, and when I met him at Angermann's I sought his acquaint-ance with avidity. Alas for the frailty of human hopes! The man was simply the critic of a Paris journal. A musi-cal critic! A brother scribbler! And I whose nails were normal, whose head was only moderately hirsute, could only shrink into nothingness beside this bird-of-paradise of a reviewer.

After the performance, at about 10 P. M., it is pleasant to stroll down the hill to the city, in the midsummer night, and if you pass by the hotel "Zum Schwarzen Ross" on the way, you will find some of the artists gathered there, who are afraid of the Angermann revelry described in my last chapter, although the place is not patronized as it was some three years ago. But there is a Wagnerian quest that draws me away from Bayreuth now; in Munich they are giving the earliest opera of the master—" The Fairies "—and therefore I take the train for that city. But I stop at Würzburg and Nuremberg. On the way from here I shall find reminiscences of many of Wagner's characters, and a run through the latter old city is the best possible prelude or postlude to " The Mastersingers."

By Hessische-Ludwig's Bahn to Würzburg. That railroad needs quinine; it has the ague in its worst shape. The train traveled as much from side to side as it did forward, but a lively American game caused the time to fly so speedily that we were nearly carried by our destination. A kermesse was being held in the city when we came, and we were glad enough to wander among the booths and the peasantry in their holiday attire. Among the blind the one-eyed man is king; among the Bavarian peasants we became princes. "Here! your highness!" shouted one vendor, "buy a beautiful surprise for your noble lady," but even that flattery caused no sale. We went, however, to a Punch and Judy show, and found that in Germany Punch remains as wicked a wife-beater as ever, although he has lost the squeak which in America is his chief charm. In Würzburg, as almost everywhere else, I found European hotel life changing and for the better. The same statement is true of many customs which I have criticised in the past, but which exist no more even in the smaller cities. The barber no longer seats you on a hard stool, twists your neck off and expects you to wash the remains of the lather out of your own ears; the sanitary provisions in hotels have passed beyond those of a Hottentot village; one begins to have candles allowed as

a necessity at night and not charged as a luxury; but the
beds, in Germany at least, are still built in the manner so
distressing to an American. Most of them were too short
for me, and I had a choice of three remedies: 1st to saw my
legs off at the knee; 2d to kick holes through the footboard;
3d, to allow my feet to hang over the dasher. To lay di-
agonally was impossible, on account of the lack of width of
the infernal machine. Besides this one has to bear the
atrocious feather-bed on top, so that one feels like a rasher
of meat in a railroad sandwich. Add to this that the head
is bolstered up high in mid-air (some of the Germans evidently sleep standing), and you can imagine that "tired
nature's sweet restorer, balmy sleep," loses some of the
balm.

While I am in a growling mood let me pay my attention
to the cigars of Germany. With a plaster on the back of
one's neck to make them draw, plugs of cotton in the nos-
trils to keep away the smell, and a very tight belt around
the waist to hold one's stomach in position during the ordeal,
they might be borne by a man of firm will and iron constitution, otherwise not. It makes little difference how much
you pay for them. I have had some at a mark apiece,
which fulfilled all the conditions. But I must add that
there are one or two stores in Berlin, known only to the
initiated, where a respectable smoke may be obtained.

From Würzburg to Nuremberg. The latter city is one
solid curiosity shop. Old streets, bridges, churches, fount-
ains—a perfect city of the middle ages dropped down into
the 19th century. There is a terrible collection of instruments of torture in the castle, frightful beyond belief, and
one of them (a charming cradle, with spikes in it to prevent
the occupant from sleeping too soundly) was used in this
century, and on an innocent man over 60 years of age! If
I had had the guide who took me around Bonn in that

chamber, I think that by the aid of the thumb-screws and a charming little arrangement for pulling out a six foot man into one eight or nine feet high, I could have found out in which of the two houses Beethoven was born. And by the way, I must pay tribute to that same guide's ingenuity, for on finding both houses labelled as the "birth-place of Beethoven" he unblushingly told me that the *son* of the great composer was born in the second. I explained to him that Beethoven was a bachelor and not an immoral one either, but he clung to his statement. To return to my Nuremburg experience.

I took my lunch in a little hostelry called the Brat-wurst Gloecklein, where they make a specialty of hot sausages and beer. It is a more interesting place than Auerbach's cellar in Leipsic (although no Goethe has yet sung its praises), for in the quaint little room, which has been a tap-room for 500 years, have sat Hans Sachs, Albrecht Durer, Veit Visscher and a host of other worthies of the past, whose names adorn the walls. After the cravings of the inner man had been pacified I made a few purchases in the city and learned another point. I desired to see some shirts, and was shown a marvelous arrangement with gorgeous ruffles on the bosom and a general loudness of style that suggested the end man of a negro minstrel show. "That sir, is an American shirt!" said the lady, proudly.

"Do they wear them like that in Boston and New York?" I timidly inquired. "Oh, yes," was the calm reply. How the fashions must have changed since I left my native land! A game of billiards at the Café Zettelmeier closed the day. The peculiarity of this game was that there was no appliance of any kind for keeping the score. You count in your mind, and the man with the longest memory wins the game. I have a phenomenal memory. The pretty waiter girl, however, prevented me from keeping my tally firmly in mind, for she wanted to know about America. "Were there waiter girls there?" "Yes, but not as pretty as she." "Ach, so! And where did I live in America?" I told her "at No. 18," and she promised to call if ever she came over, but she had not yet been away from Nuremberg, and she was afraid to try the trip. The next day I left Nuremberg and *die schöne Kellnerin*, and began a further staccato on the ague-stricken railway. But the conductors are polite enough to make up for any shortcomings of the road. They come for the tickets with "Die Billeten wenn ich bitten darf?" Fancy an American conductor saying to you, "May I take the liberty of begging to look at your ticket?" One would at once take him before a commission *de lunatico inquirendo*.

But do not be foolish enough to trust the politeness. It is only a bear who has learned to dance. Let there be any doubt about your ticket or your tip, and the veneering cracks off instantly. It is quite the same with Parisian suavity. I have seen more solid politeness in a western farmer or a Texas ranchman than in a hundred phrase-making Germans or Frenchmen.

To Munich by a train whose slowness I have already commented on. As the solemn procession moves on toward the Bavarian capital, the bells at the stations ring out melancholy signals in minor thirds. Why these bells should always be tuned to this sad interval I know not, but it was a relief to have the signal at Regensburg give a major sixth. Another comical railway custom is to give the passengers several warnings before their train starts. An official approaches the waiting room, and after ringing a bell, proclaims, in most important style, "Passengers for Regensburg, Weiden and Munich"—I gather up my parcels hastily and go to the door—" have fifteen minutes time yet!" Was there ever a more exasperating way of doing things? He shouts again later on, telling us that we have ten minutes yet, and finally the intelligence that it is "the highest time to get aboard!" With all these orations I nearly lost my train, believing his last speech an unimportant one, and paying no attention to it.

I came to Munich, as above stated, on another Wagnerian excursion. I had heard Wagner's latest work, "Parsifal," at Bayreuth; it was a great contrast to hear his first work, "The Fairies," given at Munich. The vast opera house was crowded to the doors, and it was with great difficulty that, at an advanced price, I obtained an orchestra seat.

The opera was mounted with great splendor, its stage effects being even comparable with those of Bayreuth. The management chose to make a spectacular piece of it and were wise in doing so, for it has merely a ballet plot, and one which is far too ridiculous for serious treatment. The music, although reminiscent, is much better than the libretto. The plot is a compound of "Iolanthe" and "Lurline." A young prince has married a fairy and is pledged for eight years not to ask who she is. Naturally he waits patiently seven years and 364 days, and then asks the name and address of his spouse, who at once disappears. Two children have been born to the couple, whose status, like that of Strephon in Iolanthe, is not quite decided. In order to regain his spouse, Arindel, the prince aforesaid, who has now become king, has to be tried in the most terrible fashion, and should he curse his wife, he is to lose her forever. That lady appears in his palace, with a bevy of lovely fairies in short dresses, and calmly turning the place into a fiery furnace, takes the two children of the king and throws them in the flames. The monarch does not altogether approve of this application of the Malthusian doctrine, but still refrains from cursing, not even saying "demmit!" Those two children, by the way, are afterward found safe and sound.

They are pulled about in a manner that recalls the youngsters in " Norma."

After a few other calamities are doled out to the monarch,
such as the defeat of his army, the death of his friend, the
betrayal of his palace, etc., by this most uncomfortable
spouse, the king gets angry and curses the fairy, who is
traveling incognita. She then informs him that he has lost
her forever, and getting on a cloud, drives off to fairyland.
That cloud was continually coming on or going off the stage,
by the way, and seemed to be a sort of fairy omnibus; it was
not as comfortable even as a Chicago Hansom, for when it
went up in the air the passengers clung to it very tightly
and looked most uncomfortable. Fairies and mortals mingled together in this act with the same unconcern that is
found in "Iolanthe." In the third act the king goes crazy,
and the conventional operatic mad scene is introduced. You
know that on the operatic stage the crazier a person gets
the better he sings, and this is the case with Arindel, who
after a brilliant aria recovers his senses, and being helped
by a sorcerer named Chroma (why he is thus helped is not
stated), goes through enchanted regions, amid monsters of
every guise, to conquer back his wife. The end is happy,
for the ruler of fairyland rewards his faithful love by returning his wife to him, and making him also a genuine,
imperishable, first-class fairy.

Imagine such a Wagnerian plot! It is an injustice to the
memory of the great master to produce it. As well produce
that bloodthirsty play which he wrote in childhood, wherein
he killed all the characters (some thirty) in the second act,
and ran the third act with their ghosts!

The music, I have said, is far better. If the plot could
only be worked over into something sensible, the opera
would be performed sometimes, not merely as a curiosity,
but on its own merits. There are fragments of Weber and

of Bellini and Auber in it, and I found in the heroic character of some of the soprano work more than a reminiscence
of the Queen of the Night in "The Magic Flute." Strangest
of all was it to find the conventional aria, scena, cavatina,
prayer, and mad scene in a Wagnerian work.

The opera thoroughly crushes the critics who have main-
tained that Wagner was by nature incapable of composing
tunes. The overture is in medley style and contains some
romantic orchestral coloring a la Weber, and also a pretty
march. One felt (as the old Frenchman in the story) like
touching one's hat continually and bowing to the old musical acquaintances as they went by. The number of transformation scenes and the amount of kettledrum used at each
was astonishing. The second act is the strongest of the
opera, and once in a while one gets a glimpse of the real
Wagner in it. The arias by the two sopranos are of very
dramatic character, and the chorus of greeting on the return
of Arindel is good, but Arindel's mournful reply, with a
monotonous figure in the orchestral accompaniment, is original and striking. Very interesting too, as coming from
Wagner, was the playful quarrel scene between the king's
esquire and his sweetheart. This was dainty and pretty in
every detail. It is one of the "ifs" of musical history
whether Wagner could not have composed comic opera, in
the French sense, had he practiced more in this vein. Thank
heaven, he did not!

The whole latter part of the act is melodic enough to
please the masses and was applauded to the echo. The
third act dealt chiefly with spectacular matters, fiends, imps,
fairies, and transformation scenes, yet the strongest single
number of the work is in this act. It is a beautiful and
richly harmonized prayer for quintette and chorus, entirely
unaccompanied.

The mad scene which followed was of the usual vehemently capricious character of such scenes, but contained a charming oboe solo (pizzicato accompaniment), some very tender cantabile passages, and some bold modulations that already promised the greater Wagner. A final song (Gluck's style this time) by Arindel, with harp accompaniment, is the most musical touch of the opera. It is melodious enough to whistle.

Then came the transformation scene of the finale. Never have I seen anything of the kind more gorgeously done; buds sprang up in fairyland, and bursting, disclosed beautiful children; shells opened and became chariots drawn by swans; dissolving views and tableaux a la "Black Crook" on every hand; and finally with a dazzling flash, electric lights of every color burst forth from every part of the scene at once. It was a magnificent ending which may not be described; but fancy that being Wagner! ! From "Parsifal" to this was a jump greater than from Shakespeare to Zola would have been.

Munich is a city devoted to art and beer. Vast expositions of paintings are in one part of the city, and still vaster breweries in another. In the *vorstadt* the inhabitants draw in hops and malt at every breath, for the atmosphere is impregnated with beer. Munich was suffering from the combined effects of two exhibitions and a centennial when I came there, and was having what in America would be technically called a "jamboree." Before plunging into the whirl of dissipation I determined to get as near to godliness as possible by taking a bath. In some parts of Europe this is quite a ceremony, and I was therefore not astonished to be ushered into a parlor of a gloomy looking building, and interviewed on the subject before I took the rash step. "Would I have it first-class, second-class, or third-class?" Can one ever get rid of the "class" business in Europe? I think that when the soul of the European presents itself at the celestial portal, St. Peter will inquire, "Do you want to enter as a first-class, second-class or third-class angel?" I had enough real estate gathered upon my person to desire a first-class ablution, and stated that fact.

There is no denying that the result was an amount of splendor which is not generally associated by Americans with a wash. A marble tank, finely decorated at the edges with artistic tiles, a flowing Eastern robe, scented soap and all the luxuries of the season were there, and in an hour, refreshed and buoyant, I started for the exhibitions. The great Gewerbe-Ausstellung was only a smaller edition of our "Mechanics' Fair," but choicer and more tastily put together. It needs no description, although I am sure it would be well for some of our fair committeemen to go there and study the grouping. So I went to the other end of the town to the art exposition, which was of far more interest to me. Of course I shall not attempt to give details of an exhibition containing hundreds of masterpieces of all nations. I may, however, mention that there was an American section. It was small, yet some good painters were represented.

One must not omit a visit to the great breweries in Munich, and the Café Luitpold is one of the most gorgeous restaurants of the world.

In the matter of processions we have much to learn from Europe, and most especially from such an art centre as Munich. I recall a procession I once saw in Munich on the occasion of the centennial of the dynasty of Bavaria, which was a wonder. With us on such an occasion there are half a hundred brass bands, a dozen regiments of militia, a number of Masonic and charitable societies, and a boy with a pail of lemonade. The very beginning of the Munich cortege was a surprise; instead of a drum-major strutting like a turkey-cock, there came a number of youths beautifully attired as pages, and following these a number of trumpeters in old heraldic costume. The procession was made up of many tableaux borne on great wagons, or floats, a herd of elephants, a whole host of strange mechanical devices, and blended historical instruction with artistic pageantry in a most wonderful manner. The mechanical devices, however, led to a disaster, for, as the herd of elephants came along, they were obliged to pass by a monster dragon which was side-tracked while some repairs were being made in its interior. Just at that unlucky moment the engineer turned on steam, and the hideous monster began to hiss and spit forth clouds of vapor. The result was easy to predict; the elephants, mad with terror, rushed into the crowd, and a fearful catastrophe was the result.

During that same festival season I made the acquaintance of the old conservative composer, since dead,—Franz Lachner. I found him in modest quarters, as was the case with too many of the German composers that I visited, but he received me with unaffected cordiality. A short, stubby figure, a genial face topped with gray hair, a twinkling eye that seemed to enjoy a joke, that was Lachner. He had recently celebrated his "jubilee" on the completion of his fiftieth year of service as a musical director, and showed me with delight the many addresses, the telegrams, the poems, and the laurel wreaths, that he had gathered in on that occasion. These honors are more prized by such a nature than the greatest salary that America could offer. Yet Lachner expressed regret that he had never seen our country, and then came the sad remark, "it is too late now." He sighed as he said this, and perhaps thought that the very gifts that spoke of his fifty years' service also portended the end that was soon to come. And then he spoke of

Beethoven to me, and of Schubert. It was like turning back the hands of the clock half a century and more, to converse with this man. He had been an orchestral leader in Vienna when Schubert was alive! He had composed songs in friendly rivalry with him! He was a contemporaneous composer with Beethoven! When I told Lachner that we admired his suites in America, and proved my familiarity with some of them, the ice was broken and the pleasant Bavarian ways came to the surface, and anecdote followed anecdote until the time of my departure, and then came greetings to American acquaintances, and I left the veteran never to behold him more.

Rheinberger I found more in the American style of activity, neatly dressed and dapper, full of the keenest interest in American musical matters, and thoroughly conversant with what is going on among us. He seemed to have less of the conservative qualities which were so prominent in the others. One pleasant fact I must mention in connection with these composers and instructors—they all spoke in the highest terms of their American pupils. Our country has been better represented abroad of late years than ever heretofore, and if half of what these authorities enthusiastically told me be true, we shall have a large crop of composers shortly. Rheinberger sent many greetings to his friend, Professor Baermann, in Boston, and said that he hoped to see our country one of these days. What a grand influence in the progress of our art such a man would be!

CHAPTER IX.

The trip to Vienna from Munich is not an unpleasant one,
and one can break journey at Salzburg and find a whole
museum of Mozart relics.   The town itself is beautiful in
its scenery and surroundings, but the musician finds his
greatest pleasure in looking over the rarities of the Mozart
collection.   Perhaps the most interesting single piece among
the set of autographs, scores, and relics, is a manuscript work
which Mozart composed at *seven years of age*.   A reproduction of this may be of interest to American readers, and
it may stand in place of any further Salzburg reminiscences
or views.

I arrived at Vienna in the very midst of the heated term,
and the first impression was that I had plunged into purgatory.   It was one of those days when Sydney Smith says
"a man would like to take his flesh off and sit in his bones!"
The thermometer registered 102° in the shade, and several
of the oldest inhabitants assured me that such weather had
not been felt in Vienna for twenty years.   I shall not give
the catalogue of the various antidotes which I tried against
the fervid atmosphere; even the delicious Pilsner, the best
and lightest beer of Europe, was powerless.   Suffice it to
say that perseverance brought its reward in the discovery

of the largest swimming bath of its kind in Europe, situated just beyond the Prater Strasse, on the Danube. I was struck here, as everywhere in Vienna, with the manner in which everything is systematized. The temperature of the water, and of the air, is marked upon a blackboard at the entrance to each of the four immense basins; inside is marked the depth of each; the bath doctor is in constant attendance to counsel any who seek his advice. The pleasant bath becomes a perfect hydropathic establishment.

But if the Viennese systematize in some things, they have cumbersome formalities in others. I saw a young American pompously reprimanded for taking his coat off while playing a game of billiards and adding to the crime by whistling a tune in a café. At the same time, some (but by no means all) of the cafés are what we should call decidedly immoral. Yet in every café the stranger who takes a seat near your table will make obeisance and say "Mit Ihr' Erlaubniss" ("with your permission") and when he arises to go will bow again with "Ich habe die Ehre," which is an abbreviated form of saying " I have the honor to take my leave." In two of the taverns they had a few souvenirs of Schubert, and anecdotes as well, which had been handed down traditionally, of how he used to break the dishes in sport, and how he used to tease the waiter for a long time before candidly confessing how much his score was. I went along many of his old-time walks but was not able to discover the restaurant where he composed "Hark! hark! the Lark!" on the back of a bill of fare while waiting for his breakfast, after one of his morning strolls. But of Beethoven I found a reminiscence in Schönbrunn, the beautiful palace just outside of the city. It was an old tree in the garden, with three branches separating from the trunk, about four feet from the ground. These three branches form a natural seat, and in this seat Beethoven did much of his composing

in 1823-4. In this secluded perch he thought out part of
his ninth symphony, so he told Schindler, his friend and
biographer, and so Schindler told the old musician who took
me to the spot. I climbed into the seat, but I did not write
a symphony; it would not have been quite fair to Beethoven,
for after all he was the originator of this out-door style of
musical work. I can readily imagine his working thus in
a peaceful solitude, for I visited some of his temporary residences in Vienna and they were in rather noisy localities.
It is said that once he was led, through this fact, to write
one of his most striking figures. It was in the dead of the
night, and a drunken man had been locked out of his lodgings across the way. The clatter soon awakened even the
semi-deaf composer and he listened; "Bang-bang-bang,
BANG!!" went the irate and homeless lodger, and then followed a pause; no result; again—"Bang-bang-bang, BANG!!"
until finally Beethoven was struck with the emphatic rhythm,
and down it went into the familiar note book, and that
"Bang-bang-bang, BANG!!" became the

of the fifth symphony. But my old musical friend told me
that they have another anecdote about that self-same figure
in Vienna, which is that Beethoven was drumming on the
window pane of Artaria's music store one rainy day, when
he suddenly jotted down the rhythm made by his own four
fingers. In this case I must allow the reader to take his
own choice of tales. But the anecdotes of this particular
figure are almost endless, the most pathetic being that
Schumann imagined that he heard it rapped out at a spiritu-
alist *seance*, and fancied that Beethoven was trying to com-
municate with him; the most vulgar interpretation of the
meaning coming from Beethoven himself in one of his

JOSEF RHEINBERGER,
DIRECTOR OF THE ROYAL CONSERVATORY, MUNICH.

bizarre moods. And thus Vienna is full of reminiscences of
Beethoven and Schubert, and in the great central cemetery,
(formerly they were at Währing), in this same city, they
rest together, their graves being but a few steps apart. On
the grave of Beethoven, over fifty years ago, Schumann
found a pen, and with that pen he wrote his own beautiful
symphony of Love and Springtime, the symphony in B flat.
I had been in Beethoven's tree, and had not composed a
successor to the 9th symphony, and now I looked in vain
for a pen which would enable me to follow Schumann. So
I went back to the Ring Strasse and sought my musical
friend Albert Jungmann, who was as dapper and genial as
any *Wienerkind* (child of Vienna) ought to be, and he took
me to the grand opera which is one of the finest buildings
of Vienna

The best singers of the troupe were absent, (I have
spoken of some of them in my Bayreuth chapters) but the
great chorus and superb orchestra were enough to make even
Abbey green with envy. I saw, too, an opera which
called forth all the best stage effects—"The Huguenots."
In the second act there must have been some two hundred
people on the stage, and the Princess and suite galloped on
(and sang) on horseback. The auditorium itself is one of
the finest in Europe. Its *foyer* is more elegant than that of
the Grand Opera House of Paris.

I wished to learn something of the editorial customs in so
formal a country, and therefore called upon the *redaction* of
the "Neue Freie Presse," one of the leading journals of
Europe. It is housed in a palatial mansion, but the rooms
of the editors are not nearly so commodious or convenient
as those of the American press. I had hoped to have met
here the greatest of musical critics, Dr. Ed. Hanslick, but
he had already departed for the summer.

I spoke with what in America would have been the "**ex-**

change editor," who was translating some passages from a French journal. He told me that in Europe "exchanging" was unknown. Each paper subscribes to the leading journals. "It could not be otherwise," said he, "for the prices of the papers are different!" He was much interested when I explained to him our system. I also spoke with a young editor who was occupied in editing a letter from Hungary relative to the persecution of the Jews there. As this happened some years ago, I felt that the Viennese did not crave novelty very extensively. Their papers reminded me of the placid sheet in our country, which was called, among the journalists, "*The Porous Plaster*," because it was "good for a week back." When Dr. Hanslick hears a concert or an opera, they do not expect that he will rush wildly to the office with his "copy" after the manner of an American critic, but any time thereafter he may graciously deign to record his views on the matter; it is considered etiquette, however, not to defer the criticism until the singers and audience are dead.

It may gratify some of the American reviewers to know that even this dilatory Homer sometimes nods, and that once he too, spoke of the "usual fine execution" of a vocalist who did not sing at all on the occasion the reviewer referred to.

The editors take their coffee and rolls in as tranquil a manner as any merchants, during the business hours of the morning, and I fear that not an "exclusive" murder, a sensational suicide, or even a dog-fight in the immediate vicinity, would move them then. In some newspaper offices, however, they go beyond even American enterprise in a certain direction. We think it natural to buy a "five o'clock edition" on the streets at three o'clock P. M., but in some of the German cities they date their evening edition *the next morning*, so that you can buy a Friday's paper on Thursday evening!

An Andante for Piano, Composed by Mozart at the age of Seven.
(In the Salzburg Collection.)

ɪ dwelt at the "Hotel Erzherzog Karl," and found the porter there several degrees less pompous than his tribe. Not that he did not bestow titles of nobility upon me, I should have felt hurt had he omitted that, but his gratitude at receiving a few good cigars, (as an inhabitant of Austria he had read about such things being in existence, but had never seen them) found vent in paternal advice as to everything that ought to be visited, and ought not to, in the imperial city. I am afraid that he was not in sympathy with my musical pilgrimages, and thought that my looking up reminiscences of the dead was not exactly just to the living Viennese, and when I came in sedately at 11 P. M., he looked at me reproachfully as if I were losing my opportunities. But he brightened up when I began going to the Prater on Sundays or fete days.

The Prater is the pride of Vienna, and justly so. It is practically many parks in one. First, there is the part nearest the Prater-strasse, which is given over altogether to the working classes. Here on a Sunday afternoon are hundreds of booths, whirligigs, shooting galleries, cafés, gondolas, panoramas, etc., each with an orchestra. It is like twenty Fourth of Julys rolled into one. Even the display of highly colored indigestion in the shape of cakes, candies, etc., is not lacking,

The peasantry stroll about in brightest costumes. but do not get into line and sing as on the operatic stage; on the contrary they dig their elbows into you, and tread on your corns until life seems a burden. The booth-keepers hail the advent of a stranger with more than effusive flattery, and seem to imagine that I spend my days in ceaseless shooting, panorama-viewing, and whirligiging, and the effect of twenty brass bands within hearing, each playing a different tune, and each possessing an ambitious and active bass drummer, is sufficient to shatter one's ideas about music forever. However, the bass drums, like charity, cover a multitude of sins, and I turn from "the madding crowd" and wander through beautiful forest paths until the Haupt Allée is reached. Here is again a vast crowd, but of a totally different character. It is the "Rotten Row" of Vienna. Along the broad avenue pass and repass splendid vehicles of all descriptions, containing the *beau monde* of the empire. Here even the empress loves to ride early in the morning, almost unattended. Along the sides are vast walks, with numerous benches, and also three enormous cafés, where one can sit in the open air, sipping beer or coffee, and listen to excellent music. It was in one of these cafés that I first heard the gypsy music in its purity.

It was in "Café No. 3," whither I often went to hear a really excellent military band, and to sip an equally commendable coffee. One afternoon, instead of the tubas, saxhorns, and trombones, I heard the most exquisite stringed instrument playing. Its character can scarcely be described in cold type, it was so very fervid, but I was astonished to find that the dozen of players had not a scrap of printed or written music before them; all was inspirational and free. At the beginning of each number, the leader arose with his violin and plunged into a characteristic air, in which all the others followed with appropriate, if at times unconventional harmonies. No matter how he varied the tempo, and this was caprice personified, the players kept together, and with him. The work generally began in slow and tender fashion; with quaint intervals, founded I afterwards learned, upon the Hungarian scale, which is an especially weird minor mode, running thus:

and its two augmented seconds make an anguished effect that is indescribable; deeper and deeper grows the yearning and sorrow, and then it seems to pause from very heaviness —that is the Lassan. But the piece is not done yet; suddenly, crisp and clear, there comes a phrase fiery and bold as the others were weary and plaintive; and now wilder and wilder grows the music, it is not glad, it is fierce; it is not joy, it is frenzy; it is like a horde of ancient Huns riding impetuously into battle, or a flight of furies. The frenzy mounts to delirium, and then, at the very height of it all, it comes to a brusque and capricious end—that is the Friska. I looked at the swarthy band in awe-struck wonder, and called the waiter to me. "Who are those musicians?" "Ah, your excellency [I had still some small change to disburse], must excuse it; our band is in the city to-day, playing at a ball, and we had to put up with these Gypsies instead!" That "putting up" (!) with such music cost the humble waiter his tip, although he hovered around like a guardian angel during the rest of the proceedings. I went to the leader and spoke with him in German. He was delighted to find that the "Amerikaner" had been carried along on the stream of his music, and finally grew confidential enough to tell me that there were many larger bands in Buda-Pesth. He assured me that if I enjoyed Tzigany music I must at once depart for Hungary and study it in its native purity. I was glad enough to take his advice, for although I cordially agree with the statement that

> " 'Sgiebt nur a Kaiserstadt
> 'Sgiebt nur a Wien,"

still the city was proving just a trifle too seductive for my pocket, and my purse needed change of air. Therefore, the next morning found me on the Danube river. I went in the morning that I might be able to negative that oft repeated question, "You recollect that *night* in June upon the Danube river?" and also that I might see the scenery.

I leave to Baedeker and his guide-books the description of all that, however, only adding that Strauss would have been nearer to the truth if he had written "the beautiful *yellow* Danube waltzes." On the boat I had the pleasure of meeting with a Hungarian nobleman, who gave me some information about the people and the country. Austria rules Hungary with a mild and beneficent government, but it is doubtful if it can ever win the gratitude of the wild, untamable people. With these latter everything is national; they will not speak German if they can help it; every child is bound by law to learn Hungarian; if official notices require two languages, the Hungarian comes first and there are a thousand other little ways in which the people show that they are only tributary to Austria, and are not Austrian.

All the better classes have the wonderful lingual, or philological, facility of the Russians, and speak a half dozen tongues with ease. All through Austria, as in Germany, it is soldiers, soldiers, soldiers, everywhere, and I was not surprised to see fifty cadets come on the boat at Pressburg, the great fortress, and make the journey down to the very "Iron Gates," the wonderfully picturesque Carpathian mountains, the frontiers of Hungary. They were military graduates, who, at the completion of four years' study, were sent by the government to practically study the topography of the country. Some of them took a vivid interest in American affairs, but seemed comically ignorant of them. One asked me about our army, and upon being told its minute proportions, expressed sympathy at the dangers we must suffer from Indians. On my telling him of the large army which the civil war called forth, another said, "Oh, I know about that. You were led by General Washington!" With them America was represented by one city, and even that they mispronounced in the Russian manner, "*Neff York.*"

Pesth, the Hungarian capital, is worth going a long way to see. It is modern, and it is Oriental. It is, in fact, two cities—Buda on one side of the Danube, and Pesth on the other. The latter is a city of palaces. The Austrian government is lending its aid to build up a new city by degrees, and street after street of small one-story hovels has given way to massive and vast buildings.

The Opera House, the gift of the emperor of Austria, is one of the finest specimens of architecture in all Europe, and the great street leading to the public park is two miles long, yet has not one plain or small edifice in all its length. It is one row of palaces. The contrast between wealth and poverty is far too striking to be agreeable. To see hungry and hopeless wretches in the midst of so much splendor, was an incongruity which showed that there was something wrong in the system, possibly too many palaces and too few soup houses. The oddity of the construction of the Hungarian language strikes one in the shop signs, for here they put the given name last, as "Ferenczy Josef," or "Zach Franz," which makes the city look like a directory or a voting list. I looked around for "Smith John," but did not succeed in finding him.

But I did succeed in finding, even in the courtyard of my own hotel, (the "Victoria"), the gypsy bands that had tempted me away from Vienna. They took as great an interest in me as I in them, and when they heard that I knew Remenyi, their friendship increased perceptibly. But the fact of their asking for him, and my being able to answer, may have given them a false idea of the size of our country. I recall a similar question which was once put to me in Europe, which I could not answer so well. It was in Melrose, in Scotland, and I had won the heart of the man who was driving to Abbotsford with me, by quoting a few lines of Scott applicable to that part of the Tweed, whereupon he grew less diffident and said inquiringly, "You come from America?" On my answering in the affirmative he added one more question, "did you happen to meet Robert Jones there?" It seems that the Robert aforesaid had gone to America, (he did not know to what particular country), some ten years before then.

A few walks through Pesth convinced me that the scriptural Joseph never dwelt there. He could not have got away even with the loss of his coat. Besides this, Pesth copies Vienna in the servility of its treatment of strangers, and the frequency with which little fees are extracted. I dread to think of the number of royal and princely titles and deep and humble bows that were showered on me, and the equally great number of small coins which went to keep up my patent of nobility. It is a little at a time and often. A couple of dollars would unhinge the spinal columns of all the waiters in Pesth, and the flexibility of their backbones is marvelous.

The poor gypsies! I saw a dozen being marched up to the fortress (prison) under guard. They were arrested as thieves, and among them were thin, little, brown-skinned and large-eyed children of eight and ten years old. There was no complaint, no grief even visible on their faces; they went with a matter-of-course air that was even more pitiable.

Desiring to see Hungarian life in all its phases, I went into a large café of the lower order to see the peasantry and soldiery in their convivial moods. The men were in their quaint costumes, with a short, oddlooking skirt or petticoat, and they looked fierce enough in spite of this adjunct of feminine finery. They sang Hungarian songs with terrific vehemence, and seemed not in the least akin to the good-humored Austrian peasant. One of them grew enraged at the fact that his waitress left him and attended to my orders, with no very evident haste to return to his side. He

GRAVES OF BEETHOVEN, MOZART AND SCHUBERT, CENTRAL CEMETERY, VIENNA.

watched the trend of events with a scowl for a few minutes, and then came over to where I was seated. He began a long, and doubtless very eloquent, oration in Hungarian before me. It was somewhat on the "Ye call me chief" order of elocution, and the gestures were largely made with clenched fists. Unfortunately I am totally ignorant of the Hungarian tongue, and when my orator paused I scarcely knew how to return thanks, but raised my glass as if toasting him. This seemed to excite him greatly, and he pranced around as if to mingle dancing with his recitation, and wound up the exercises by throwing his cap on the floor before me. By this time the host and three waiters were interested in the proceedings, and the orator was wafted up the stairway into the outer darkness, and then I was informed that it was simply a defiance which had been breathed upon me, and that the dance aforesaid was an invitation to fight, with an "R. S. V. P." attachment. It was too late to look up my challenger, although I rather expected that he would look me up, assisted by a few friends, on my homeward way, but I heard no more of him

Ofen, or Buda, on the other side of the river, contains the finest situated palace I have ever seen. High up on a great hill, almost a mountain, surrounded by walks and terraces innumerable, it is the most romantic spot of the city. Below it is the bazaar, lined with little shops, and near by is an enormous Turkish bath which would make America pale with envy. It is about of the same size as the New York Custom House. The whole town of Buda is essentially Hungarian, and Orsova, farther down the river, is almost Turkish in life and customs.

I have not found the hotels in southeastern Europe so expensive as I had imagined. To be sure the bill itself is the slightest part of the proceedings. There are the various india rubber contortionists I have alluded to, who bow their heads to the dust as they insist upon carrying your sacred umbrella or carpet-bag, and there is also a pompous creature called the portier, who sometimes wears gold lace enough for an ambassador, but is not averse to receiving gratuities.

But in the hotels of the Danubian principalities the entomology is free and is at the same time large and varied. One can study it without leaving the house. If it were charged for the bill would be tremendously augmented. In Vienna the hotels are excellent, however.

In Buda I was seized with the idea of surprising a few friends at home with Hungarian newspapers, which I knew no one in America, except a few imported inhabitants, could read. It was simple enough to buy these, for all the shopkeepers spoke German, when they could make a sale by it. But that was only the preliminary step; I had to send them off in wrappers, and newspaper wrappers seemed to be unknown in Hungary. By the time I had stated my wishes at the post office, the entire postal force of Buda were gathered around to assist. An attempt to stuff the journals into the largest envelopes in the office, failed ignominiously. Then string was attempted, but there arose some official objection to this (what it was I could not ascertain) and then two clerks set to work cutting strips of brown paper under my direction and four more set off in search of the paste pot. It must be remembered that Buda is not a puny village, and the illiterate character of some parts of Hungary, and the few papers that are dispatched may be judged from this event. When finally the addresses were written and the parcel delivered to the chief official, who had betrayed the greatest concern in the matter from its inception, he read them and said, " These are all people of Neff York." "No," I answered, "but they are all in America." " But that is the same thing," said he and turned away. It was useless to explain that the people of Chicago, Boston, St.

Louis, Cincinnati, etc., etc., did *not* live in New York. I left, serene in the conviction that I had sent the first newspapers to America from that particular post-office (I may state in parenthesis that they arrived all right), and strong in the belief that if ever a New York alderman visited Hungary he would be received with more honors than the president of the United States.

CHAPTER X.

Adelsberg — Florence — Venice — a concert two miles
long — the reception of the queen — music on the
grand canal — rome — naples — pompeii.

From Vienna to Adelsberg the movement went *piu lento*,
for the Italian and the Austrian trains are not especially
rapid.   But this was rather an advantage than otherwise,
for the scenery through the Semmering Pass is worthy to
rank with any in the world.   The American mountain
scenery is, undoubtedly, equally grand, but is not so full
of incessant changes, and the deep green of the heavily
wooded mountains, and the lighter, yet velvety green of
the valleys, the quaint little bridges, the white towers of the
churches, the tiled or thatched cottages in the little villages,
form contrasts that make an artist's paradise.   The Cave or
Grotto at Adelsberg is, of course, the great attraction.   Not
so vast as Mammoth Cave, nor so beautiful as Luray, it is
more accessible, and its columns and chambers are in more
fanciful shapes.   An altar, a pulpit, a shrine, a lace curtain
and a parrot are all marvelously exact, and it is difficult to
imagine that nature was the only sculptor.   A vast ballroom
(also natural) is used once a year—at Whitsuntide—by the
peasantry for a festive gathering and dance.   A stream flows
through the cave, with the usual rapid mountain current.
It emerges from the mountain miles away.   A few years
ago some peasants from the village determined to trace its

course, and getting into a small boat started from the interior of the cave. It came very near being a voyage into eternity, for after going a few miles they found that they could neither go forward further nor return, on account of the rapidity of the stream. Three days later they were fished out by a cordon of boats with long ropes, very hungry and very frightened, but none the worse for their bold attempt.

In Adelsberg I encountered a first-class specimen of Italian ignorance of America. A young gentleman, apparently of good family, after a series of questions about the United States, expressed great surprise that I was not *an Indian!*

From Adelsberg the movement went *presto* to Venice. Before reaching the Queen of the Adriatic there was an encounter with an Italian custom-house officer, whose chief efforts seemed to be devoted to preventing me from smuggling six infamously bad cigars into Italy. I at first thought that this might have been in the interests of the sanitary condition of the smokers of Italy, but subsequent trials of Italian cigars convinced me that this was not the case.

One plunges into the typical life of Venice at the outset, for you must take a gondola from the railway station to the hotel. The canals, of course, are at every threshhold, and an American *enfan terrible* who rushed out to play in the street, the morning after our arrival, was fished out of the water only after he had imbibed several quarts of it.

At Venice I began to taste the sweets of hard earned repose. There is nothing so conducive to the *dolce-far-niente* feeling as lying back in a gondola with one's feet on a cushion, one's head on another, and listening to the musical call of the gondoliers as they shoot through the narrow water lanes that branch out from the Grand Canal, (which is, by the way, about the only gondoliers' music in the city). As I was thus tranquilly dreaming, I saw my gondolier stop rowing and take off his hat; I had just time to rise up and take off my sombrero as a richly ornamented gondola passed directly by my own; it contained a most beautiful lady dressed in white, a face and figure which possessed dignity, repose and elegance—the queen of Italy. She had but just arrived in Venice, and on my return to the Hotel Danieli I heard that the municipality was to give her a serenade that evening. I became aware of the fact in another manner also. When there is a féte the city abolishes the regular gondola fares and allows each boatman to get the highest price he can. A young American residing at the hotel desired me to come to his aid in engaging a gondola. As an example of the Italian business system the succeeding interview may be instructive. Having intimated my desire to obtain a noble boat, a swarthy boatman informs me that he is the possessor of a magnificent gondola, just such as my highness needs. The boat is examined and proves reasonably satisfactory. " How much?'' " Thirty lire, most noble.'' I laugh a scornful laugh and say that I do not wish to hire the whole fleet, but only this one boat. "How much will you pay?'' "Thirteen lire.'' Now the gondolier assumes an attitude of bitter anguish, as if my words had cut him to the heart. I do not heed this, but walk slowly from the wharf. Now his pain is shaped into words, and he calls out "Twenty-five lire!'' "Twenty-three lire!!'' "Twenty lire and say no more about it!!!'' in an ascending minor key. I still make no reply, and he says "farewell'' in a manner that convinces me that it is an official dismissal. Scarcely have I reached the next set of steps leading to the water, when my arm is touched. It is the gondolier, who has rapidly put all his grief in his pocket, and desires to commence negotiations on a new basis. This time his premise is "Fifteen lire, and drinks for the two boatmen.'' Finally a bargain is made on a temperance plan at fifteen lire, (the lira is about twenty cents), and all are satisfied. I am glad to say that the boatmen received their *pourboire* as well at the close of the evening. The regular rate would have been about one-half of this price, but the gondoliers deserve the extra pay. The Grand Canal, just below the Museum, is about twice the width of Broadway, in New York. Into this space, on the occasion of fétes, the gondolas pack themselves so solidly that one could walk from bank to bank as on a bridge; yet there seem to be none crushed in and none upset. The skill of the gondoliers is amazing to the uninitiated. The serenade to the queen took place in a barge decorated with lanterns, rowed by twenty men, and containing an orchestra and solo singers. The programme was a long one in a double sense, since it extended over two miles of the canal, the barge moving from place to place at the conclusion of each number, accompanied by the vast mass of gondolas, while almost every boat displayed bengola lights of various colors. The scene was one of fairyland, and it was one which even the Venetians do not have very often. The following is the programme of pieces, with the names of the places where each was performed, and is something of a curiosity in musical peripatetics:

1.   Fondaco dei Turchi—Marcia, Reale, orchestra.

2.   Traghetto S. Stae—Sinfonia nell'opera "Aroldo" di Verdi, orchestra.

3.   Ca d'Oro—"Se tu m'amassi," melodia di Denza, Signorina Pucci.

4.   "Attila" di Verdi, Signorina De Benedetti.

5.   Banca Nazionale—*a*, Giuramento nell' opera. "Orazi e Curiazi" di Mercadante scuola corale; *b*, "Una notte d'amore," duettino di Campana, Signorine Malliani e Zuliani.

6.   Municipio—*a*, Sinfonia, nell'opera " Zampa" di Hérold, orchestra; *b*, "Dormi pure," romanza di Scuderi,

Sig. Scandiani; *c*, Aria nell'opera la "Favorita" di Donizetti, Signorina Petich.

7.　R. Corte d'Appello—"Vieni al mar," barcarola a due voci (parti raddoppiate) di Errera, Signorine De Benedetti, Malliani, Merini e Petich.

8.　Corte Dell'albero—"Delizia," romanza di Beethoven, Signorina Malliani.

9.　Ca Foscari—"Dimmi che m'ami," aria di Palloni, Signorina Tivoli.

10.　S. Samuele—Duetto per mezzo soprano e baritono nell'opera "Favorita" di Donizetti, Signori Petich e Scandiani.

11.　Belle Arti—Divertimento per cornetta, sopra motivi dell'opera "Lucia" di Donizetti, Professor Cavazza.

12.　R. Prefettura—"La Zingara," ballata di Donizetti, Signorina Pucci.

13.　Grand Hotel—"Vorrei morir," melodia di Tosti, Sig. Scandiani.

14.　Dogana—Cavatina nell'opera "Lucia" di Donizetti, Signorina Merini.

15.　Giardino Reale—Coro d'introduzione nell'opera "Isabella d'Aragona" di Pedrotti, scuola corale.

Naturally, in an open-air performance, there was not the nicety of expression and shading that one would find in a concert hall, but the vast crowd, both in the gondolas and on the banks, were so quiet that no part was lost. The queen came out at about 10 P. M. in her gondola, and it was astonishing to see the seemingly solid mass part right and left to allow her to pass. I was sorry, however, to see how little enthusiasm was awakened by her presence. Italy seemingly forgets what progress has been made in twenty years, and is full of a rather vague radicalism, which does not know entirely what ends it aims at

The concert came to a sudden close in a thunder storm.

At the eleventh number the air began to grow chilly, and sudden gusts of wind to blow fiercely. In an instant the whole scene changed; the boats suddenly began to scatter, and all went flying up the side alleys, making the shortest cuts for home. A great deal of good humored shouting and rapid rowing followed, but still no collision and no accident

The next evening I went to the Lido, the summer resort of Venice. Again it was an open-air performance, where the singers seemed to take no heed of their voices. The chief part of the performance was given, not by the throats, but by the legs of the performers, and consisted of a three-act ballet, with a stupid plot and dull music, but a picturesque finale. The chief charm lay in the fact that one could eat ice cream and drink coffee or wine during the entire evening.

How thoroughly music permeates the masses here cannot be imagined by those who do not hear it. I found one street singer who sang, with his own guitar accompaniment, songs by Tosti, Mattei, and other leading Italian composers, to the ordinary street crowds.

I shall not attempt to describe Venice itself in any manner. Our own painters have made almost every American familiar with its appearance. I need only say that the atmosphere is at times as clear as crystal, and at times has a delicate Indian-summer haze about it that adds to the dreaminess of the place. The Hall of the Doges is about the only place where gold and gilt effects are all around, yet never a taste of tinsel or tawdriness is felt.

The guide who took me through this palace was a character in his way; he began each discourse to the party he was piloting with "Sirs and Ladies!" as earnestly as if he were a mediæval knight addressing a tournament audience. When he came to the great two-handed sword with which one of the doges used to probe the infidels, he re-

marked "Now-in-the-days is no sir can swing" and then
nearly beheaded a couple of harmless tourists by shaking it
around in a very wobbly and uncertain manner. But I
fear that he was not always as truthful as George Washington in his cherry-tree days. He was taken from his pedestal by a tourist from the state of Ohio, but who was just
then in a state of perturbation.

The party were just leaving the prison beneath the palace
when the gentleman desired to be shown the little window
of the cell with an island somewhere in the landscape, which
he had read about in a recent poem. The guide with the
omniscience of all his tribe took him upon the Bridge of
Sighs where there was a window, but no island, (I suppose
that he would have afterwards have ferried him to San
Giorgio where there is an island but no window, and
averaged things up in that manner) but the tourist protes-
ted emphatically that this window was in a cell, not on a
bridge. The guide was crestfallen for a moment at the
idea of there being something in the doge's palace which he
could not exhibit, and seeking an aged janitor began inquiries in Italian, about the "piccolo finestra." The janitor declared in the same tongue, that there was nothing of
the kind in the prison, upon which the guide rose to the
occasion and said to the Ohioan, "Ah, yes! I know all about
zat weendow! Eet was here once! Eet is destroy in ze revolution of 1848!!" That statement was enough to have
saved Talleyrand himself, but when a personally-conducted
tourist is aroused not even the fabrications of a veteran
guide can stop him. "No," he replied, "I read about it
in a letter from Europe, last year. There are three trees
upon it!" A light burst upon my brain then. I thought
of the lines

> "And on it there were three tall trees,
> And o'er it blew the mountain breeze.'

and asked, "Are you not thinking of the Castle of Chillon?" It was even so! That sapient traveler had endeavored to see a Swiss island from the heart of Italy. The guide tried to smile his thanks and scowl his rebukes alternately at me and the other man, but his confidence had been severely shaken and he gave very few "Sirs and Ladies" after that.

A point of especial, yet melancholy interest to me in Venice, was the Palazzo Vendramini, in which Wagner died. I was fortunate enough to find a servant and a gondolier who had known Wagner, and from them gleaned a few interesting facts about the Venetian vacation which had such a tragic ending. The Italian musicians were disposed to honor Wagner, but scarcely knew how to set about it. One day, as he approached the square of St. Marks, where the band was playing, the leader saw him and at once began a potpourri from "Tannhäuser," but was astonished to see the master clap his hands to his ears and make off as quickly as he could. It was one of those public disavowals of his earlier works in which Wagner sometimes indulged. I heard many tales about the sumptuous style in which the study of the palace was furnished during Wagner's sojourn. He frequently had it refitted according to the work on which he was engaged, for Wagner was greatly influenced by externals. In this same study he met his solitary death. As there are so many false accounts of this event it may be well to give the details here. Wagner had planned for an excursion on the fatal day, but not feeling in the mood for it in the morning, he countermanded the gondola and set himself to work. On his "gray days," as he called the days when he was out of sorts, he generally dined (at mid-day, in the German fashion), quite alone, that he might not inflict his ill humor upon those whom he loved. On this day he took his meal in the study. No one was allowed to cross the threshhold of that sanctum, and when the servant

(Betty Bürkel) heard a violent fit of coughing, followed by groaning, she did not dare, at first, to enter. In a moment, however, she heard Wagner call her name, and rushed to him at once. He had just strength enough to gasp out, "My wife,—and the doctor." Madame Wagner was at his side in an instant; in a few moments the spasm passed, and his wife thought that he was sleeping in her arms, but he was dead. The few words given above were his last.

Just before leaving Venice I saw a most peculiar arrest. All the Venetians swim like ducks, but the police regulations enforce a bathing suit if the ablutions are taken in the public canals. A sturdy workman had plunged in regardless of the police and of bathing tights; he had, however, trusted too much to providence, and he was dismayed to find an officer standing guard over his scanty wardrobe on the bank when he desired to revisit terra firma. He left his clothes to the State and swam up the canal, but the police were on their mettle, and finally, as he saw two officers getting ready to swim in after him, he decided to avoid a naval combat by coming ashore and surrendering himself. Here a vehement conversation took place in the midst of an admiring crowd of both sexes. The man was in the costume of Adam, before the fall, (not that I suppose that Adam wore a summer suit before the fall), but even that did not quench the interest of the fair *Venitiennes* in the matter, which was finally ended by the swimmer being marched, *puris naturalibus*, to the nearest police station.

From Venice to Florence ; but *bella Firenze* needs no eulogy of mine. I might as well write about the discovery of America as about the beauties of the Venus de Medici or the Fornarina of Raphael. But one piece of advice to the flying tourist may be given: in the Uffizi and Pitti galleries are miles of paintings; do not try to see them all unless you have at least a month to spare; you will only achieve a chromatic nightmare; go rather to the Uffizi gallery, and having seated yourself in the *tribuna*, stay there all day. In that room is the cream of the entire art of Florence, and this at least you *can* digest and carry home with you to beautify your life forevermore. The great trouble with the lightning tourist is that he is bound to see it *all*, and the result is that nothing is retained. In George Washington Phipps that eminent playwright, Mr. Bronson Howard, has not overdrawn this species of human flea, and it is a more pitiable species than even the gentle and sheeplike "Cookie" who follows his leader patiently through the European mazes. From Florence I went directly to Rome, reserving Milan for the return trip.

Of Rome, too, it is necessary to say but little, since I have promised to give no statistical information, and Baedecker can give all the necessary raptures about the old buildings and churches, and the romance of the city has been told all the way from Hawthorne, to James, and Marion Crawford.

In Rome I was forcibly impressed with the lack of communication of one city with another in Italy. Some of the hotel keepers were afraid to receive visitors from Naples, as they feared that the cholera might be brought from there. Meanwhile Naples, (not half so far off as New York is from Boston), was enjoying the best of health. Along with this lack of communication I found another feeling, which is more deplorable for united Italy. Each city is jealous of the other. Florence, Rome, Naples and Milan all dislike each other. Really, united Italy is a far-off matter yet. But the government acts wisely in allowing all possible liberty to the opposition. Even the republicans can sputter with comparative safety. I was sorry to hear an American in an after-dinner speech in Italy express the hope that the country might soon be a republic. Not every nation is fit

at once for self-government.   The French republic of 1793
was very different from that of 1896.   If one only looks
back at the Italy of twenty years ago and compares it with
that of to-day, instead of only looking at the flaws of the
present nation, it would be easier to let well enough alone.
It seems hard to be dissatisfied with the Hercules who has
cleaned the Augæan stables, because he has not yet made
them as neat as a Dutch cottage.

About Rome, as about Naples, there are many falsehoods
circulated, and Roman fever will be a bugbear so long as
"Daisy Miller" is read.   The fact is, that if one will take
reasonable precautions with regard to sudden changes from
heat to cold, and will sleep with closed windows, there need
be no fear.   But it is really difficult for the stranger to take
care of himself amid the thousand and one wonderful sights
of Rome.

The excavations are being pushed forward rapidly
by the government, and constant additions are made to
the valuable antiquities.   Among these is a representation
of the Temple of Jerusalem, (on the base of a drinking
cup), with some emblems which Mr. Forbes, the antiquarian, claims to be Masonic.   I will leave this point to be
discussed by the fraternity, along with Hiram Abiff.

I had an apt illustration of the deceptive size of objects
in St. Peter's, in Rome.   A lady, after expressing her disappointment at the size of the edifice, was charmed with
what she termed some "lovely little cherubs" at the side.
I went and stood beside them, and found them to be three
or four inches higher than myself !   These little cherubs
were six feet and a half high!   So I find that my size will
not debar me from going into the cherub business in Rome.

Everything in St. Peter's is so symmetrical that no mortal being can appreciate the size of things; the colonnade
outside, breaks the first impression of immensity and sub-

stitutes that of symmetry, and Moses' pencil with which he
is writing down the law, although it is about ten feet long,
does not impress one as more ponderous than an ordinary
stylograph, and looks as if it would not provoke half as
much profanity as the latter.

I was more impressed with the polyglot confessionals
which lined the church; here at least was something vast
which the human mind could comprehend. Every language
of the civilized (and some of the uncivilized) world was
there. I think that if my cherished emigration agent had
come down from Hamburg to confess the theft of that railway time table, he would have found a priest ready to hear
him and absolve him in Welsh. But one must beware of
the churches, in a temporal and strictly hygienic sense.
Many a tourist gets heated in the streets of Rome and then
spends an hour or so in this or that church. As a rule he
might as well spend the time in an ice chest, and he need
not wonder, the next day, if he is sick.

It has often been said that to *feel* the antiquity of Rome,
one must visit the Coliseum by moonlight. I felt more impressed, however, by the view on the Appian Way, in a
summer sunset. The tomb of Cecilia Metella was tinged
with the warm, glowing color; the vast circus of Maxentius
was half in twilight; everything was still with summer evening tranquility. It did not take a great stretch of fancy
to shape the shadows that came gradually down upon the
Appian Way, into the ghosts of the old Roman life. It required a greater stretch of fancy to imagine the cruel
" thumbs down " of the Coliseum which consigned the unfortunate gladiator to his execution. How many a general
had camped out on that road, waiting for the dawn when
he might enter Rome in triumph! How many a captive
waited there in anguish, before his dreadful walk in that
same triumph, a walk which often ended with decapitation

on the Capitoline Hill. The Coliseum represents the brutal sports of ancient Rome, but the Appian Way is its history.

If the tourist in Rome desires to make sure of returning to the Eternal City at some later time in his wandering career, he can attain this result in a very simple manner. It is done by a brief incantation. He must go to the beautiful Trevi Fountain at midnight, and after drinking a glass of its water must throw the glass over his shoulder, into the basin, a proceeding which is good for the dealers in crockery ware, and can do the tourist no harm beyond the chance of catching malarial fever by being out so late. This same Trevi water is very sweet and pure, yet not too hard for washing purposes. The Roman is splendidly supplied with water and for this he owes thanks to the ancient dwellers in the city, for imperial Rome built aqueducts enough to supply a nation, and these are used by the present inhabitants. In the house of Mr. S. Russell Forbes, the celebrated antiquarian, I found two kinds of water laid on, and this is the case in many of the better class of houses. The second variety of water is the cold Aqua Marcia, which comes from the Marcian hills far away, and which is just a trifle dangerous to the overheated pedestrian.

Apart from the regular sights, I found considerable pleasure in going about among the antiquarian stores in Rome; but I must warn intending purchasers among my readers *never* to buy without the assistance of an expert. The manufacture of antiquities is one of the most paying of Italy's modern arts, and when we consider that there are counterfeits dating back even to the fifteenth century, one can imagine that the chance of obtaining relics of very " uncertain date " is quite large.

But not only the purchase of antiquities, but every kind of shopping is a difficult matter to the American in Italy. It is totally different from purchasing what you want in

America. Beware of showing eagerness to acquire any special thing in any Italian shop, for the price will ascend in direct ratio. If it is only a necktie there will be seven or eight falling cadences in the price. On the other hand, some American buyers, exaggerating the fear of this custom, have let excellent offers pass by unheeded, to their unavailing regret, after leaving the country. But it is well to distrust the courier or guide who offers to help you in making your purchases without charge, for he will receive his stipend in the shape of a handsome commission from the shopkeeper. I had a startling instance of this in Venice once, when helping a friend in the purchase of some of the silver filagree bracelets for which the city is renowned. The shopkeeper came very nearly down to a fair price, but there all further efforts to " bear " the market failed, and the reason soon came to the surface, for after a moment's hesitation he turned to me and inquired, in Italian, "How much do you expect in this?" After that it was easy to conclude the bargain, but my friend was astonished to receive a good part of the purchase money back from me, that evening, for I could not refrain from tasting, even temporarily, the sweets of a courier's existence. There are some honorable exceptions to the above rule, but they are like angel's visits, few and far between.

And now I hasten southward to seek the most beautiful, the most interesting, and the most dirty city, outside of Rome, in all Italy. The old proverb, "See Naples and then die" has had a rather intimidating effect on many travelers who believe that the latter part will be the legitimate outcome of the first. Never were mortals more mistaken. With reasonable precautions, an avoidance of the water and of the terribly odorous alleys of the place, Naples is as healthy as New York, and ten times as varied and beautiful.

The tables of mortality show a different tale; but one must recollect that the mortality is among the children, (of whom *forty per cent.* die), and that these, even with this drain, remain as numerous as flies in mid-summer. Why these die is easy enough to explain. Early one morning I walked through one of the numerous alleys, about six feet wide, teeming with traffic, reeking with smells, and almost without sunlight; seeing a tailor's shop, I took occasion to have a slight repair made in order to view the place; there was but one room, about eight by fifteen feet, in which were the tailor's implements, the household utensils, (the Lares and Penates were humble enough), three persons were busy at work and six, including two children, still in their beds. One of the men, awakened by the sudden entrance of a stranger, turned around in his bed, raised himself to his elbow, and gazed at me for a moment with a languid interest; but I was a complete failure as a sustained attraction, and he turned around very soon and went to sleep again. The atmosphere in the place was at a pressure of about 70,000 pounds to the square inch, and reminded me of the Danish cheese factories. After that sight I understood the mortality. To be sure, many of the trades are pursued just outside the door of the domicile, but here, too the air is bad, and they only enjoy about fifteen hours even of that. I shudder to think of the other nine hours. Naturally disease and immorality follow, yet not so much of the latter as one would suppose, for the Neapolitans have something of the submissive religious principles of the Irish, whom they resemble in more ways than one. Never was there a more light-hearted, good humored race. I saw boys of seven or eight years of age, working at the most fatiguing manual labor, yet smiling and joking even at their task. The northern and central Italians tell you that the Neapolitans are not Italians at all, and when you ask what they may be, the answer is "They are Moors." It is not unlikely that the Moorish blood has mingled with four or five other currents to make the Neapolitan. Such a population never was seen. There are about 800,000 souls (providing that each inhabitant has one) in Naples and its immediate environs. The city is a narrow ribbon, extending in a semi-circle along the banks of the bay. It is almost impossible for it to broaden, since steep mountains are at the back, but with facilities it can lengthen, and there is a scheme on foot which ought to relieve the overcrowded alleys of their tremendous pressure. Mr. A. G. Caprani (of the Hotel Royal des Etrangéres) gave me the first details of the plan of a metropolitan railroad, which seems to be the crying necessity of the city. It is to combine the tunnel and surface with the elevated system, since the topography of Naples demands all three. Tunneling is a matter of the greatest ease in southern Italy, since the tufa stone cuts like cheese, and then hardens on exposure to the air.

Signor Caprani was the kindest of friends during my visits to Naples, and he is an ideal host to all Americans who come to this city. He was much interested in some comparisons I drew between Brindisi and Naples (for I believe that Naples can be made the chief port of Italy for *all* commerce), and as we became better acquainted he determined to give me a public breakfast, to which he invited the leading English and American residents who were in the city in the summer time. One most prominent Italian was present, however; it was the owner of the famous *Lacryma Christi* vineyard, on Vesuvius. The real *Lacryma Christi* is about as rare as the real Johannisberger, and when I state that this gentleman brought a few bottles of this precious vintage with him, it may be judged that his passport to American citizenship on that occasion, was not rejected. At this most pleasant breakfast, which at my request was cooked

entirely in Milanese style (with Risotto, maccaroni and the
Vesuvian wine), I had the pleasure of meeting a genial
English doctor—Mr. Berrenger—(who told me that eighteen
years of Naples had not been unhealthy to him), and
also Mr. Lamont Young, to whom the great railway will
owe its existence. At the invitation of the latter gentleman
I visited his villa, the most beautiful in all Naples, once
owned by King Ferdinand I.—the Villa Lucia. The noble
mansion rests on the summit of one of the high hills back of
the city, and we sat sipping tea in the glow of a tropical
sunset, with Naples gleaming far below us. Villa Lucia
interested me far more, however, in another sense. It is the
home and laboratory of an inventor and scientist. Mr.
Young (also an Englishman, who has by choice become a
Neapolitan) showed me many of his plans for the development of Naples; but it was especially interesting to note the
cautious way in which he developed the various steps of his
railroad scheme. First he took, at his own expense, a cen-
sus of certain of the districts through which the road is to
run, and which it intended to relieve; next he cut a tunnel
on his own grounds to demonstrate the expense of this part
of the work; then he had geological surveys made, and in
this manner he has made tentative efforts to introduce the
scheme. It is not an easy matter to do. The Neapolitan
is content to leave things the way he finds them. In any
other city of such size one would at once say that the plan
was sure to be a gold mine to its projectors; in Naples, who
can predict? Will the Neapolitan ride in the steam car when
he has the chance? I have seen numbers of people in southern
Italy who never entered a railway train in their lives, and
who never intend to. Many of the Neapolitans of the lower
class live in their little alleyways as if they loved them, and
scarcely care for anything like travel, even to the suburbs.

In Naples I also met the agent of the Pullman Car Co., Mr. Wildhagen, who told me of the difficulties he had encountered in accustoming the southern Italians to a comfortable mode of traveling. Now these obstacles have been surmounted, and I watched the departure and arrival of trains in the cars of which passengers had no more discomfort than in America.

To illustrate the ingenious ways which are necessary to overcome Naple's undeserved bad name, I need only mention Mr. Caprani's mode of setting the public mind right upon the climate question. On every letter leaving his hotel he stamps the record of the thermometer and barometer at the time of departure. There is no question about the fact that Naples has a great future. Already the question of bad water has been settled by the commencement of great aqueducts, which are to bring splendid water from mountains forty miles away. When better drainage and transportation facilities follow, Naples will be the New York of Italy, and its environs the most beautiful pleasure resorts of the world. I earnestly wish that the first forward step might be the formation of a "Society for the prevention of cruelty to animals." Such an institution does exist, but it is a mummy beside our society with the long name. The poor donkeys are murdered by inches. They are loaded beyond credence. I saw a high heap of brushwood moving along the road one day. Wonder-struck at the miracle, I walked around it and was rewarded by seeing a thin tail sticking out of the heap. The mystery was explained; somewere beneath the heap was a donkey. This deduction was confirmed by the fact that the driver soon came to that part of the heap to kick. On my remonstrating, he calmly told me that a donkey was *not a christian!*

I have spoken about the swarms of children, let me also

speak of the hosts of beggars. At every turn there is some one to waylay you. They do it so frankly, and with such a business-like air, that it has the charm of naïveté. At Torre del Greco, on my way to Mt. Vesuvius, I saw a man and boy very contentedly seated under a tree. As soon as the elder saw us, he rose hastily, tossed his hat to the boy, and lifted up his voice pathetically, "*Sono, povero, signor! una piccolo soldo.*" But one cannot give even *soldi* to every beggar, and as this one did not inspire my confidence, I drove on in silence, whereupon the irate gentleman ventilated the hope that Vesuvius might fall down on my head. It was a vivid contrast.

I noticed that some Neapolitans did not speak to the beggars, but made signs. I asked Signor Caprani what these signs meant. He taught me to make two or three of them. The next day I practiced my new accomplishment with telling effect. A beggar began his song at the side of my carriage (never walk when you can ride, in Naples), whereupon I put my thumb near my chin, and wiggled my forefinger; the mendicant looked at me for a moment as if I were a new and strange sort of native Neapolitan, and then, knowing that blondes did not grow in southern Italy he made up his mind that my gesture was merely an odd coincidence, and began all over again, whereupon I put four fingers under my chin, and waved my hand; on seeing this he silently withdrew. I had told him first, "I have nothing for you," and then, "You said all that before!" Not only the beggars but the cabmen can do business by the signal code. You approach and point to the cab with the little finger: "I want a short drive for half a franc." The cabman shakes his head—"No;" or gives it a little side jerk—"Get in!"

Naples has no real pleasure ground for the people, so they transform the whole city into one; but there is music in the evening at the new embankment, where you can walk for nothing, but you must pay two *soldi*, (a *soldo* is a cent), for a chair, and can listen to rather poor dance music. Posilippo is the finest suburb of Naples. One can reach it by tramway (horse cars) and enjoy glorious views of the bay and of Vesuvius. There are restaurants here where one can sit in grottos cut into the rock, or tufa, and sip light wine at an absurdly low cost. There is much architecture at Posilippo that astonishes a stranger, since many of the houses are not built, but excavated, being entirely *of one piece of stone!* Many of the Neapolitan houses are gayly painted, red and yellow being predominant colors, which gives the whole place a rather stagy appearance. The colors soon fade, and are absorbed, and "spread" into the tufa as into a blotting pad. Sometimes the entire architecture is painted on the house, arches above the windows, statues, cornices, columns, etc., being all the product of the painter's brush and not the sculptor's chisel. When these begin to fade the resemblance to stage scenery is very marked. In one country place I saw an entire dead wall of a house made lively by numerous windows, blinds, curtains, children looking out, etc., all painted on the stone. I must state that all the Neapolitans assure me that their city has made immense strides since King Bomba has been set aside. It is refreshing to see such a city grow, for once it was the abode of tyranny and intolerance; one of the strongholds of the past begins to take place in the ranks of the present, but the progress must naturally be gradual. I cannot close the cadenza about Naples without speaking of an occurrence at the post office there, when I mailed a letter to America. I registered it without difficulty, when suddenly the official asked, "Where are the five seals?" On inquiring into his meaning, it was discovered that registered letters must have five seals to secure their safe condition. I was about to comply with this regulation when the gentleman said, "*Scusate, signor,* I see that this goes to America. Letters to South America and Africa are allowed without sealing wax, since the melting of the wax spoils other postal matter." I thanked him, but said that this letter was not for South America, but for the United States. "That's all the same thing," he responded, "since it has to pass the equator, anyway!" That was an unexpected and original lesson in geography.

Of Pompeii it is unnecessary to speak *in extenso,* since every detail both in print and picture is in every large library. It may be borne in mind by the reader that only about one-third or one-half of the city is as yet uncovered. In America it would have been unearthed many years ago, nor would Herculaneum be suffered to retain all of its mystery, as it does to-day. When all the treasures have been gathered we may know something about the music of the ancient world, for it is probable enough that a musical library of some sort will be discovered, and then we shall no longer rely upon the three doubtful manuscripts of ancient Greek music, (discovered in Messina in the 16th century), for all our knowledge of the pre-christian system of music.

It is pleasant to go to Pompeii from Naples by coach, or on foot, for the road through Portici, Torre del Greco and Torre del Annunziata, is a varied and interesting one. But do not stop to look at the maccaroni factories, for it will cause you to have unpleasant memories while eating that species of food thereafter. The veil of mystery had better remain over the processes, the appearance of the workmeñ, and the number of dirty children who roll around in the product before it gets to market. Besides maccaroni, the production of children seems to be the chief industry of these towns. If "a babe in the house is a well-spring of pleasure," as Tupper says, then these people had better "let well enough alone," for they are nearly drowned out with their numerous "well-springs."

CHAPTER XI.

Casamicciola—a terrific earthquake—scenes in a de-
vastated country—the death of an English pianist
—the fatal termination of a concert—a life saved
by Chopin's funeral march—Pisa—Milan—Lake Como
—an impromptu musicale.

It was in July, 1883, that one of the most terrific catas-
trophes of modern times took place, only a few miles from
Naples. I was then in that city, and in my capacity of
foreign correspondent to the American press, was supplied
with a permit to visit the island of Ischia, where the dread
calamity had occurred. This chapter will sing a very melancholy minor strain in consequence, for the sights on the
island were the most dismal that I ever witnessed. Armed
with my permit, it was not difficult to reach the island,
although the journey in a small boat, crowded with soldiery,
surgeons, ambulance corps, etc., was uncomfortable enough.
On passing the port of Ischia I looked in vain for any signs
of the calamity. The beautiful island was crowned with
lovely vineyards and rich mansions in a manner which
showed undisturbed prosperity. Rounding a point on the
west side of the island, all was changed in a moment.
Casamicciola had been to Italy what Newport is to New
England and New York. Vast hotels, beautiful alleys of
trees, drives, great bathing establishments, had made it one
of the most attractive summer resorts. It nestled on the

HOTEL DES ETRANGERES, CASAMICCIOLA.

AFTER THE EARTHQUAKE.

slope of a hill which stood in front of a semicircle of high but richly cultivated mountains. Of all its architectural beauty scarcely a trace remained. At the water's edge were what seemed to be elegant residences, but, on approaching, it was at once evident that the interior was one mass of crushed masonry. Farther up the slope, the beautiful streets were more entirely obliterated; chasms yawned in the middle of the road; few walls even were standing, while amidst the débris one could see pathetic indications of the fashionable pleasure resort—bits of lace, a once elegant bonnet, now draggled and blood-stained, fine engravings still hanging on a single wall which stood above one of the heaps of death. Even the natural scenery was partially effaced; a whole vineyard had slid down from a hill above the town and added its débris to the general crash. At 9.50 on Saturday evening, July 28, 1883, the city was a flourishing watering place; fifteen seconds later it was a terrible cemetery, with many of the living buried with the dead.

I saw two clocks taken from the ruins which pointed to the hour of destruction with silent accuracy. It was due to the hour of the shock that so many were killed. Many had retired for the night, and I saw some of these, still covered with the bedclothes, who were mercifully killed before awakening. Others were in their drawing-rooms listening to music, or reading, when the sudden bolt fell. I spoke with many regarding the manner of the shock. The lower classes were naturally imaginative and spoke of balls of fire and fearful darkness, and other phenomena, which probably had no part in the catastrophe; but some of the guests of the place told me that a shivering, rumbling sound was heard, then the side of the hill fell down, then the earth seemed to rise upward, followed by a side motion (it was this twitch which crumbled all the houses), then followed a moment's absolute silence, and all was obscured by dust, and then the babel of shrieks and lamentations burst forth. I fear that my pen can do only scant justice to the scene, but the result has not been exaggerated; the dead numbered over 3,000 in Casamicciola alone. In coming so soon after the disaster, I had the advantage of speaking with many of the survivors, although their grief and agitation was yet scarcely under control. One of the most pitiable of these I met on the boat going to the island, Mr. Dombré, syndic (or mayor) of the city, who was rich the day before and was now almost reduced to beggary in his old age. He owned two of the largest hotels of the place. In one of them—the Piccola Sentinella—lay thirty-six dead guests, and the whole was merely a set of useless, crumbling walls. One was astounded, on looking at the size of these edifices, that in so hazardous a country (it had a disastrous earthquake two years before, in which over one hundred were killed) the inhabitants should dare to build of stone. Yet they seem to have done so, and possessed some buildings as large as the greatest hotels in the cities of the United States. Now the government has prohibited the building of any but wooden houses in the future.

The government did not come out of the matter with any great credit, since there seems to have been a reprehensible delay in sending troops to the island.

Even when I left the scene, there was a small force entirely inadequate to cope with the calamity, among the ruins, and these, strange to say, took their midday *siesta* (from 12 to 3) as if the occasion did not demand especial haste. As a consequence many who might have been rescued died under the ruins. The careless manner of grappling with an emergency was evidenced by the fact that, after a cursory examination, an officer reported that there were only dead dodies under the ruins, and these already decaying, and the whole town was a very dangerous place, for sanitary reasons and because of crumbling walls, and that it would be advisable to strew plenty of quicklime and temporarily close that part of the island. This would have been done, too, but for the arrival of the humane king, (what a grand man King Humbert is!) who ordered that the work of excavation should go on at all hazards. Only a few hours later two persons were rescued alive and without a scratch of injury. It was a strange rescue. One of the soldiers came to notify me that they had heard moans near the Villa Verde, and he supposed the *reportorio Americano* would like to assist. I did so with hearty good will, for it was a relief to be active with so much misery all around. It proved to be a young lady of noble birth, from Germany, and a tailor of the place. She had been thrown from her chamber, he from the office of the hotel, into the cellar, where a pillar had lodged transversely over them, saving their lives. As we assisted them to the surface the lady was calm, although tears were on her cheeks, but the tailor in the twinkling of an eye, became insane; "Where was his shop? He had promised a coat that day! He was a man of his word! Had we taken his cloth?" and so he went on, growing more furious each moment, until he was led away under restraint, by some of the soldiery. Yet the lady said that while imprisoned, he had been the more prudent of the two, and had even groped around to see if food or drink were within reach, and after finding a few tomatoes had given her some of them, advising her to eat that they might sustain their strength should their imprisonment be very long. What would have been the fate of these, had the island been closed as the officer suggested, and the quicklime strewn? These are two of the many lives King Humbert has saved in his career.

The next day the scene on the island was a strange one.

Booths for the sale of necessities of life, tents for soldiers and relief committees, men driving frightened cattle from boats to the improvised slaughter house, ominous piles of quicklime, wonder-struck children and care-worn parents— these made up a picture which would move any heart. There were very few of the survivors of the richer classes on the island, since they naturally would fly from such a scene.

Starting up the curving street which ascended the hill, the terrific odor at once showed the danger, in such a warm climate, of such excavation. A kindly officer broke off half of his piece of camphor and gave it to me to use. The first large edifice was the grand bath, now almost unrecognizable. In this place one gentleman, a photographer named Sommer, saved all his family and many others, by presence of mind. There was music in the covered hall in the centre of the establishment, and many were sitting around listening to it. When the shock came, Mr. Sommer called all around him in the centre of the hall, which was covered only by a large sky-light; some, after a few seconds, called out that the ground was opening, (as in fact it *did* in some places), and trying to rush to the street, were killed; those who remained with Mr. Sommer were all saved, only being slightly cut by the falling glass.

Speaking of the music of that fearful evening calls up one of the most pathetic incidents of the event. A young pianist, von Struvé by name, had been invited to assist at a musical soirée, and a young lady who had not intended to attend, had been persuaded to assist with a few songs. Every one in that drawing-room was instantly killed, and the body of the young pianist was found seated at the instrument, with the music, (a volume of Chopin), open on the rack. The young lady was found dead near by.

I brought away, as a souvenir of the dreadful concert, a

bit of that music, with the pianist's name upon it, as repro-
duced in the accompanying illustration. The concert took
place in the Hotel des Etrangéres, or the "Piccola Sentinella," as it was more generally called, (see illustration),
and we entered the place by means of ladders placed against
the second story windows. The way in which the history
of the strange concert was preserved was most peculiar.
Mr. von Struvé had not given any music on any occasion
during the season, alleging as sufficient excuse, that he was
at the island for rest and did not desire, therefore, to turn
from recreation to piano playing. The solicitation of friends,
however, at last prevailed, and he consented to give just
this one musical evening. Oddly enough (could it have
been premonition?) he began the musicale with Chopin's
"Funeral March." One of the small circle of friends, who
did not care for such sombre music at a pleasure resort, arose
and left the room and went into the garden. This was his
salvation! Chopin's "Funeral March" saved his life! It
was this man who told the soldiers of the concert, who
guided us all to the spot, and who gave the details narrated
above.

Passing farther up the slope, the way becoming more difficult, I turned aside into a vineyard, where I found five
families of peasants, huddled together without a hut or
shelter of any kind. They complained bitterly that the
system of relief was not yet well organized, and that the
soldiers had been excavating only in the fashionable quarters, leaving the large part of the city where the working
class lived undisturbed. How true this was I could not sa-
tisfactorily ascertain. An officer assured me, however, that
the men could not do more than was being done, that the
poorer portion of the city was buried deeper through being
in the valley under the vineyard, and that the soldiers were
much abused by an excited, half-crazed peasantry, who even

accused them of stealing valuables, when in fact the poor
fellows had to work the first day almost on empty stomachs,
because the food was needed for the people. He admitted,
however, that the military had been ordered there very late,
but that was not the soldiers' fault. The latter fault, I may
say, seems to have been due to much red tape on the part of
General Mezzacapo. The prefect of the province, Count
San Leverino, has been unremittingly active. But I could
not but incline to the belief that the soldiery had no thorough
system, when I saw them leave their work during a shower
and seek refuge under the trees, when I observed that
there was no system of relief gangs, and that some houses
had not been approached since they fell in, and that the
labor was wholly suspended at night. The next house that
I passed told a mute story. One corner room remained in-
tact, and here I saw neat damask window curtains, handsome
pictures, and a table which was still spread. All the inmates were dead. I cannot begin to describe the débris
farther up the road. Sleeping and reclining chairs, paintings, wearing apparel, a piano, of which not a string was
broken, although the case was entirely demolished; every
article told of what the city had been.

One of the most frightful wrecks of the city was the
Hotel et Pension Villa Verde. As I approached I saw the
gaily painted signs, announcing the hour of table d'hote,
the various medicinal baths, and the different attractions of
the place. Back of these signs was a solid heap of masonry
in which lay almost every inmate of the hotel. I was
joined here by a party consisting of Messrs. Mella and Dal
Ferro of the Roman News, Mr. Wildhagen of the Pullman
car company, and Mr. A. G. Caprani of the Hotel Royal
of Naples, but I was soon obliged to leave them because
the fearful sights and odors caused them nausea, Mr.
Mella only continuing with me. Just beyond the Hotel

Fr. Chopin's

Sämmtliche

Pianoforte-Werke.

Kritisch revidirt und mit Fingersatz versehen

von

HERRMANN SCHOLTZ.

PRÉLUDES

und

RONDOS.

LEIPZIG
C. F. PETERS

Verde I found a house which seemed to have been a large structure many stories high. Everything was down as far as the second story. Here, from a vast pile of rubbish I saw a man's foot protruding. Calling some of the soldiery I had an opportunity of noting some of the defects of the system of excavation. After exposing the body from the ankle to the knee they decided it was too solidly buried to recover, and calling up two boys with baskets of quicklime, they filled up the cavity. Meanwhile an officer had arrived with a list of the inmates of the house, and had checked off one name almost at haphazard. A soldier told me that his brother, sister-in-law and two nieces lay under this heap, and with no more emotion than if he were pointing out the beauties of the landscape. The house was called the Villa Marcatelli. But I found a vivid contrast to this apathy in a young man named Severio Monti, who told me that his father and mother were lost in the crash, he himself escaping unwounded. He spent the night and part of the next day in furiously digging in the ruins for their bodies. His greatest fear was that they might be buried alive. At last he found his mother's body and he tells me that he cannot explain his emotions on finding that she had been instantly killed. He felt almost as much joy as if he had found her alive. His father he was unable to find.

It is strange that one could think of eating amid such scenes; nevertheless, we were glad to be shown by this young man to the hotel of his uncle, which was only about one-quarter in ruins, and was about the only house of the place that had escaped. It was called the Hotel Bellevue, and proved an oasis in the desert. Here our little party met again and, with some Italian officers, partook of a frugal meal. The proprietor seemed to take the misfortune very stoically, but not in as apathetic a manner as some of the other inhabitants. At the conclusion of the repast, he absolutely refused all compensation for the meal, saying that business should begin after the dead were buried. Meanwhile we were his guests.

After this there was but a repetition of the old story—death, death, death on every side. At the hotel of the Gran Sentinella I met a man, half crazed, who invoked the vengeance of heaven upon the soldiers, who, he said, had done nothing but drink and steal since they reached the island. In the midst of this tirade, an Italian captain stepped up, trembling with rage, and demanded a single proof of the assertion. He turned to me and said, " Our soldiers came here late, it is true, but they worked, and are working, faithfully and honestly. The first day they were starved; they had not even a crust of bread; what wonder if they seized a few bottles of wine to sustain them.'' But in answer to my question about the suspensions of work, he was obliged to admit my criticisms. The soldiers did not work at night. One of the rich inhabitants offered to furnish electric lights at his own expense, but the officers thanked him and said they could not accept the offer without ''higher authority.'' Red tape could go no farther than this. At noon each day the entire soldiery took three hours rest in spite of the fact that there were still living beings in the ruins. All this was confirmed by the officer, who was forced to admit the truth of it.

While talking with him, a private came up to announce the discovery of another victim. We went together, and found the body to be that of a fashionable lady, finely dressed, with a brilliant ring on the left hand. The ring was put in alcohol; the body, only half unearthed, covered with quick-lime, and the name of Rose di Clustere erased from the list of missing and placed in that of the dead. The list will, however, never be complete, for many were not on the hotel books. Saturday night was the worst possible moment for such a calamity, since many had gone to the island to pass Sunday with their friends, and these must have swelled the population at least by eight hundred, and these eight hundred will never be thoroughly accounted for.

I cannot add to this chapter all the anecdotes and incidents of that ten hours' visit. Every moment brought some new pang, until I began to undertand the callousness of the people. Arrived at the beach, after I had gathered most of the important details, I found there was no certainty as to when a boat would leave for Naples. Even the highest official, the secretary of public works, did not know. This official was very cordial, promised to send details of further excavations to me at Naples (which he did not do), and assured me on his personal honor that there was no possibility of a single person being any longer alive under the ruins. Somebody had said that but a few hours before a few unfortunates demolished his theory by stepping out without a scratch.

At last I found a government boat, which took me back to Naples. Here again everything was excited and feverish. Vesuvius was in a state of eruption, and the Neapolitans began to fear that even they might not be secure. Yet a most wonderful sight, an indirect consequence of the earthquake was to greet me the next night in Naples.

I was resting after the exciting events just described, at the "Hotel Reale," which is situated on the new embankment, just opposite the Castle dell'Uovo, and from the balcony of which one can see the long crescent of the beach, stretching away for miles towards Vesuvius. I had gone to bed quite exhausted, but was awakened at about 2 A. M. by the most indescribable of sounds; it was the voice of a vast multitude. What could it be? With visions of earthquakes and disasters upon me, I sprang to the balcony just outside my chamber window. Then I beheld a most unexpected sight; it was a moonlight night, and the beach was as distinct as if it were day, and upon it, and the embankment, were gathered 300,000 people, (this was the estimate of the journals the next day), and the mighty crowd was agitated as the waves of the sea. What could this mean at two o'clock in the morning? It meant one of the most audacious schemes of robbery ever planned, and a hoax beside which Hook's celebrated Moon Street hoax was nothing; a trick which deceived an entire city. A small band of thieves had gone from house to house at midnight, stating that Professor Palmieri, of the observatory on Vesuvius, had predicted a great eruption and earthquake by three o'clock in the morning, and bidding the people save themselves. Immediately all Naples was in an uproar. The memory of Casamicciola was upon everybody, and with one wild impulse all left their houses and sought shelter by the seashore. Fancy the effect in a city of the size of Naples! Of course, in a few minutes a dispatch was received from Prof. Palmieri denying that he had made any prediction, but it took some hours to get this news disseminated among the people, on the principle that a lie will travel around the world while truth is putting its boots on to pursue it, and in those few hours there was rich plundering for the band, who were, I believe, never discovered.

Great is the power of Italian imagination. The day after my visit to Casamicciola the Popolo of Rome contained the following telegram: "Several American correspondents were here yesterday, and expressed complete approval of the energetic measures taken by the government at Ischia." To my own knowledge there was but one other American on the spot, and if there was any approval in our sentences it must have been because of our poor Italian. But enough of this gloomy subject. I left Naples regretfully, and passing through Rome, made straight for Pisa, which I found the most uninteresting city of Italy. Having seen the tower lean to the best of its ability, and having heard the echo in the Baptistery, I could meditate on earthly vanities during the rest of my stay. Perhaps my judgment is warped by the fact that I came to the place at 4 A. M., after an all-night ride. A custom house officer of some kind met me at the gate, and asked me if I had anything to declare. I declared that I was cold and sleepy, whereupon he laughed, and told me to get to bed as soon as possible.

Perhaps, in a semi-musical work, however, the echo should not be so summarily dismissed. It is a refined and musical echo, which has probably studied Richter, and understands harmony, for when the guide sang certain notes singly, it gave back a neat assortment of triads and seventh chords which it had made up out of the raw material. A man could, in this place, sing a duet, or a trio, with himself without much difficulty. There are different theories as to what made the tower of Pisa lean so much. I believe I discovered the cause when I saw an American relic-hunter trying to chip off a piece of the building to carry away "as a souvenir." The tower probably did its utmost to fall over on one of these relic-gatherers, and a very sensible tower it was.

At Milan the musician is chiefly interested in La Scala, which is by no means an attractive looking opera house. Whenever I have had the fortune to see it, it has seemed dingy and faded. But its acoustics is quite another matter; there is probably no other edifice of size in the world, except the Albert Hall in London, where every sound is so well garnered up and delivered to the expectant ear. It will strike the American oddly at first, that an amount of tremolo is tolerated, and even desired, in Italy, that would be hissed in our country, but this is a matter of taste which falls under the head of "*de gustibus non est disputandem.*"

Some of the singers flicker in their tones as if they needed quinine for vocal ague. Of course the artistic traveler will go to see Leonardo da Vinci's "Last Supper," and will feel disappointed to learn that it has been retouched from time to time to prevent its fading out. One may feel that this makes it about as original as the boy's jack knife, which first had a new blade inserted, and then a new handle, but after all we have to do the same thing in music, and set additional accompaniments to Bach and Handel, so that when we hear a modern performance of "The Messiah" it is not always easy to say what is Handel, what is Mozart, what is Adam Hiller, and what is Robert Franz.

But Como! lovely, sweet, incomparable Como! I shall not soon forget the *andante tranquillo* which fell upon the *allegro* movement at thy shores! I felt that if there had been a Pauline within reach who understood the United States language, I should have quoted Bulwer to an alarming extent. The very beginning of my visit there was auspicious. The American flag was hanging over the door of the Hotel Britannia as I entered. A large number of foreigners were staying here, and that evening we had fireworks and a serenade. The latter was memorable for the most energetic trombone playing I ever heard. The wild luxuriance of that trombone player's powers will not soon be forgotten. The concert would have been perfect and the ensemble well balanced if that emphatic musician had been on the other side of the lake.

I cannot describe the quiet, restful charm of the lake. It is of a vivid green color and is surrounded by hills which remind one of the Scottish lochs; but the languid, hazy atmosphere lends a charm which is altogether absent from the latter. To take a boat and row over to the smaller lake of Lecco, from Cadenabbia, and to linger around the lovely villas which fringe Bellaggio, is little short of paradise; but unfortunately paradise cannot be described in earthly type. The golden afternoon effect—the midday is kept as a time of siesta in all Italy in summer—was heightened by peasants going home from their work, singing by the way, exactly as the peasantry do in Boucicault's dramas.

The following evening we had a *fete* on the lake in true Italian style. A large barge—gayly trimmed with lanterns, and containing a piano, fireworks, wine, cake, and soloists, among whom, by special invitation, was myself— put out from the shore. A programme of music was gone through with in this *al fresco* manner, the singers being Senorita Curti of Buenos Ayres, Signor Mella of Cadenabbia, and myself; several pianists and choristers were also on board the barge, and contributed numbers. It was said to have been very pleasant from a distance, but taken from the near point of view, it had its drawbacks. The lights drew hundreds of insects which were inhaled and exhaled by the singers at loud notes, and which crawled down their backs at *pianissimo* passages; the lanterns occasionally took fire and added vehemence to the high notes of the soprano; the tallow, dripping from the suspended lights, formed fantastic patterns on the dresses of the singers. I shall go to future water-serenades as a passive member.

Yet the spontaneous character of these fetes is charming. This excursion was planned in the afternoon, in the evening we started out from Cadenabbia, and we had not sung two numbers before there were signs of activity in Bellaggio, on the other side of the lake. Out came the boats, a moment after in swarms. Each brought its quota of fireworks along and Roman candles and colored fires soon punctuated the musical numbers. Nevertheless a quiet, moonlight row on that corner of Lake Como, called Lago di Lecco, is preferable to all the manufactured enthusiasm of water festivals.

CHAPTER XII.

Switzerland—the great organ at Luzerne—zither music in the alps—climbing the chapeau bas—the romantic mule—a ride beset with dangers—up the
righi—a musical acquaintance—zurich—chamounix
—geneva—schaffhausen.

At last I am out of sunny Italia, and rest under the folds
of a republican flag. In Switzerland the motto is "Liberty,
Equality, and Cash Paid in Advance." The last is the
most important part. The refreshing coolness of the atmosphere is fully equalled by the refreshing coolness with
which the natives of this place lay on the tariff for strangers.
But of that hereafter.

At the frontier we are told, by the railway officials, with
much emphasis, not to leave our seats until the customs
officer has examined all our handbags. I prepare to dis-
gorge soiled collars, cuffs, bad cigars, tooth brush, nail
brush, everything, but when the smiling Switzer comes to
me he says: "Don't open your bag! You have nothing you
desire to declare, have you?" This is as leading as any Sunday school question, and I answer promptly "No," and
enter into the Swiss republic.

Of the three lakes of north Italy, Como, with Lago di
Lecco, seems the fairest; Lago Lugano is undoubtedly
grander, but has not the dreamy repose of the former.
Lugano itself, although in Switzerland, is a thoroughly

Italian city, having Italian inhabitants, Italian buildings and Italian smells. From here the traveler towards the north crosses the Alps. This part of the journey again defies description. As I went through the passes on the slow-moving railroad train, a thunder storm passed over the peaks. One cannot imagine a more stirring sight than such a storm in these mountains; echoing reverberations from every side; the swollen torrents begin to bring down stones, and small landslides occur. Meanwhile men are busy all along the road clearing away the dangerous débris, and ready to signal the train should any great obstruction occur. The time of running through the St. Gothard tunnel (one of the longest in the world) was twenty-one minutes. The air throughout was pure and cool, thanks to an excellent ventilating apparatus.

Luzerne was the objective point of my next foray, and here it poured all day and night, and the great lion seemed peculiarly sad, viewed from under a dripping umbrella, while the glacial garden was a succession of little pools. Switzerland in the wet is a regular damper to one's hilarity. Finally, driven by the rain, and having heard so little music during the past season, I went to the church to hear a concert upon the great organ. The instrument has some beautiful solo stops, but unfortunately it has an organist (with an unpronounceable name) who is so sentimental that he uses almost nothing but these, and the effect is like a meal composed wholly of sweatmeats. He took to the *vox humana* as naturally as a duck to water. In American church organs the *vox humana* generally sounds like a goat with the ague, but here, fortunately, it *did* resemble a human voice, and the effect was not altogether bad. The most musicianly work of the organist was done in the Vorspiel to "Lohengrin," but then, as if he repented him of having given some good music, he immediately followed it with

"The Storm," the most sensational piece ever written. It was bad enough to give lightning flashes on the piccolo, and roars of thunder on the pedals, but it was worse to give Wagnerian phrases between the flashes, on the corno and trumpet stops; it sounded for all the world as if a cornetist were out in the fields practicing selections from "Tannhäuser" and had been struck by lightning—a righteous punishment. Another favorite trick of this organist was to jump from a deafening fortissimo to an inaudible pianissimo, but there are so many organists and pianists at home who do this that I was quite used to it.

At the end of the thunderstorm in the church, I went into the rainstorm out of doors, and in spite of the lowering skies, departed the next day for Interlaken. The scenery along the new railroad over the Brunig Pass is something beyond description, and the lake of Brienz is quite as fine, but as the guide books do the necessary rhapsodizing, I pass it by in silence, and only state that I ended this stage of my journey on the mansard roof of the two-storied railway which runs to Interlaken. This is one of the tiniest railroads imaginable, its whole length being only a few miles; but what it lacks in length it makes up in height, each car being about twenty feet high. I could live at Interlaken about twenty-five minutes before going into insolvency; I was therefore perfectly solvent when at the end of twenty minutes I engaged a carriage to go to the Grindelwald. The driver promised everything; he saw that I had my doubts about the weather, and he promised immediate sunshine; he anticipated my misgivings about finding rooms at the destination by promising princely lodgings at pauper prices; he painted a picture about as glowing as Claude Melnotte portrayed to Pauline—before marriage, and put on so much *couleur de rose* that the sun seemed to burst from behind the clouds. Once started a cloud fell upon his brilliant prospects; he had a daughter in Lauterbrunnen; he had not seen her for many days; would our noble highness consent to his going to see his child and compensate him for the trouble? He didn't put it just that way, but that was what it boiled down into. I am not naturally hard-hearted, and consented to the re-union of two loving hearts at my expense. Besides I wished to look at the Staubbach, that wonderful fall of 1,000 feet, which was just then especially fine, because of the recent rains.

Therefore, while he looked at his daughter, I looked at the fall, and both were satisfied. After this came a long drive, with the same optimistic driver, to the Grindelwald. Here I committed a fault which no experienced traveler should do; I allowed my Jehu to persuade me as to what hotel to put up at. He told me the rooms at the Bear Hotel should cost but three francs *per diem!* So indeed they did, but the " extras " put the rooms out of sight. There was the mystical "service" charge, two francs a day; the equally dark charge for " lights," one franc, and a dozen other equally incomprehensible debts. But as the air in this Alpine district was worth about ten cents a breath, I consider that I made a profit in spite of this.

I hope that I am not giving my readers the impression that I am a traveling skinflint (if they could hear the number of times that I am called "your excellency" and "your highness," this idea would at once vanish), but the constant succession of flea-bite charges annoys an American more than the extortion of a good sum taken at once would. Let me explain: We are walking to the glacier on the Grindelwald, for example; there is a guide (necessary) who gets four francs; then we meet an infant who stands in our path and sings dismally about the joys of Alpine life (tip); then her elder sister with *edelweiss* (buy); then a boy with smoky quartz (swear); then a cripple with outstretched hat (give);

then, as we emerge from a gorge, we are met by a female with a placard stating that these gorges cost half a franc to look at (settle); then comes a man with a long horn and sells us the echo at another half franc (liquidate); finally we are at the cave in the ice, out of breath, for it is a strong climb, when we pay just one more half franc apiece to go in. Is that the end? Nay, misguided reader, for in that ice cave, in the heart of the Alps, sits a female, apparently several years older than the glacier; she has with her a prehistoric zither and a cracked voice, and she makes our existence there unendurable, for which we give her one franc. On our return trip all the army above described (and this is no fancy sketch) is on duty to do it all over again, but the iron has entered into our soul, our heart is hardened, our pocket empty of small coin and our retainers are dismissed this time without guerdon. For all this, these petty beggings and demands do not rob the Alps of their grandeur, and after all the season is very short, a half franc is only ten cents, and the people are very, very poor, so I feel half ashamed of the above growls.

I begin to suspect my suave driver, with the parental feeelings, of duplicity; for he is engaged the next day, and when my guide is negotiating with a good team for my return to Interlaken he says, "Why not take Seppl?" "He's only got one horse." "But don't you know what a fine one he owns." And so when I engage Seppl I expect a sort of Nancy Hanks, and am rather distrustful when I am given a steed that probably once belonged to an undertaker and was thoroughly used to funeral processions, and had never got over his early habits. Nevertheless we get to Interlaken in due season. We are more than satisfied, for the sun has come out, the white peaks are all glittering, and we are to have a grand day to go back, over the Brunig pass and ascend the Righi.

At Luzerne I found a perfect colony of Americans. The place seems to grow in favor with our countrymen every year. Its atmosphere is cool and clear; it is within reach of many beautiful spots, affording opportunity for numerous excursions, and, with all the extortion of the Swiss, it does not come nearly so expensive as an American fashionable watering-place. Concerts every evening at the hotels, and a fairly good French opera troupe.

I will not speak of the well-known railroad up Righi-Culm, but will only mention the fact that after a delightful ascent the clouds came, the rain fell, and chilly, damp and uncomfortable, I sought refuge in the drawing-room, where I met a young pianist from Vienna—Miss Gisela Lorinser, who, in a succession of strains by Chopin and Schumann, banished the discomforts of the trip. This young lady played me several of her own compositions. They do not cherish the female composer so much in Austria as we do in America, so she told me. I never felt the delight of the freemasonry of music so keenly as in the pleasant hours in the midst of a pouring storm, spent with an enthusiastic artist almost a stranger.

At Giessbach I began to realize that I had indeed left Italy. The thermometer settled down to forty degrees, with an evident desire to stay there. The ponderous feather-bed covers which I sneered at in Germany, here became a sweet boon. I crawled out into the keen atmosphere, from under my feather mountain, in the early morning, with feelings of the liveliest regret, but an Alpine sunrise is not to be missed, and I saw it.

Less grand was the illumination of the falls at night. The cataract comes down about a thousand feet, and all along its course are set bengola and lime lights. The sight is a strange one, although it lasts but a short time   The scenery around Giessbach is more impressive than that of the White Mountains, and fully as accessible.

Interlaken is more beautiful still, for the pure white peak of the snowy Jungfrau is contrasted with the vivid green of the valleys and lower mountains. We may have grander scenery in Colorado, but we have nothing which exactly compares with this striking contrast. But to the traveler who comes here, I must recommend the proverb, "Put money in thy purse." A large number of wealthy English families habitually resort here, and have brought things to such a pass that even if one does not consider Mallock's question, "Is life worth living?" one must at least confess that living comes very high.

I went back to Interlaken to meet a young American who desired my company to the Wengern Alps. On my second arrival there, however, I avoided the very expensive *Hotel de L'Ours.*

On arriving at the pretty little Hotel du Glacier at Grindelwald, I formed the rash resolve to ascend to the Ice Cave and Mer de Glace, this time on horseback.

> "The horse was brought, a noble steed,
>   A Tartar—"

(I had indeed caught a Tartar) of the very worst kind of breed, who, when I had mounted him, proceeded towards his stable in a vehement manner. I pulled at the rein, and vociferated "whoa!" with various expletives to add force to my command, but it was in vain. Suddenly the truth flashed upon me—that horse did not speak English. I called a boy who was standing by, noting the proceedings, and took a hasty lesson—price ten sous—in the Swiss tongue. From the instructions of my philological professor I gathered that it was considered good style to say "E-e-e-e" when you wished your steed to go, and "H-a-a-a-y" when the animal was desired to stop. This brought me on a speaking acquaintance with my horse. I was now able to indicate to him that I desired to ascend the mountain. I know the exact moment when this flashed upon his mind, for he started with a suddenness that seemed to loosen the very soles of my boots. From that moment my interest in the scenery ceased. Across planks which spanned mountain torrents, up paths which seemed to be perpendicular, and down banks which would be called precipices in New England, that horse safely bore me. His angle was not the same two seconds in succession, and I alternately sat on his ears and on his tail in a manner which kept the average all right. The chasm at the Grindelwald is grand, but by no means the finest in Switzerland. The echo is a delusion and a snare. At every available point a mercenary Swiss approaches you with a pistol and demands money. He is a sort of licensed highwayman; he does not put the pistol to your head, but on receiving a franc, goes into a gorge or a cave, or a chasm, and fires a volley that you may hear the echo. With the exception of the echo at Mont Blanc, every echo I have heard in Switzerland is inferior to our own home-made, United States echoes. The echo on a still day in Rockland harbor, Maine, can discount the echoes, at a franc apiece, of Switzerland. Higher up the mountain I took a temporary farewell of my steed—I was without guide —leaving him at a little hut where they sold an internal terror called *kirschwasser*, and clambered to the Ice Cave again. Here I found quite a party of tourists passing in and out. The Ice Cave is simply an artificial passage and chamber hewn out of the glacier. The strange blue color of the ice in the interior is well worth viewing. This time there were *two* Swiss girls in the cave singing folk-songs with a happy "*Jodel*," and playing on the zither. They pretended to enjoy the cool atmosphere. Believe them not, their affection is centred on the purses of the visitors. When the tourists are gone, they hasten from the cave and warm themselves and drink *kirschwasser*. On the other side of the Wengern Alps I unexpectedly found my brother who had taken a run down from Schaffhausen, and who induced me to visit that pleasant and restful city with him. It was not exactly on my route, but in a real vacation tour it is doubly pleasant to demolish one's own plans occasionally and go to places which one had not intended visiting. On the way we stopped over at fashionable and lively Zurich. Here much of my time was spent in a cab (not always the best way to see a city), for I did not desire to bankrupt myself by staying long in a fashionable Swiss resort. I was searching for my old music teacher Carl Gloggner (once of the Leipsic Conservatory faculty), a man not unknown in Boston, and one whose greatness and worthiness is only fully comprehended by those who went beneath his rough and brusque exterior.

He died several years ago in Zurich, and some hours of search and many inquiries at the cemeteries did not result in giving me even the small satisfaction of standing by his grave. Rip Van Winkle's "Are we so soon forgotten after we are dead?" was borne in upon me with telling force. But I forget again; allegro movements ought not to indulge in many *mestoso* or *doloroso* passages. I found a cabby who agreed for a stipend to show me the city, which by the way, I already had seen. Such scrupulous attention to detail has seldom been found. As he was engaged by the hour, and Zurich has few remarkable points, he elongated his material to the utmost extent. He stopped with much decision and regularity at every beer brewery and informed me that the liquor within was of especial excellence, and could be bought by the glass. At last I had pity upon his evident thirst and allowed him to pull up for refreshment.

In the hostelry I found a reminder of my Italian trip of
a few years ago in the shape of some of the long, thin, black
and poisonous cigars, with a straw in the center ("Cabagero
Infamia" would be a good name for the brand), which I had
once attacked in Rome and Naples where the inhabitants
have the temerity to smoke them. Spite of the dissuasions
of my brother I drew the straw from the centre, and sending some farewell messages to friends and relatives in America, lit the affair and began to smoke!!! —— ——
—— —— —— ***** ! ! !

When I recovered my senses I was in a railway carriage,
on the way to Schaffhausen. I had survived.

During the stop at Winterthur I saw a good illustration
of European ideas of the dignity of woman among the lower
classes. A man and woman were promenading together,
chatting. The former had his hands in his pockets and was
puffing a pipe; the latter was dragging a heavy cart, filled
with potatoes. The conversation was necessarily desultory,
as the lady had to pull pretty hard, and this occasioned
grunts and pauses in her remarks. It pays for the continental peasant to marry, because after the ceremony he can
make his spouse do the manual labor he would otherwise
have to do himself.

Swiss railways can never be described without knocking
the type into pi. The train which carried me to Schaffhausen had delirium tremens, and after each violent attack
would pause for many minutes to recover.

Schaffhausen certainly deserves well at my hands, for it
became to me a haven of rest during a rather eventful European tour, and for a week I vegetated within its ancient
walls, and came there to do it again the next year. Alpine
tourists make of Schaffhausen a port of entry and exit, and
having glanced at the falls of the Rhine, dash on to "other
climbs." It ought to receive more attention than it does

from the traveler, for it is full of interesting antiquities, and although a small place now (15,000 inhabitants) it has seen better days, somewhere in the middle ages.   I could speak of more than one interesting old building "fallen from its high estate," and become a tailor shop, a barber saloon and what not, but I prefer to speak of the people, and of life in a small Swiss city.

Don't believe in pastoral simplicity as regards small cities and villages: Sardou's " Nos bons Villageois " is a true bill (much truer than the foul King Lear of village life which Zola has inflicted upon the world), and even the small cities reproduce its colors.   Schaffhausen has its bickerings and quarrelings with the rest.   A few examples: A few years ago a popular Catholic priest settled in the city, and the municipal authorities helped him in founding a chapel of his faith.   The good priest died and had an ugly and cantankerous successor, who embroiled himself with the entire Protestant community, whereupon the authorities aforesaid fenced up nearly all the roads leading to the chapel, and the zealous worshippers have to go a long way across lots before they can come to their altar.

A wealthy manufacturer, not knowing how to expend his money, build himself a mausoleum, with a large double sarcophagus of stone in it.   His wife, dying soon after, occupied half of the costly premises, but alas for human steadfastness, the Crœsus married again and then died.   Wife No. 2 planted him in his stone tete-a-tete, but turned the previous corpse out into a more plebian resting place, holding cavity No. 1 in reserve for her own demise.   It is a plot for a novelist, only no one would ever believe it happened, that is unless he revolved in Schaffhausen circles.

I am afraid I appeared eccentric to many of the Schaffhausenese, for I took a bath in the Rhine, which they said no one but a crazy Englishman would do, with the water at icy temperature; but in my case it was ignorance rather than foolhardiness. I could never get accustomed to the different modes of recording the degrees of heat and cold. "How is the water to-day?" I would ask the fair maiden who attended to the preliminaries of the ablution. " Thirteen, mein Herr," was the response. Of course, I knew that it wasn't thirteen degrees Fahrenheit, but was it Reaumur or Celsius? There was no use inquiring, for I did not know which of the two was the higher, and by the time I got into the cold, green water, and came out of it blue, I was ready to say with Mercutio—"A plague on both the houses," and anathemize any thermometric system which countenanced freezing the marrow in one's bones.

But I had warm enough receptions to make up for this chill. To the pretty Hotel de Poste, where I stayed, there came a Gesangverein, a singing society of Herrisau, and they insisted that I should join in their revelry. They did not sing quite as well as the Apollo Club, (although quite well enough), but they had a heartiness in their musical work that was attractive, and they applauded my own solo in a manner that disarmed criticism, while at the close, the light, fantastic brogans moved gayly in a dance. The next day they all had what the German student calls "hair-ache," a term of much deeper significance than "headache," which they all blamed to the quality of Schaffhausen wine, maintaining that the above malady could not be acquired by any amount of Appenzeller. For myself, I found the wines of Switzerland very innocent and very sour.

I found the inhabitants of Schaffhausen addicted to the seductive game of billiards and I made the discovery in a mortifying manner by playing one rainy afternoon with a stranger who must have been a Swiss compound of Schaeffer and Ives, who made impossible caroms with the greatest of ease and who took me into camp with a grace and dex-

terity that astonished me.   I learned subsequently that he
was the champion of the canton.

The next day was fine, (Switzerland in a rain storm is
about as bright as the celebrated picture of the negro looking for a black cat in a dark cellar at midnight), and I
walked out to the Rhine Falls at Neuhausen.   I would
advise the active traveler who seeks these falls, to live as I
did at Schaffhausen, and then go on foot to the more fashionable Neuhausen.   I went in a circuitous manner, (let no
enemy connect this with the revelry mentioned above),
stopping first at Dachsen, where I sat in a restaurant amid
the cornfields and vineyards and sipped my coffee and pufied
my cigar, and found that peace which passeth all Cook's
tourists' understanding.   Then I walked through the fragrant fields down to the banks of the Rhine, where I found
the quaintest of ferries in the shape of a small flatboat and a
smaller boy, who responded to the incantation of "uebergeh,"
("go over"), uttered in a choking voice, with as many consonants and gutturals as it would hold.   The Swiss always
break up the German language into gasps and grunts which
would send a Hanoverian into convulsions.   After the
crossing of the Rhine a delightful ramble through the
woods brought me to the falls, which were especially fine at
that season, as the Rhine had not been so high for years.
They are, of course, not a Niagara, but are rather comparable to the falls at Trollhatten, in Sweden, and they are
illuminated at night with bengola and electric lights, as is
done at Giessbach.   But I cannot say that the waterworks
are much enhanced by the fireworks.

I found adventurous boatmen ready to take me up to the
foot of the falls for three francs, and accordingly made the
short but exciting trip.   The spray was all around me, the
noise was tremendous, and like Southey's Lodore waterworks, there was a "splashing, and dashing, and crashing,"

until I thought of the chances of an upset, and furnishing an item for the Swiss newspaper reporters, especially as I had just seen one of the boatmen drink a quart of fiery wine. I felt sure that in such a case they would misspell my name and get the circumstances all mixed up, perhaps stating that "the Rev. Dr. Elison of Boston, New York, has been drowned." We got safely back to terra firma, however, and I found on walking back to Schaffhausen, the lower part of that city inundated. The heavy rains had so swollen the Rhine that it had entered many of the dwellings, from which the inhabitants were making a hasty exit. The floods had done great damage to the crops, and where the dividing line between existence and starvation is so slight as in Switzerland, even a partial failure of the harvest causes great distress. The climate in the northern part of the country is not a very healthy one, neuralgia, earache and toothache being prevalent; nearly half of the population had wads of cotton wool in their ears, and the other half had swollen and bandaged cheeks, and the general result was not cheerful.

I made a little side tour to Basle, during this part of my vacation, and to get there was obliged to cross a small portion of German territory. Why the customs officers should gaze all through your baggage when you leave Switzerland for Germany (especially when they had been so courteous when I entered the republic) is a mystery to me. The official ransacked my entire portmanteau, and gazed at my soap-box as if he were not quite sure as to what it was meant for. After he had viewed all that could be seen from the outside he asked me if I "had anything to declare." I wanted to declare him the biggest nuisance on the border, but forbore; otherwise the railroad station at Schaffhausen is a tranquil one. The employes sing forth the names of the stations to which the trains go in a stately Gregorian chant. After the station master has sung "This train goes to Basel, Freiburg, Waldshut, Offenburg, Appenweir, Mannheim and Carlsruhe," you feel like chanting "Amen," so religiously has the gazetteer been warbled; and then the train does not go, for a good while at any rate, and peace and tranquility reigns again.

Basle, Bale or Basel, whichever you please, (for I can offer an assortment of correct spellings) is a brisk commercial city; it affords little to the traveler, however. Some of the peasant women wear striking costumes, surmounted by tremendous black bows which stick out from their heads like wings. If you were to saw their heads off the result would be a very ugly cherub (a la Raphael) in black.

We returned from here to Schaffhausen again, indeed Schaffhausen, in Switzerland, became our base of supplies. From that city, as from a beleaguered fortress, we made sorties over the neighboring and more expensive country, and when our enemies, represented in this case by the hotel landlords, had captured almost all our munitions of war, we beat a hasty retreat to our cheaper resort, and saved our few remaining ducats. Dear, dear Switzerland! how much more I should have enjoyed your views if I had not been kept busy in diving into my pockets for francs at every turn.

But finally growing bolder, and new remittances having arrived, I determined to push toward the valley of Chamounix, stopping at various points of interest on the way.

Lausanne, a pretty terraced city on the borders of Lake Leman, charmed me most, because its houses resembled those of New England. There came a touch of sentimental homesickness when I rowed out on the placid lake the next day, with the Castle of Chillon on the horizon, and the blue mountains all around, which was relieved somewhat by my making rhymes as follows:

LAKE LEMAN

If we two were together
  Beneath these tranquil skies.
Lulled in the drowsy weather,
  The past dream might arise;
A dream of memory golden,
Amid the ruins olden,
If we two were together
  Beneath these tranquil skies.

If we two were together
  Upon this lotus shore,
With noiseless dip and feather
  I'd ply the boatman's oar;
Across these ripples rowing,
From earth to heaven 'twere going,
If we two were together
  Upon this lotus shore.

If we two were together
  The scene would lack no more;
No grief the soul would tether
  And mar this alien shore.
But now the waters gliding
Seem but a gulf, dividing;
Since we are not together
  The scene can charm no more.

After that I felt somewhat better, and the malady gradually disappeared, although the remedy was a desperate one.

Chillon itself is altogether beautiful from the outside, but
it needed many grains of salt to believe all the stories told
us on the inside. The pillar with Byron's name carved on
it, was of course visited; also the second one beyond it,
where Bonnivard was chained. The poem of the "Prisoner
of Chillon" is rather imaginative when viewed on the spot.
If the prisoner ever climbed up to that little window and
looked on the three trees on the island—which are still there
—he must have been too tall a man for the pillar to which
he was chained. This was the island a fellow-tourist once

endeavored to see by looking out of a prison window *in Venice!* It cannot but remind one of Artemus Ward's famous imprisoned knight, who, after pining in his dungeon for twelve long, weary years, was struck by a happy thought—*he opened the window and got out!* I had trouble enough in lifting an enthusiastic tourist up to the little window, which is ten or twelve feet above the floor, and the wall is too solid to cut any footings into it.

At the door of Chillon's Castle, "damp and cold," I found the eternal vendor of souvenirs—busts, pictures, carvings, canes, scarf pins, brooches and rings, all branded "Chillon." I had been tempted and fallen (into the hands of the dealer) so often that my gripsack resembled that of a commercial traveler for a notion house, and I could have gone into the wholesale souvenir business when I returned.

But I met one American young man in Europe who was in worse case. He had been around with his little hatchet knocking corners off all the various cathedrals, palaces, etc., which he had met in his devastating career, and his bag was as heavy as if he were traveling with samples for a cannon foundry. Something must be thrown away, and the poor young man was perplexed as to whether it should be the "brick from Knox's house in Edinburgh," the "piece of marble from Milan Cathedral," the "piece of the wall from the Tower of London," or some other piece of choice but heavy purloining.

As for myself, I have kept all my purchases except my alpenstock. These broomsticks are generally the most cherished part of the tourists' luggage. They walk the town with them, they eat with them, and I verily believe some sleep with them. On the alpenstock is branded the record of the tourists' exploits. It costs fifteen centimes to brand each name. One tourist showed me with pride his stock with the record—"Chamounix, Mer de Glace, Mauvais

Pas, Chapeau, and Grand Mulet, Mont Blanc;'' he having made all these ascents. As the price of branding is so reasonable, I had thought of having my broomstick labeled ''Himalaya, Popocatapetl, Pike's Peak and Erebus,'' and carrying it back to America.

From Lausanne my pilgrimage took me to Martigny, where I was much impressed with the size of the gorges and of the mosquitos. The latter would make the same kind of birds in New Jersey blush for shame, and when they present their little bills they almost rival the hotel-keepers. But the gorge of Triente, which opens at Martigny, is ''gorge-ous.'' One cannot see any bolder cliffs or stranger chasms anywhere. Like everything fine in Switzerland, it is fenced in, and one must pay a franc to see it; but, on the other hand, one does not see ''Rising Sun Stove Polish'' or ''Castoria'' painted on the finest portions, as with us. The customary echo highwayman and the souvenir fiend flourish here, as elsewhere.

I have alluded to the Martigny mosquito; I must also pay a word of tribute to the Martigny flea. He is not nearly so numerous as his Neapolitan or Roman brethren, but he has more business enterprise and a more roving disposition. It is interesting to watch the tourist, engaged in conversation, suddenly start as if a thought had struck him. It is, however, not a thought, but an insect. I have discovered, by pursuing this train of thought, why so many ballet dancers come from Italy. The people there are accustomed from early youth to stand on one leg and scratch with the other.

From Martigny, over the Téte Noir Pass to Chamounix. In this pass one finds the most impressive scenery imaginable. Precipice follows precipice; chasms, torrents and cliffs, in overwhelming profusion. But the ride is a very fatiguing one, the horses being unable to go faster than a walk, and the jolting being kept up all day. In a word, let me say that Switzerland is a country which no one not in robust health ought to dream of seeing. Also, in planning excursions to different points, the traveler must bear in mind that the magnificent proportions of the mountain scenery and the clearness of the atmosphere lead to great mistakes as to distances. Mont Blanc itself seems much lower than some of the peaks by which it is surrounded.

One of the favorite excursions from Chamounix is over the Mer de Glace to the Mauvais Pas and the Chapeau. It is an exciting and beautiful trip. Early in the morning a party is formed, with guides, mules, alpenstocks, etc., etc. The line of march is then taken for Montanvert, which lies high up on the mountain, and is attained only after a circuitous ride of two hours. My mule in this trip was a decided improvement upon the horse of Grindelwald. He was sure-footed and untiring. At Montanvert, the Mer de Glace, one of the finest of glaciers, lies below one's feet. It is absolutely necessary to have an alpenstock in traversing this portion of the trip, and it is also advisable to have heavy hobnails struck into one's shoes, if one desires to go easily. The glacier is diminishing year by year, and there is not a doubt but that at some future time a valley or a chasm will be in its place. On the other side of it one of our party discovered the remains of a snow avalanche, and we both rushed down to the bank and started a lively snowball fight—in August. But while it was cool in the vicinity of the snow, the ice sea, and the torrents,—which consist of ice-water the year round—it was decidedly hot on the rugged path leading to the Mauvais Pas, or "bad step." Yet the risk of this trip is exaggerated; any reasonably sure-footed person, who is not nervous, and can bear a little fatigue, can make the excursion. The steps are cut in the side of the rock for a distance of about a quarter of a mile, and a slip would send one down the precipice were it not for a single hand-rail on the inside, which the cautious traveler must clutch as he crawls along. I was warm enough when I arrived at the little inn on the other side, and calling for milk—which was of a richness unknown to America— and brandy and sugar, I compounded a restorative which I believe is not unknown in Chicago, New York, and Boston. Half an hour's farther climbing brought me to the spot where the mules were tethered, they having been sent around by a lower path from Montanvert. Some obliging tourist had kindly exchanged mules with me, which is as permissible as changing umbrellas, and had left in the place of mine a ruminative, absent-minded animal who did not inspire me with any great degree of confidence. The descent of a mountain on horse or mule back is always more difficult than the ascent, and I found that the narrow paths, some of them only two feet wide, running at the edges of very deep chasms, were eminently calculated to make a man sorry for his past sins. In the midst of one of these narrow passes my mule gave a stumble that made me conclude that my series of reminiscences had come to an untimely end, and set each particular hair of my head bristling. I shouted the most emphatic "H-a-a-a-y!" ("whoa!") that had ever been heard in the Alps, and astonished the animal so much that he recovered himself. On examination it proved that a large stone had "balled" in one of his fore hoofs and had caused the unexpected mishap. It took nearly ten minutes to wedge out the rock, when this was done I found myself far in the rear of the party, the rest having gone on down the mountain.

Then that mule began to make my life wretched in a manner which obliterated the memory of all past animals that I had ever ridden. He had an eye for the picturesque, and would walk along the edges of high cliffs and gaze down pensively at the valley below in a manner which, under other circumstances, I should have called really poetic, but which at that moment seemed to me cold-blooded foolishness. He always kept at the extreme outer edge of every path, so much so that his two outer legs seemed to tread npon air only. Occasionally a stone would give way and go rolling down, down, and down, in pleasing intimation of what might have been my fate if the beast had pursued his wanderings in search of scenery a few inches farther. I gazed in that mule's eye to see if he was despondent, or had ever been crossed in love, but I found no trace of suicidal intent on his stolid face, which reassured me somewhat.

I took a partial revenge when we got to level ground by making him gallop nearly all the way to Chamounix; but even here he had the best of me, for his gallop was of such an indescribable nature that it was impossible to adjust one's self to it, and I seemed to be riding an animated earthquake. But a good sitz bath and a hearty supper removed all traces of my hard day's work, and then I had the hobnails removed from my shoes, and the guide stole my alpenstock, and I went out of the mountaineering business for good.

That night, while resting in the parlor of Hotel Couttét, I looked over the visitors' book, extending back to 1860. In these books one finds the impressions of many a poetaster. Here are a few of the gems culled from the volume:

First—Politico-patriotic:

Alexis Janin,	
Edmund S. Dicky,	New Orleans, Aug. 31st, 1862.
Albert C. Janin,	Confederate States of America.

"We are probably the first to plant upon the soil of Mont Blanc the Confederate flag, glorious emblem of valor and independence.'

" *Vivat, Crescat, Floreat.*"

There was a Confederate flag sketched above, which some one had almost obliterated, and written "Treason " across.

Second—Witty:

> John C. Waters, England.
> " Man proposes, and—woman accepts."

Third—Poetic (?) and religious:

> Wm. B. ———,
> " Amid such a grandeur of Nature, how small indeed is man!"

How beautiful is a sunrise upon the Alps! The white hills lie shrouded in a cold, steely hue, when, suddenly, the uppermost peak begins to glow, like a strange, red star, or like a pimple on the nose of a pale tourist. It is a glorious scene. I know it is so, because it was described to me by a reliable tourist who had arisen at an unseemly hour to look at it. As for myself, on that particular morning, I devoted the early-worm-catching hours to sleep.

I needed it, for after ten hours' daily climbing and mule riding, the love of the beautiful becomes sensibly diminished.

The day after we had crossed the Mauvais Pas, a lady proved that it deserved its name by fatally injuring herself there. It seems that she turned her ankle and pitched headlong down the precipice. Every year Switzerland and Savoy have their category of Alpine accidents, and pleasing pictorial representations of the subjects are displayed in the store windows to encourage the tourist to go and do likewise.

The next day, after doing the Chapeau and the Mer de Glace, I started for Geneva. It was a long ride of fifty miles by dilligence, but I must say that it took no longer than some of the European railways, and was scarcely more uncomfortable. The scenery all the way was magnificent, and the road as smooth as a table.

Arrived at Geneva, I found its little suburb of Chéne-les-Bougeries all ablaze with excitement, since it was celebrating a communal féte, and the erection of a new town hall.

Flags were suspended from every house, and I was delighted to find several American ensigns floating in the breeze. In such a féte in Switzerland the first thing to be thought of is a rifle match. In Italy it is music; in France, dancing; but in Switzerland no great rejoicing is complete without a shooting competition. This particular match was a large one and continued three whole days. I grieve to say that some of the celebrants had been gazing at the festivities "through a glass, darkly," and corkscrewed their way around in such a manner that the target keeper must have felt nervous when it came to the shooting.

Returning to Geneva by tramway, I found that my baggage had not yet arrived. As I had given it into the hands of the hotel porter at the diligence office, I felt deeply wounded at his lack of interest in my well-being, and, calling the head waiter (at the Hotel de la Paix), I proceeded to deliver a short oration in French, at a pressure of 260 pounds to the square inch. The quality of my remarks and of my French moved the waiter so much that he went to a small youth near by, who was in no wise connected with the matter, and after demanding my portmanteau, and not receiving it, began vigorously boxing the ears of the unoffending young man. Strange to say, even this did not produce my luggage, which eventually turned up at the diligence office, but at least it gave me an insight into the discipline of the hotel. The same evening, at table d'hote, I saw the same head waiter administer gentle correction to a young subordinate who was passing knives and forks around. A comprehensive dig in the back caused the poor fellow to drop the entire tray, and stand a picture of dress-coated and white-gloved misery.

Geneva itself affording so little to see, I went again on Sunday evening to the féte at Chéne. It was an interesting sight. The villagers had got along comfortably in their three day's uproar, to the end of the imbibations of the second day. The mayor had made a speech, which was probably the "greatest effort of his life," and had invoked Tell, Winkelried, Minerva, Mars, and Cæsar, to watch over the destinies of Chéne-les-Bougeries, and was now allowing the destinies to drift along by themselves a little while, while he enjoyed the vintage of his native hills. I, too, sat down at a table near by and tasted the pangs of a bottle of Swiss wine. From the fact that the bottle only cost half a franc (ten cents) I judge that Chéne has not yet learned to milk the foreign tourist. The same fact was borne in upon me when I strolled among the booths and found pistol galleries in operation at one cent per shot; teetotums at two cents a chance; side shows of various marvels at an average admittance fee of three cents, and many other popular recreations at correspondingly low figures.

Music was being discoursed in the centre of the place, and a veritable dance on the village green was going on in which the ladies were distinguished by the vehemence of their pirouettes. The evening closed with a very respectable exhibition of fire-works and the illumination of the green with an electric light. Everybody seemed very good-humored, and if I *did* see some slightly intoxicated people, I must add that elsewhere I had met but three drunken people in all Europe. The next day I went through the usual boredom at Geneva, the chief relief being a look at the cathedral and the Duke of Brunswick's monument, both of which seem perfect crazy quilts of architecture. I also had a plunge and swim in the lake, which is as clear as crystal, and as lovely as the whole chain of Swiss lakes, but is as treacherous as it is lovely, for it changes very suddenly from enchanting placidity to a heaving agitation, like a beauty in a temper, and it has swift currents that would drown any swimmer.

I left Geneva by the Lyons & Mediterranean railway and came directly through to Paris. In this journey the fact was again made apparent that the railroads in Europe often make no arrangements for the comforts of passengers on long tours. The carriages are packed as full as they will carry, and the passengers pass the night as best they can. Are there no sleeping cars?

Yes, but the few possessed by the road were "at the other end" that night!

One can imagine that at times this system leads to deplorable results. I know of one case where a Cleveland lady took her husband, who was just convalescing from typhoid fever, from Rome to Vienna. On arriving at the station to take her berth, she was informed, just as we had been, that the *wagon-lit* was not on hand that night. She traveled for thirteen hours, supporting her sick husband, in one of the miserable subterfuges called first-class carriages. She died herself, poor martyr, soon after (and because of) that terrible journey.

As for ourselves, for I had "chummed in" with a jovial American party, in that little railway compartment we determined to make the best of it. A game of whist, some jolly singing, a pocket flask, etc., proved that Americans generally can imitate Mark Tapley under rather difficult circumstances. When the question of sleep came before the meeting it was disposed of as follows: Two were laid tenderly on the floor, four were dovetailed on the seats, and two—a young Chicago lawyer and a Cleveland banker— were hung up high in mid-air on the baggage racks; and soon snores coming from the various latitudes told of the fact that Morpheus had taken several of the party into his kindly arms. And the next morning, scarcely a bit the worse for the night's discomforts, we all entered Paris.

PARIS GRAND OPERA HOUSE,

FRONT VIEW.

CHAPTER XIII

PARIS—A TURKISH BATH—A SUAVE BARBER—TWENTY-FOUR
HOURS OF TYPICAL PARISIAN LIFE—A NIGHT IN PARIS—A
COMMUNIST GUIDE—A FEARFUL RIOT—A CHARGE OF THE
FRENCH SOLDIERY—LOUISE MICHEL—INTERVIEWS WITH
FRENCH COMMUNISTS.

On arriving at the most beautiful city of the world I did
not, at once, plunge into the vortex of dissipation, but,
feeling that I had two or three Swiss farms concealed about
my person, I sought a bath and a barber. Paris contains
the most elegant Turkish bath in the world—the Hammam.
It was doubly necessary, for Switzerland is like unto America with but the difference of a letter—it is " the land of
the flea and the home of the brave!" The same shampooer
who endeavored to tie me into a true lover's knot a few
years ago was there, and had lost none of his enthusiasm,
for he pounded me as vehemently as if he were a French
gendarme arresting a female socialist. Jean, who took me
in charge, is the most energetic of all shampooists. Here
is a literal account of what he did. He set me to stewing
at 150 degrees Fahrenheit and then, repenting of his mercy,
he came back and placed me in a purgatory of 200 degrees;
after I had almost sweated out my immortal soul he remembered where he had left me and came back and laid me out
on a slab and pounded me. Then he rubbed me in the regular manner, after which he took my arms and tried to tie

them in a knot behind my back, failing in this he tried to
tickle my left shoulder joint with my right arm; then he
laid me face down, and stood upon the small of my back,
and having me thus at his mercy, he took my right leg and
introduced it to my left arm. I begged him to allow me
to send some last words to·my family, to make my will, but
I suppose my voice was drowned in the cannonade made
by the cracking of my joints, for he callously, but energetic-
ally went on. But after I had been showered and sprayed
from every direction, after I had plunged in the delightful,
tiled swimming bath, after I had lain, half dozing, on the
Turkish divan in the "dim, religious light," coming through
stained windows fit for a cathedral, I forgave Jean; I even
gave him two francs and went again and again to undergo
the same process. After it I feel as hollow as Mammoth
Cave, and search for a beefsteak. No Frenchman knows
what a true beefsteak is. You may call for " Biftek a
l'Anglaise," "Biftek gras" or whatever you please, the result is a wafer of meat, fried, with plenty of butter. I shall
always honor James G. Bennett, Jr., for flinging one of
these trifles in the waiter's face, for this repartee caused one
restaurant, at least, to know that the ideal beefsteak is different; and now for the barber.

European barbers deserve a chapter by themselves. I
have already alluded to a couple of varieties; in Italy and
sometimes in Switzerland, the chief trouble with the tonsorial artists is that they will set no price upon their scraping;
" Whatever you please, your excellency," is the usual formula, which generally ends in their getting considerably
more than you please, and twice as much as their regular
price. The French barber is of another sort and generally
has a female accomplice, disguised as a cashier. This fair,
young lady greets me. I have no fear; she will not shave
me—not with a razor. I mount a winding stair; I meet the

artist. He speaks English!! I am lost!! He begins gently: It is a pity that one so young should be bald and gray! It is, but I have borne youth and baldness from infancy. If I use his brilliantine my mustache will curl of itself! I wish he would take a dose of his brilliantine, and curl up and die, but I say nothing. He has a large stock of lotions, hair growers, etc., on hand, and he is determined that the opportunity, and I, shall not slip through his fingers.

He compliments my French! ("Trust him not, he is fooling thee"), and finding me rather apathetic on that subject, takes on a more severe and warning vein. He tells me my skin is delicate and tender (it is as thick as a rhinoceros hide), and predicts a strange and hideous eruption unless his lotion is used. He says my hair is coming out rapidly, but that it can be checked and a generally youthful appearance regained only by a mystical pomatum which he makes. He offers to relieve me of more diseases than Job ever possessed if I will but take two bottles of his preparations, and as I will not, he grows colder and colder, and the shave, which began in tenderness, ends in rasping.

I am offered everything from shampoos to eternal youth before I escape down the winding stair and face the beauteous damsel again. One shave, one friction (!), one *coup de peigne* and several other things, which are mysterious, and which I probably didn't have, are charged to me—two francs, and I fly.

The next day was very varied, much of the time being spent in voitures, driving to various points of interest. Many were the pourboires to the hackmen, who certainly deserved them, for their earnings are small enough. This pourboire business must shock a prohibitionist, however. Possibly you have heard of the conscientious Englishwoman who always gave the fee, but renounced the object, saying —" Non poor boire—poor mangay!"

Among the places visited on the second day was Versailles, and to economize time at this and other places of note, I engaged a guide who turned out to be a real, live Communist. I was struck at the very outset with the fact that he seemed to possess a large amount of rather unwieldy information. In fact, he was staggering under a larger educational load than he could conveniently carry. His description of the paintings which he showed me was at least graphic. "Look," said he, "upon the 'Raise of Lazarus.' Look upon the astound which is pictured upon all around. Even Lazarus is astound at himself."

He gradually confided to me his pain at the indignities heaped upon Louise Michel. His grief at this seemed so vehement that he several times tried to drown it in the flowing bowl.

It was difficult to induce him to part with me. There was nothing high or low in Paris that he did not know thoroughly about, and which he did not desire to show me. At last, on the way to Versailles, he was so overcome by his emotions, and libations to Bacchus, that I left him asleep at an inn table, while I went on alone.

I do not think he is cut out for one of the future rulers of France, and for the sake of that lovely country, I hope that neither he nor any like him may ever bubble up to the top again.

At the post office my registering a letter for America caused the genial clerk to air his knowledge of our tongue. He pointed to the elevator and said, "Ha! leeft! Angleesh, no good is better!" to which lucid remark I yielded a cordial assent, and then went away to think it over. Dined with Mr. Moffett of the New York Herald in a quiet *pension*, but at the table met Father Ryan, a literary priest, (not related, however, to the great southern poet-priest), who speaks pleasantly of John Boyle O'Reilly, Father Corcoran, and other Boston friends. The world is small, and I had a further experience of this in meeting a man from the other end of it almost directly after. The Maronite archbishop of Damascus, (Dahdah is his name), was lying ill in the priests' hotel in the Latin quarter, and as my friend was to interview him, I went along, and in the invalid's apartments (he was very glad to see us, by the way), I was for the time being in the Orient, as eastern servants and Damascene surroundings proved. The dignitary spoke very discouragingly of the spread of christianity in the east, and with great contempt of the morality of the Mohammedans. Such interviews as these show the cosmopolitan character of Paris thoroughly.

If I started out to describe Paris, to give the dimensions of the Place de la Concorde, to name the pictures in the Louvre, to tell the height of the Column Vendome, my readers would await my return with shotguns in their hands, and I should deserve my fate. No! this chapter shall be of a widely different order. For the sake of science I became a veritable night owl, and studied Paris for nearly twenty-four hours at a solid stretch. "The proper study of mankind is man," and I have studied Paris men, (and women too), with a persistency that will meet its reward in a better land —probably the United States. In the pursuance of an economy which is always a marked characteristic of the modern journalist, I went to Paris by night service, (on the principle of the eminent traveler who always traveled third class—because there was no fourth), and then to the Hotel Bergére, which was neat, economical, clean, and above all, central. I forgive the wicked *blanchisseuse* who pounded my underwear to fragments and then charged me double price because of the blue streaks left in the shirt fronts, and speak this good word for the hotel. After all fatigue of past travels had vanished, I started out in search of my

Parisian types, 6 A. M. How still some of the portions of Paris were! It was about the only time I had seen the restless city almost at rest, and this was only in the more fashionable quarters, for when I came to the Faubourg St. Antoine everything was in full life; the workmen in their blouses hurrying to their labor, the cheap restaurants in active operation, and the groceries and provision stores well patronized.

The boulevards again presented another aspect. House-maids were hurrying homewards with their purchases for various Gallic breakfasts, and the long sticks of bread, a yard or two in length, carried under their arms, made an odd impression upon me. The cafés generally were yet closed, save in the by-streets, where one of the lower class showed open shutters, and a garçon with sleepy eyes and dirty shirt was sprinkling sawdust among the tables on the sidewalk. The only customers I saw were of two kinds: firstly, a Parisian swell, who had evidently been out (or at least away from home) all night, and was taking some *amer picon* to steady his nerves, and who was still in a dress coat and light tie, but whose rumpled attire spoke of the fatigues of the search after enjoyment. The other was the confirmed absinthe drinker, who was bound, like Ixion to the wheel, to the ceaseless practice of his habit. I watched this one narrowly. He had evidently passed a feverish night and was now in search of his regular relief. He did not sit at a table on the sidewalk; that would have involved delay. He passed at once into the café and took a large dose of pure absinthe. A short time afterward he emerged an altered man. The tremulousness of his gait had temporarily passed; his face, though hollow, had something of fire; he had obtained a reprieve; he had pushed the inevitable a little farther away from him. Decidedly my first types in gay Paris were not gay. Then followed more life. A walk to the

Gare du Nord brought me in time to note the passengers of the incoming English trains; but this, save for the custom-house examination, was not vastly different from an American depot at an early hour, although one could tell by the faces of the passengers that the channel passage had been a little rougher than usual. The newsboys and newsgirls in the city, and at the depot, were folding and arranging their papers; but different from their American *confreres*, were mute. It may be mentioned *en passant*, that the newsboys form no such an element in Paris as in America. The chief sale is at the kiosks, or regular stands, and the only shouting done is by newsboys of a rather large growth (from twenty to fifty years), who cry various papers, such as L'Anti-Prussien, L'Anti-Berlin, and other small journals which only live to fan the smouldering fire of hatred which exists in France against Germany, although the " *Intransigeant*," which is larger, has a great sale by boys and men. I now begin to feel the effects of the morning air, but even though I am hungry, I do not think of breakfast, for I cannot get it. In the swell cafés I will find only sand, looks of scorn, and dirty towels, while in the small ones I can get only coffee and a roll, but no true Frenchman will give me any meat until nearly eleven o'clock. Never mind, I can go out to the Bois de Boulogne, and take a stroll in that magnificent piece of woodlands.

Perhaps at this morning hour I may find a body or two suspended from the trees, for the suicidal Frenchman knows of but three modes of exit from the world—jumping from a high window, throwing himself into the Seine, or hanging himself in the Bois de Boulogne. Fortunately I find nobody, dead or alive, but if I came at 4 P. M. I should find all the remnants of the high world that are left in Paris, for that is the fashionable hour. You will see that all the way from carriage driving to suicide, matters in Paris go in ruts;

even the theatres have their special nights when the "upper ten" turn out. At last, however, I come to a little side street where a tidy restaurant, which is open at this early hour for its workingmen patrons, is situated. A *biftek* is obtained, which the cook insists on slicing as thin as a wafer, but which is palatable nevertheless, and which, with some delicious bread and butter, is washed down with a bottle of claret at a ludicrously low figure. Through the open window I watch the vivacious shop girls, some with hats, some without, going to their daily work. All are intelligent looking, and all are chatty and cheerful, while a few are beautiful. It is another Parisian type. But as to the *grisette* of fame and story, she is a delusion and a snare. She does not exist. I have sought her in the haunts where all the novels have placed her (as you will see later), and I have not found her. For the benefit of this history I was ready to enter into a flirtation with her, if I had discovered her, but this hardship was spared me.

So the chief part of all this early morning life was that of the working people; not unlike the life in New York at the same hour, but more cheerful and neater in appearance. At nine the business on the fashionable boulevards began, and by ten oclock the fashionable restaurants condescended to serve breakfast. The Café Anglais and others began to fill up with young-old and old-young men, who dallied with their food in a very *blasé* manner.

And now, perhaps, one could get a bowl of excellent *bisque* of some sort at the Café Riche, which is famous for this kind of thing, although it is as innocent of true beefsteaks as every other French restaurant. Do not tarry too long here if you desire to keep any money in your pocket. The café may be called Riche, but it speedily makes its patrons poor.

By eleven o'clock I found the Avenue de Boulogne, which

was formerly the Avenue de l'Impératrice, an attractive spot. Many young Parisians were taking a morning horseback ride along its broad course and into the Bois de Boulogne just beyond, and the bright looking *bonnes* with their juvenile charges began to spring up as if by magic. I looked to see if the typical soldier would follow the typical *bonne*; he did not; another delusion of youth was gone. And now came the large Athenian-looking building called the Bourse, the stock exchange of Paris. I was a trifle early for the best of this life; but what I did see was interesting enough. There was about the same confusion as in an American stock exchange, and all spoke together just as they do at home. One young man appeared to be the leading spirit of that day, and seemed far less excited than the older men around him. A calm nod or a quiet word seemed to reach its object with him as thoroughly as the wild gestures or vehement expressions of the older speculators, It was a type of young Paris which is beginning to affect English ways and manners, and which begins to study boxing and "sport," and be led around by a "bouledog."

It was now noon, and the sightseer could go anywhere and find points of interest. He could go shopping at the Bon Marché, the "Au Printemps" or the "Maison du Louvre," (the three great establishments,) or along the Avenue de L'Opera, if careless of his purse. But let me plead with him not to go into the places marked "English spoken here," for this more generally means "English cheated here." I well remember finding a *carriage* with the sign "English spoke," and as I concluded that the "spoke" referred to the driver and not to his cab wheels, and as I was pleased with the quaint imitation of the fashionable stores, I engaged him—by the hour. His "English" was a delusion and he himself a snare. At the end of forty minutes, "How much?"—"Eet ees four franc, and ze pourboire!"

"No, dearest," said I, in the sweetest Lord Fauntleroy tones (I called him " dearest " because he emphatically *was* the dearest), " it is two francs, as the gentleman standing over there will tell you, if you have forgotten." The " gentleman over there " was a *sergent de ville*, a police officer, and all at once the floodgates of memory were opened, and the Jehu with the "English spoke" remembered the tariff, but the funniest of all was that he gave a pleasant little laugh as he took the two francs and a half, said, "I haf meet you too late!" and touched his hat respectfully as he drove away.

But I digress; I am going around Paris. But now so many paths are open! One can go over the Seine and look at the Latin quarter, but in summer it is like the poorer part of every other city; it only wakes in fall and winter. If I pass along any of the great thoroughfares now I shall find all Paris abroad. How many strange and interesting types there are. Even the street cries are individualized, and one huckster sings his wares in melodious measure, while another attracts the attention by blowing a short melody at intervals on a musette. There is your Parisian *flaneur*, who stops at the shop windows or sits down at a table on the sidewalk and dawdles over his glass of vermouth or absinthe. There is a dangerous chance that if you sit down at one of the café tables alone you will have more female society than you desire inside of five minutes. But I can mention an infallible way to get rid of persistent beggars of all descriptions and both sexes in France. Simply shake your head in a puzzled manner and say "*Sprechen sie Deutsch?*" They will leave you more rapidly than if you told them you had a combination of cholera, smallpox, and diphtheria.

The boulevards are Paris to many Americans, and not unjustly so, for they reflect every phase of the seething life of the metropolis, they are essentially French, and therefore doubly attractive to the American. Every man admires (for a certain time) things that are exotic. I had a proof of this in a French boot store, where I was upon the point of buying a brilliant pair of patent leathers, when the dealer to clinch matters, said: "They are the finest American leather!" and showed me, on the inside, a stamp, "New England leather" with an American flag waving over it. That settled it: I had not come to Paris to buy American leather; I had bowed before the French calf too long for that. The painful part of it all is that I am firmly convinced that the leather never saw America, and that it was only the exotic idea gone rampant. Speaking of French calf, I saw an American calf at the barber's recently. The tonsorial artist was about 20 years old, and the shavee was earnestly asking him if he had fought in the Franco-Prussian war! He must have been about one year old when it took place, but I suppose my compatriot ranked him with the infantry!

But now I have become a trifle weary with my peripatetic investigations, and cross the Seine to one of the delightful swimming baths on the other side, pausing by the way to look at the second-hand book stalls along the edge of the embankment which possess a never ending interest to the antiquary. Then to the English café and bar (rather a dissipated place) in the Rue Scribe where I find a waiter who gives me a pathetic account of how he was struck by John L. Sullivan on his way back from his French defeat. Our charming Bostonian was a trifle drunk and more than a trifle sulky, and the garçon got no fee whatever, but a little local celebrity as the man who was hit by "our John."

America is known abroad chiefly by two things—its dentistry and its drinks. But put not your trust in the latter. Every café has up its sign, "Boissons Américains." These cafés are, however, entirely innocent of the mysteries of

cocktails, punches, sherry cobblers, and other American institutions. The sign generally simply means that the proprietor has bought a bottle of rye whisky. But this bar
was of another order, and had graduated in the higher school
of American art. It was a sort of thirty-third degree of an
irrigation asylum. While eating an English chop, which
had so shrunk in the making that it seemed nothing but a
suggestion, I watched one side of Anglo-American existence.
There was gambling, but it was not of the exciting order
where a fool could part with the whole of his money with a
degree of "soonness" not contemplated even in the proverb.
A number of Englishmen, whose horse talk led me to believe them jockeys, were shaking dice for five-franc pieces.
I waited in vain for one of them to ruin himself, and go out
and throw himself into the Seine, thus giving me a para-
graph that would brighten up my chapters like a New York
gas company. When I saw one party lose forty dollars I
had great hopes; but when, instead of sacrificing himself to
help me along, he simply fell to swearing, I left in disgust.

And now, it being long past noon, I felt that I could show
myself as a boulevard *flaneur*, without being considered a pariah. It would puzzle Webster and Worcester to exactly
define the verb *flaner*; it is something more active than
loafing, and less energetic than strolling or promenading.

It is a difficult art to acquire, the faculty of dawdling
along the broad sidewalk, sitting down and sipping coffee,
ice or absinthe at a café, looking in at every shop window,
reading every poster on the kiosks, and, in short, doing
nothing in the most skillful manner. Of course the slightest event draws a crowd. I joined one large gathering and
beheld a few boys playing peg-in-the-ring, another and saw
two men mildly chiding each other, a third and found a
lad selling puzzles.

I dropped in at the Café de la Regence, and found it the

same chess resort as of old, when Morphy used to play every day at one of the tables. With a quiet game, dedicated to the goddess Caissa, I refreshed myself from my wanderings and started anew on my journey "twice round the clock."

After this it was past three o'clock, and I went to the Parc Monçeau. At four o'clock, what is left of the best of Paris may be found, in the pleasant months, either here or at the Buttes-Chaumont, listening to the music of military bands. The latter place is the best to visit, for its scenery is beautiful, spite of the fact that it was once the Tyburn of Paris. Intermingled with the auditors I saw a type which must be mentioned, however unwillingly, in a description of Paris.

With slim and graceful waist, with eyes of unnatural brightness, lips too deeply red, well-fitting and graceful dress, *bien ganté* altogether, was the "strange woman." It was probably the beginning of her moth-like day, and, she would flutter around the glare of the city for the next ten or twelve hours.

And now I bethought me of the possible close of her glittering existence, and my thoughts and footsteps turned toward the mysterious temple which ought to be the shrine of the goddess of the dark side of Paris—the morgue. It was comparatively untenanted when I arrived there; a body of a man, evidently of the working class, and some fifty years of age, lay extended upon a slab, with a slight stream of water trickling over the face. There was no opportunity to soliloquize over "one more unfortunate," although had I been a day earlier I should have seen a sight to thrill all susceptible readers. A gentleman named Mielle, of an anatomical turn of mind, had enticed a friend into his house and practiced carving. He also took his friend's valuables to pay for his trouble and the wear and tear of the knife. The latter certainly felt very much cut up about it, and the

morgue authorities put the slices on exhibition to improve
Parisian morals

I cannot see that any good object is served by the facility
of admission to this place.

Going back to the hotel, I stopped at the American
Exchange, to get a bit of United States to contrast
with the sensationalism which characterizes France. It
is a pleasant thing that, since we have developed into
a traveling nation, we have taught the tourist nation
of the world—England—many points of comfort, and
chief among these are the exchanges, where, in the midst
of a foreign land, one can sit under an American flag,
read the American papers, look at American faces, and
talk about home. No British consulate can afford this
to the Englishman, and no nation has as well organized
tourists' headquarters abroad as we possess in the leading
European cities. You must pardon my patriotic enthusiasm,
and remember that the farther one gets from home the
more it bubbles. At the hotel I joined forces with a young
American, and started out for exploration of Paris by night.
The early evening in Paris presents nothing vastly different
from any other large city at the same hour; the working
classes are returning home, the boulevards are thronged
with promenaders, and the aristocracy are dining. For
the time being we voted to join the ranks of the aristocracy,
and driving to Marguery's, we were soon dining under the
supervision of a gorgeous being who plied us with all luxuries from turtle soup to Hamburg grapes and black coffee,
while we watched the constant flow of life along the boulevard; and here again we could notice the French working
girl, on her homeward way. She does not dress as showily
as her American sister; she frequently goes bareheaded, but
is neat, and as full of chatter as an English sparrow. She
may not earn much, but I believe that she enjoys life.

When the stream had assumed another phase, and the toilers, the late shoppers, and the idle promenaders, the most innocent *flaneurs*, had disappeared, and the laughing, chatting pleasure-seekers of the night began to appear, we made our plunge into the vortex.

Paris life resolves itself into a formula as regards its amusements; that is, there is a special night which is by common consent devoted to fashion in each pleasure resort; Saturday night the circus, Thursday night the Eden Theatre, etc. And now we were again *embarras de richesses;* the amusements at the various houses tend all the way from the Comedie Francaise to the Folies Bergéres. At the Francaise you have the best company of actors in the world, and all the traditions of French art are faithfully adhered to. But the American auditor will not readily accustom himself to the sing-song style of delivery used in the rhymes, and he must bear in mind that in all the classical plays of France, rhyme is used as blank verse is with us. This becomes unbearable when applied to Shakespeare, and "Hamlet" would make the skeletons of Shakespeare and Bacon dance a *pas de deux.*

The Folies Bergéres is the other extreme, and will be mentioned later.

As a well-behaved journalist I know that I have not time to sit out any theatre performance, yet I gravitate toward the Eden Theatre simply because the way is attractive, (let some moralist make a point here), and in a few minutes I am looking at the time-honored ballet of "Excelsior," which they seem determined to give in Paris until the *corps de ballet* die off. The theatre is especially brilliant on this night, and the Oriental (but tawdry) effects of the architecture of the *foyer* are set off by elegant costumes (not any of the female portion of the audience are in full evening dress, however), and there are several leaders of the "half-

world" present, who appear not especially beautiful of
countenance, but attractive in manner and conversation.
One *entr'acté* is sufficient and we make a dash to the Folies
Bergéres. This is the Mecca of a great many American
travelers of the male persuasion, who fondly imagine that
here they have found the wild life of the metropolis. This
is a mistake, or at least, if it be true, the whole of it pro-
vokes only disgust, and certainly demands pity from every
thinking person. The performance here is of good order,
for a variety show, but the attraction for the travelers aforesaid is in the constant stream of promenaders in the lobby
and in the restaurant attached. But there is to be a students'
ball to-night, and we may not stay long here when the spirits of all the French novelists for the last half century are
beckoning us to the Quartier Latin. So off we go, in a carriage now, stopping only long enough at a *café chantante* to
see that it is Tony Pastor spiced up and translated into
French, and finally arrive at the orgie sought for. All is glare
and glitter here—thousands of gas jets, a brassy orchestra,
a large dance floor, a large and well patronized café and restaurant. It is impossible to deny that the whole is attractive
at first. As every dance seems to be a grotesque quadrille,
and as the male dancers seem to be performing all the antics,
I cannot get a lingering suspicion out of my mind that they
are hired to do it, and that shrewd Paris is speculating on a
bygone attraction. I find no students, no grisettes, no bo-
hemianism; only vulgarity and a certain amount of bacchanalian excitement. This impression is rather intensified
when two females, dazzling in lace and satin, quarrel over
a partner and come to blóws. A fierce and repulsive encounter follows, which all crowd to witness and none try to
check, until the victor is left in torn finery, mistress of the
field; then the dance is resumed. As *entr'acte* between the
next dances, two men have an impromptu encounter, in

PARIS GRAND OPERA HOUSE,
SIDE VIEW.

which some blood is shed, not in the romantic duel style, but prosaically—from the nose. Shades of all the romancers! Is *this* the wild, devil-may-care Paris you have described?

But the general hilarity increases with the increased amount of drinking, and now the women outvie the men in vehemence of gesture and action. It becomes not enjoyment, but frenzy. There is no stretch of fancy required to imagine these creatures dancing the Carmagnole, instead of the Cancan, or reveling in blood instead of champagne. We leave the place a little after midnight, and find our patient cabman ready for further investigations. One of the half-drunken dancers comes to our carriage and asks to drive across the Seine with us. As we trot off with a quiet refusal she screams a request to our driver to upset us. There may be gayety here, but we have not the keenness to discover it.

We need rest (my companion and I) after such an excitement, so we go once more to the Boulevard des Italiens. Do not imagine that because it is considerably after midnight we shall find it deserted; on the contrary, the crowd of promenaders is so great that one can scarcely move along; far greater is this throng than that on Broadway, New York, at 3 P. M. on a fine day; only Paris can show us such a sight at one o'clock in the morning, and every morning at that! An hour later and things are quiet, but the more dissipated revelers are still awake, and if you want proof of it, we can go to the Brasserie Moderne, around the corner.

The Brasserie Moderne is a beer saloon on a very large scale. There is still a great glitter of gas lights, but there is no gilding, and no attempt at such elegance as we found at our haunts in the earlier evening. Champagne has been replaced by beer, and the whole tone is lowered. It is no longer the aristocracy, but the democracy of dissipation. Yet we find faces here a little tired, and I fear looking a little

hungry, that we had seen in the early part of the evening in
higher quarters. Is is difficult now to keep to ourselves,
for these parodies of gayety come each instant to beg a
drink, lunch, anything. But we have laid out our programme, and although pleasure, and even interest, have
evaporated, we shall go a step lower still, and so to the Café
Frontin (as old Pepys would say), where an hour longer of
this life is allowed, which is the last. It is now nearly
three in the morning, and still this place is thronged, and
will continue so until the lights are put out. All the faces
here are of lower type; sifting after sifting has taken
place, until the lower grades only of Parisian dissipation remain. I will not attempt to describe such a place, for it
could point no moral and adorn no tale; but I felt that many
a life had gone just exactly the round of our journey—not
in a night, but still in a fearfully rapid time—and felt, as I
did at the end, that Paris was not really as gay as it was
painted. Of course this gives only one part of the picture,
but this is a very large one in Paris, and gives color to almost all that is written about the city. And now, at 2:45 A.
M., we sought a healthier atmosphere in the great markets
—the Halles Centrales—which we reached just in time to
see the beginning of the wholesale trade for the day, which
was done simply by ringing a bell and declaring the market
open for wholesale transactions. The carts came rolling in
from the country, and it was pleasant to see the ruddy faces
and to smell the grateful odors of the fruits and flowers. A
few cafés in the immediate vicinity had just opened, and we
found several of the peasants in blouses taking a light repast to begin the day. The retail market would not begin
until five o'clock, so there was a constant influx of wagons,
and of market, and country men. A woman was going
around among these with a coffee-can strapped to her
shoulders, and selling a mysterious mixture at one sou a

large cup. I draw the line at bad coffee, and so I did not investigate this, but I joined a group of rustics who were gathered about a large kettle, where another woman sold a sort of broth and bread at ten centimes (two cents) a bowl, and, in the interests of science, partook of the humble fare. It was at least warm, but it was not as strong as Sullivan, and reminded me of the Irishman's soup, which was made by boiling a quart of water down to a pint to give it strength. Among the company at that festive board was a *sergent*, who was taking his meal with an evident relish, and also taking some interest in me. He commended the soup, he commended the weather, he was satisfied evidently with himself and the world, and possibly, with true politeness, he thought he was cheering some foreigner who had been wrecked in Paris and was reduced to penury and weak soup. And now it was broad day; our round had been completed, and we walked—we had dismissed our *voiture*—to our hotel. There was still plenty of life in the streets; persons connected with early traffic were hurrying to their work, and a few had evidently not yet finished their round of pleasure. Two of these asked us to assist them with cab fare to get home. They were evidently unable to walk, and as it was the end of our round, we assisted them to end theirs. And so our last two types of Parisian existence, as the first two, were not pleasing, and in a state of combined melancholy and drowsiness we sought our beds.

If I have devoted something of space to the wild side of Paris, it is on the ground of this being a leading feature of its existence. If I were writing from Florence, I should speak of art; from Leipsic, music; from Nice, gambling; and I could not give a French "Hamlet" with M. Hamlet left out.

Paris is beautiful, Paris is intellectual, and Paris is a home of true art, but the dangerous elements are there, all

the same, and once, at least, I saw them seethe up to the
top of the cauldron.   I had arrived in the city on August
7th, 1888.   Almost upon arrival I met a motley procession
of men and boys with broomsticks, near the Louvre; "C'est
la grève!" I was told.   The strike!   So then even in gay
Paris there was hunger and discontent.   I was not averse
to comparing the wolf of Paris to the wolf I had once seen
show his teeth in Trafalgar square in London, but I had a
more indefinite idea of a French mob, and somehow, a belief that they became more frenzied and turbulent than in
colder England.

Nevertheless the next day found me equipped for the
fray, in the oldest clothes I had at command, and with a
conviction that there was to be trouble, for had I not read
that morning, (Wednesday, August 8), an inflammatory
appeal in the *Homme Libre* saying that "the revolutionary
committee, and the old members and combatants of the
commune, and the family and friends of the deceased, in-
vite the populace of Paris to assist at the obsequies of
Citoyen Emile Eudes at 10 o'clock precisely." .Who was
Emile Eudes?   He was the general of the terrible commune
of Paris, the editor of the "Freeman," the socialist agitator;
and this announcement, coming in the midst of grave labor
disturbances, meant that the scum was to have a full opportunity of bubbling up, that communism was to have a chance
of gathering and shouting and possibly fighting, without the
government having the power to prevent the meeting.

I was soon in a cab, and feeling sure that no trouble would
take place at the house of mourning in the Rue Reaumur,
ordered the driver to tap the procession at the Rue du Temple.   Here I found crowds of excited people, but not any
of the dangerous elements as yet.   The shops were beginning
to close—an ominous sign.   The procession came; not in
the best of order, but still impressive enough.   The striking

workmen carried great wreaths of red immortelles, the revolutionary committees had red rosettes and red banners in-
scribed "A Blanqui," for a flag of any color may be carried
in a Parisian procession if it has an inscription, but to carry
a plain red or a black flag is sedition. Yet there, in the
rear part of the procession, is suddenly upreared—the red
flag of anarchy! I leave my carriage and push toward the
spot; it is difficult to come near, for the press is terrible;
there will be room, and to spare, in a moment. I see the
flag near the carriage in which sits Henri Rochefort with
two children in black, the daughters of the dead agitator.

He evidently deprecates this defiance of the law and rises
to speak; he implores them to respect the safety of the two
fatherless ones with him. The bearer of the seditious emblem becoming angry, beats the banner down upon his hat
and shoulders. The driver finally forces his way out of
the procession and drives Rochefort away, through a side
street. For a moment I think of following; but a few steps
and I see a scene which holds me fast. A shot is heard, and
then another, then yells and tumult indescribable as the
crowd surges back and people begin running up the surrounding streets. The soldiers and police have made an
ambuscade without a word of warning, some with revolvers,
most with sabres in their hands. They are hacking and
hewing their way to the flag. A charge with fixed bayonets
takes place. An excited lieutenant screams out, "In the
name of the law—disperse!—disperse!—give up your flag!"
A gendarme seizes the staff and breaks it. The procession
is cut in two, but some of the combatants rally.

I see some throw bottles and decanters from a café, which
they have evidently forced open, at the heads of the soldiers;
one quite near me is cut and bleeds, and tries to improvise
a bandage with a newspaper. Some of the crowd attack
the military with tables and chairs taken from the café above

mentioned, which seems to be an improvised arsenal for the mob. A bomb is thrown into the midst of the mass of military, where it might have killed friend and foe alike had it gone off, which it fortunately did not.

A French soldier clubs his musket and aims a decisive blow at my head, which fortunately only reaches my chest, but causes me to speak French more rapidly than I had ever done before, and explain that I am an innocent journalist and musician, who does not intend to harm the government of France, if it behaves itself. When I recover my breath, and find myself unmolested, I push for a place of safety, which I find just back of the hearse. On my difficult way thither I see an earnest, gaunt female in black, tossed about like a chip on the waves; she clings to me as I go, and we both finally pull out of the turmoil. It is a tall woman with a veil of crape on her head. The expression of her countenance is something far more awful than grief. She astonishes me a little later by making a wonderful speech at the grave. It is the most dangerous yet the most earnest woman in France, the *Vierge Rouge*, the "Red Virgin"—Louise Michel.

But the flag is gone, and the head of the procession moves on, and as I see that the riot is nearly done, for the police are already marching off with prisoners, I, with one memento of the row in the shape of that solid knock in the ribs, struggle out of the crowd in order to be at the cemetery in time for the interment—for all this scene did not take ten (possibly not five) minutes. I am fortunate enough to find another *voiture*, and drive to the gates of Pere-la-Chaise. The cafés are closing here too, but I manage to get a glass of wine and have the good fortune to meet with Mr. Cleveland Moffett of the New York Herald, and through the rest of the day we join forces. The correspondents are all on deck to-day, for we soon meet Ives of the London Times and Bonsell of the New York World. I do not present the most heavenly appearance in the world at this time, for my hat is crushed in, my collar is trying to crawl down into my vest pocket, and my shirt has perspired itself into a rich coffee color, and at the close, if I do not resemble "Ajax defying the lightning," I certainly feel like a jackass defying the thermometer, a role in which I decline to appear again. Mr. Moffett and I, however, move through the ranks of police and military into the cemetery.

I cannot tell how strange that resting-place of the dead seemed that noon of August 8. Fierce looking men in blouses and in rags are there; even women have scrambled up to the top of some of the higher tombs, and all are shouting: "Vive la Commune! Vive la Grève! Vive la Revolution Sociale!" I heard but few shouts for Boulanger. We are fortunate again, for as the procession comes up the avenue, the seven red ribbons running from the hearse being held by seven prominent communists, we push close to the foot of the coffin and are allowed to pass without great trouble, although of course, still tossed and pressed by the tremendous crowd, estimated at 20,000.

There is no music in the terrible procession, and no religious emblem of any kind, only the large red wreaths carried by the societies. We push on toward the open tomb, into which the coffin is hurriedly lowered some 10 feet. The crush and tumult has now increased so greatly that many of the trophy-bearers cannot come near the tomb. One of them calls to me and flings his great wreath of immortelles into my hands, with a request that I place it in the grave. This insures my place more than ever, for I look disreputable enough for any deed, and I have now a semi-official duty at the front. But our position is more precarious than even in the Place Voltaire during the slaughter, for sometimes the crowd becomes unmanageable and we are in danger of all being pushed into the deep hole. I have heard of men having one foot in the grave, but I have no ambition to have *two* feet in it, and another man's grave at that!

And now the services begin. M. Vaillant speaks, but no one can hear a word, not even I, four feet away. Arnauld follows; a genteel, refined looking man, with eyeglasses and a gray moustache. His words are well chosen, and seem to indicate a man of culture. Decidedly in the party of anarchy extremes meet. Even he is not listened to (the French reporters acknowledged ignorance of the speeches the next day), and the noise is dreadful. But now the woman at my side lifts her voice, and the roars are hushed; right or wrong, Louise Michel is a woman who will command attention. What fierce power! What intense brevity! "He had no church but the church of humanity; he had no creed but to help us disinherited ones; he had no faith but that of liberty!"—those words, with the impressive, spontaneous manner in which they were said, ring in my ears yet, and were more dangerous than a dozen red flags to the cause of conservative government; and the crowd burst forth with one wild shout of "Vive la Commu-u-u-ne!" dwelling on the last syllable as if loth to relinquish it. Vastly different were some of the other speeches, which were read from manuscript and sounded like commencement-day essays.

M. Felix Pyat won attention, however. Gray-bearded and gray-haired, with blazing eyes and vehement manner, often beating his breast, he also spoke for " the great army of the disinherited." " Citoyens!" he said (for the revolutionary appellation is the only one tolerated by the communists)—"Citoyens! not these immortelles, not these; the immortality of man, of liberty, shall speak for this dead hero!'' An excitable communist at the end of the speech seized on M. Pyat and embraced him and kissed him over and over again in that slobbering fashion which is in vogue among continental Europeans. '' The commune is coming soon, very soon,'' was the substance of Dr. Susini's tirade, and a shout of '' Vive le drapeau rouge!'' followed.

There had been dignity in at least some of these speeches, but things tapered down rapidly. M. Elie May spoke well, but the ridiculous element soon crept in, even at the side of the open grave, for a striking coachman named Moore must needs get on a bench and recite some doggerel verses on liberty, equality and fraternity, of interminable length and absurd bombast. Some laughed, some applauded, but no one seemed to remember that a funeral was going on. The sweltering heat and the ferocious surging of the crowd caused many to faint, and some had a narrow escape from being trampled to death; but at last it was over; that coachman's rigmarole was the benediction, and the crowd began to disperse. Near the gate of the cemetery we found large detachments of the Garde Republicaine drawn up, with loaded muskets, ready to cool off any too fiery enthusiasm that might have been kindled by the speeches.

Nothing but a stoning of the police and a few broken heads resulted, however. I heard rumors that over 100 were wounded, some mortally, in the riots connected with the flag, but this can probably never be accurately known, for many were carried off by friends. The rest of the day, as a fitting appendix to the proceedings in Pere la Chaise, I spent in interviewing some of the leaders of '' the revolution.'' M. Jules Brisson, the editor of "Le Parti National," was found in his sanctum and spoke freely. He said that things were not unanimous, that the leaders were afraid to displace the ministry of Floquet for fear that Jules Ferry would come in. That would be out of the frying pan into the fire. He believed that the rioting was incited by Orleanist, Napoleonic and German money! He thought the day was a triumph.

I went to the Bourse de Travail, the labor headquarters, believing that some of the leaders might be found there, but found instead a platoon of the Garde Republicaine with fixed bayonets, and a placard over the door, "La Bourse de Travail est momentanement fermée." The police were keeping the crowd in motion. It was the Trafalgar square business (of which hereafter), translated into French, only instead of " Pass along, please," it was " Circulez Messieurs," whether they pleased or not. I must compliment the French journalists for enterprise; three hours after the events described above, they were out with a column of interesting details of the matter—although they did not get the speeches. The "local" work of the Paris journals is as good as the "telegraph" work is bad, but 'then to the average Frenchman there is no news outside of Paris. He believes Paris is the world. In one of the schoolboy essays of the morning, a speaker stated that " the eyes of the universe are on Paris to-day," and he but voiced the Gallic idea, not only for that day, but for every day, including Sunday.

I had an interview with one of the representative communists in the evening. M. Elie May is the head of one of the largest and most zealous of the seditious societies. Intelligent in face and manner, charming in speech, he but impressed me how easily a sincere man who brooded over the misery of many of the race could be led into Utopian ideas. He said that communists did not desire absolute equality of property, but that the great disproportion must be abolished. Starvation and wretchedness must be made impossible. There must be a universal republic in which all must labor. Would this come? Yes, within ten years.

Eventually they all hoped, he said, for a United States of

Europe, in which all the nations but America would join. Our own United States was their model; they desired nothing better than such freedom and order. Alas, and alas! it was an idealistic picture; he did not know how this very freedom, this opening of our doors to all the world (except to the Chinese, who have no political influence), was debasing our own fair land and breeding a dark future. He did not see how the divided counsels of his followers, their lack of practical experience, and blind hatred of power, would destroy more comfort than it ever would build up. He did not see that an illiberal liberalism (which communism certainly is) is the most autocratic form of government. He did not see that some of his very followers desired license rather than liberty. He only saw that many people were starving and other people were rich, and was impatient to right this wrong. God save France! And yet such false prophets may do good in the end. Agitation is always the best course for those who have wrongs to be redressed, even if they themselves know not the best ways of redressing them. "August 8, 1888" proved that in Paris, at least, the upper classes are dancing on a volcano, and that the elements which existed in 1793 are not yet entirely obliterated.

CHAPTER XIV.

THE GREAT EXPOSITION AT PARIS—A MUSICAL DAY—AN AL-
GERIAN CONCERT—INTERVIEW WITH MASSENET—UNEXPEC-
TED JURY DUTY—A NIGHT AT THE OPERA WITH MASSENET
—THE GRAND OPERA—SYBIL SANDERSON AND EMMA EAMES
—ART IN PARIS—AN ANNAMITE CONCERT.

The next year I again found myself in Paris and at a bury-
ing party, for Felix Pyat, the socialist mentioned in the preceding chapter, was dead, and I confidently expected another
little fight on the occasion of the funeral. A few boys
feebly shouted " Vive la Commune," a few red flags were
waved, and that was all, where the preceding year a terrific
mob of 20,000 stood. Instead of long lines of cavalry and
infantry, a few policemen were in Pere la Chaise, strolling
about as if they were there for their health. Why was it
so, and why did even the trial of Boulanger attract only a
hundred or so to hear it? Because Paris had a new toy;
because so long as the exposition was open all the Boulan-
gers in the world could not excite the city to revolt.

Yet the exposition was far, far more than a toy. To have
the world placed in a condensed form in a few square miles of
space, is the grandest object lesson imaginable. *Ten cents*
(for the stores sold the tickets at that price) admitted to it
all, or very nearly all, for the side shows were inconsider-
able. There was one characteristic of the great fair which
only Paris could present, and that was the cosmopolitan and

EMMA EAMES,

AS JULIET.

polyglot character of the public itself; and the " street of habitations'' was a proof of the avidity with which the orientals seize upon an excuse to come to Paris. For example in " a house of the time of Sesostris " I found an Egyptian beauty, not of the time of Sesostris, who sold me some Egyptian cigarettes before I had time to escape. In the ancient Arabic dwelling there was a sign " English spoken,'' which somewhat marred the ancient effect, and after all, the inhabitant only spoke broken English, for he stuttered. In another ancient Arabic house I found upon the table of the bazaar some regular peanuts, or southern "goobers,'' which here were called " Kacaguettes.'' What's in a name? I suppose the Cairo boys eat Kacaguettes and throw the shells from the gallery of their theatre, the same as boys do in New York. In the Russian house I went in for a regular Muscovite meal, and took a bowl of Russian soup. " Bortzsch '' it is called and it is as full of cabbage as of consonants. It is made by stewing all the vegetables you can gather, together with meat and vinegar, and then adding some sour cream! ! Liszt used to be very fond of this dish, but I did not (as he) produce any *poemes symphoniques* after it; I felt more like a set of Rhapsodies Coliques. However, a glass of Vodki, and a slice of cake, also made with cabbage, called Pirok, made me feel like a first-class nihilist, and some qvass (a sort of cider that has gone wrong) confirmed the impression.

While I am on the subject of foods let me speak of a few of the various odd dishes which were obtainable: Roumanian sausages, Arabian candy (tastes like cold cream), Viennese sausages (a dream of delight, and also of dire dyspepsia), Tunisian cake ('tis grease, but living grease no more), and so on *ad infinitum*. As to drinks a toper could get drunk in forty different languages in the road leading to the Esplanade des Invalides. Not to speak of fifty kinds of beer (from Norway, Holland, Austria, France, England, etc.,) one could get Spanish wines, Hungarian wines, Norwegian Aqua Vit, Egyptian Raki, Indian Arrack, Russian Vodki, Polish Kümmel, Roumanian Slibovitska (like brandy with castor oil), Tsuoika (the same but worse), Swiss Kirschwasser, Amer Picon (this was distributed gratuitously and the kiosk was crowded), American whisky, and then at the end of the avenue (the largest street of bar-rooms I have ever seen) the faithful investigator could find the police station.

I was saved from a drunkard's grave by hearing a drum rhythmically beating at the end of the avenue. Tracing the sound to its source I stumbled upon an Algerian concert in full blast. It was genuine enough in all conscience, and there was percussion enough to have made Mr. Theodore Thomas fall down in a fit had he heard it. A really beautiful girl was executing a coquettish dance with a mirror when I entered, going through all the pantomime of the toilet of face and hair, and admiring herself as she did so. After this a negress executed a scarf dance of no especial merit, when suddenly a demented oboe broke loose with a series of shrieks that shook my nerves so that I will never be the same man again. These explosions were but the prelude to a song which was not without its charm (in fact it was the one musical feature of the concert) having tender and sad intervals, sounding somewhat flat of our scale at times, and yet not being the scale of nature either. The song was marred by the fact that it had about 153 verses. The lady told me in broken French afterwards that it was the song of welcome of a maid to her returning lover; that lover must have been kept standing a long time. All this was like the Midway Plaisance of our own great Exposition, but it was less exotic in Paris; the picture was not only larger, but better suited to its frame.

As I came out from the concert I heard some one calling "Effendi! Effendi!" As I was not aware that I was an effendi (I am, however, a regular Boston effendi, living in the West End!) I paid no attention, but kept on. Soon however, an Arab plucked me by the arm. He had seen me taking notes and wanted to go down "in the book." His name is Isaac Ben Yeir and he evidently understands the value of India-rubber advertising. Another swarthy gentleman standing by, on learning that it was to go to America, begged hard for the same privilege, but his name was Raphael Levi, which sounds more like a son of Chatham street than a son of the desert, and I suspect him of fraud, particularly as he gave me an Egyptian cigar, which I imprudently smoked. If that was a real Egyptian cigar I know a way by which the country may be wrested from its conquerors. Let the Dervishes advance upon the English troops smoking those cigars! Yet I bought a few of them for they look innocent, and I may sometime be at a supper with my brother critics.

I have already animadverted upon the habits of the European in having every mode of travel divided into classes, very often with no other distiction between them than that of price. Even the toy railroad at the exhibition played at having "classes." A first-class ticket allowed one to ride on a blue seat, while a second-class passenger must ride on a yellow one, whether it suited his complexion or not. By the way, it was a spiteful little road, for while it printed warnings not to put out head or legs, in Latin, Arabîc, Chinese, Japanese, Malay, Hebrew, Spanish, Dutch, Italian, and a dozen other tongues, it carefully avoided posting up even a line of German. The Germans might put their heads out and get them smashed, and welcome.

In the Rue de Cairo (the self-same one that afterwards

came to Chicago) I saw the dance of the Almehs. The usual clatter accompanied the wrigglings of a beautiful, large-eyed brunette. Very suggestive are these dances, yet they seem in keeping with the sensuous beauty of some of the dancers. But why did this particular child of the Orient take all the romance out of the affair by producing a large bandanna, as she resumed her seat, and blowing her nose with frightful vehemence! Before I thought her a siren; now she lingers in my memory rather as a fog horn.

Some men achieve greatness, and some have greatness thrust upon them. My temporary greatness all came through opening the wrong door in the Trocadero. A great competition of the leading male choruses of France, for a prize of honor awarded by President Carnot, was to take place in that palace (in the exposition) and I had gone thither to see how the French male chorus compared with our white-breasted Apollos of Boston. I managed to get into the wrong corridor, and after wandering through a labyrinth of passages, boldly opened the first door that came to hand, and found myself in the midst of a jovial party who were lunching in the most convivial manner; it was the jury of awards (musical) who were thus fortifying themselves for the task which awaited them. A sudden thought came to me that possibly my friend of Bayreuth, M. Lamoureux, might be among them, and addressing myself to a pleasant-looking, stout, florid, gray-headed gentleman who happened to be near, I gave my card and asked for the famous conductor. No, he was not there, but M. Oscar Comettant, the celebrated musical author (for it was he) was quite at my service, and would not hear of my withdrawing. He wanted to present me to a brother journalist, and one who delighted to speak English.

A moment more and I was in conversation with M. Emile Devaux, editor of the Echo des Orpheons, who from that moment became my "guide, philosopher and friend." He watched over me like a guardian angel, and determined that I should miss nothing of the event of that day if he could help it. First of all, he introduced me to M. Massenet, the president of the jury. M. Massenet is active, genial, and as I had expected from his music, very spontaneous. The task before them, he said, would prevent his showing me any hospitality then, but would I call on him the next day at 6 P. M., and did I desire to come to "Esclarmonde?" He would send me a couple of tickets!

I was invited to sit with the jury (of course without having a vote) and left the lunch room with them. But my guardian angel, known to men as M. Devaux, decided that there was something better for me. I saw him speak to some attendants, who immediately disappeared carrying a table covered with green baize. Soon after he ushered me through a little side door, and I found myself on the stage of the Trocadero, alone, in presence of an audience of about 4,000 people. The audience, who had been kept waiting over the appointed hour, burst into applause as I appeared, thinking that I was the beginning of the show, as I certainly was in one sense. I resisted the temptation to deliver a speech in French, and marched to my green table, on which were pen, ink and paper, with the dignity becoming an American newspaper correspondent, and looked as benignant as if I were the founder of the entire contest.

Fortunately the jury soon followed, and the attention of the audience was drawn away from me, to such gentlemen as Massenet, Faure, Pougin, de Lajarte, Lory, Comettant, Widor, and others, who composed it. All through the preliminary contest I sat at my table taking notes, and trying to appear as if I had the prizes in my pocket, and would present them presently. The contest was a notable and a peculiar one. About thirty of the leading male choruses of France were there and were divided into four groups, all these being examined simultaneously in four halls of the palace. When the best societies had been selected, (one from each group), these were to compete for the *prix d'honneur*. Two selections were sung by each society, one being left to their own choice, the other being a *choeur imposé*, a chorus which had been chosen by the committee, and which each club was obliged to sing. This chorus was the "Kamarinskaia," by Laurent de Rillé, one of the best chorus composers of France. I was introduced to M. de Rillé, who is a short, slightly-built man with wavy gray hair, and that nervous and high-strung look and manner which tells of genius and sensibility.

He gave me a copy of the chorus alluded to. It contains two beautiful Russian airs, as well as some delightful work in the French school, with very effective contrasts. Also, Thomas' "Nuit de Sabbat" is something that would make a hit at our club concerts, if the tenors could stand the work. This fact struck me during the entire *concours,* the tenors were used unsparingly, and often in a demi-falsetto. Some of the finest tenor choral work I ever heard was at this contest. M. Massenet told me afterwards that there is a difference even among the tenors of France, the finest tenor voices coming from the department du Midi, while the robuster voices came from the department du Nord. But the basses seemed weak in every instance, nothing like what we hear at a Cecilia or an Apollo concert. As each club sang, an attendant stood behind them holding up their banner. Most of the clubs were in full dress, but some had simple uniforms. There were more swallow tails than I had ever seen gathered together before, for a Frenchman appears in full evening dress whenever he does anything exceptional or public, even if it occurs at 6 A. M. Each club intoned three times, to make things quite sure. During that contest I heard the "Kamarinskaia" sung six times, and the "Nuit du Sabbat," (a weird, uncanny, but dramatic, affair), four times, and I can now sing either of these with one hand tied behind my back; I think I hum them in my sleep. The choruses were of widely differing sizes, from 40 to 160 members, and many sang without notes.

At last four champion societies were chosen, and then the real contest began. But before this we went out and got refreshments. During this interval the late M. Ambroise Thomas, then head of the Conservatoire and the most honored composer in France, came in and assumed the presidency of the jury. I was at once presented to him as a wild journalist fresh from the New World, and was welcomed with dignity. A tall and stately man, whose form was a little bent by years and labor, whose gray locks made him appear like an ancient prophet, the formal courtesy which he possessed fitted him well, even if one was more warmed by the friendly ways of Massenet. His keen gray eye was most attractive, and showed a man thoroughly in earnest. He became quite lively, however, when I spoke of our Boston singer, Lillian Norton, and, after the contest had ended, he alluded again to the noble voices which came from America. He said, on being told that Mme. Norton had graduated at the New England Conservatory, and on my questioning him regarding his own conservatory, that he believed that we should encourage our native talent by prizes, just as they do in France. He added that there were good pupils at the Conservatoire from America, mostly in voice, and spoke with some enthusiasm of American sopranos. He regretted that there was nothing he could do for me, since he left Paris on the morrow. The next day there came to my hotel his card *pour prendre congé,*—his politeness had been punctilious to the last.

But now I went along with him to the jury. I cannot

tell whether the public regretted losing me or not, but I left my table on the stage and sat with the musicians aforesaid, at the opposite side of the hall. Gloriously did the four champion societies sing, but finally it narrowed down to two. "Les Enfans de Paris" and a society with the strange appellation of "Le Cricksick de Tourcoing." It seems there is a stream called Sick Creek, in Tourcoing, (department of the North), and this society had adopted it as their name. The award was difficult to make. Never did two clubs sing better, or more evenly. The committee were puzzled. "I never was so perplexed in my life," said Arthur Pougin to me, as he borrowed my pencil to vote with. Besides this a very pretty girl in the gallery distracted the attention of the jury, and no Frenchman is ever too old or too busy to notice a beautiful maiden. It was a *mauvais quart d'heure* for the singers, after they had finished; they crowded to the front of the stage, a striking picture of full dressed suspense. None of the vast audience left, and you could have heard a pin drop, (particularly if it were a linch pin or a belaying pin), while the judges were deliberating. Finally the verdict came, eight for "Les Enfans de Paris," seven for the "Criksick of Tourcoing." "The Parisian society has won," stated the secretary, "but" —but not the butt of the wildest goat would have stopped the shout from the Parisians,—"But! but!! but!!!" shouted the secretary, finally becoming audible, "the contest has been so exceptionally close that the secretary of the interior orders an equal prize of honor to the Tourcoing society also " Then both societies left the palace, waving their banners and singing pæans of triumph.

The next day the promised fauteuils to "Esclarmonde" at the Opera Comique were sent to me, and at 6 P. M. I went to see the composer as agreed. I found M. Massenet at the piano, playing an arrangement of his new opera. A handsome man full of life and motion, bright black eyes, a chubby, good-humored and attractive face, a pointed black moustache, black hair brushed straight back from a fine forehead —*voila* M. Massenet! I spoke of the new opera at once, and asked him which of his works he liked best. "Every father likes his last child best," said he, "and just now I prefer 'Esclarmonde.' " He played a few airs from this, finally becoming enthusiastic and singing as well, in full, clear tones. He asked about his works in America, and when I told him of the warm reception of his suites there, he began to play that part of the "Scenes Pittoresques," where the cracked village bell calls the peasants to church. He spoke of Miss Sybil Sanderson (our own American prima donna), as the ideal of " Esclarmonde," which was in fact written for and dedicated to her. "You have seen the monsters that sometimes appear in 'Traviata,' for example? It is difficult to find a heroine to fit a part. Well, when Miss Sanderson sings

'Oui je suis belle et desirable.'

[and M. Massenet sang the phrase at the piano] it suits the case exactly!"

Of American music he knew little, but spoke enthusiastically of MacDowell's works that he had heard, and mentioned some of Chadwick's, of which he had read the scores. " Where did they study? " he asked, and then suddenly he became very emphatic and excitedly earnest, speaking most rapidly and in an evident state of enthusiasm. He urged the necessity of forming our own composers, and at home; he spoke of the bane of rules alone which crushed out individuality; he cited the two contrasting cases of Grieg, who had retained his individuality spite of study in Germany, and Gade, who had lost his and become a reflection of Mendelssohn. He cited the case of a Swedish pupil who studied with him up to last year and then came back and wanted more, and told me how he had sent him home to become an individuality, to look at his blue skies, green fields and vast mountains, and put them into music; and all his words were aglow with patriotism and lofty inspiration.   When I said that perhaps our mixed races militated against the evolution of a true national school, he shouted: "It must be!   I have not seen your country, but I have seen pictures of your great Niagara, your deep forests, your vast plains; they ought to inspire music.   And then your beautiful women!   Look in their eyes and find your inspiration." [It is singular that Wagner too had a thought similar to this, and that his "Centennial March" was evolved by it.]   "And it must be no copy either," he added earnestly; "the American school must be eclectic."

I have given this part of the interview with much care as to exactness, for I consider these views of a most eminent French composer as both important and just.   *Du reste*, our conversation need not be so exactly quoted; he expressed almost a certainty of coming to America; he is fond of conducting; he was at work upon a new opera of which M. Richepin furnished the libretto; he inquired about American poets and poetry; he spoke of Miss Sanderson's high note as being very wonderful (it is G in alt, and pure as a bell) and finally gave me a pass to go back of the scenes at the Opera Comique, saying that we could meet on the stage after the third act.

The evening, therefore, found me at the theatre listening to "Esclarmonde."   I will not write about this in detail, for it has been fully reviewed on the occasion of its earlier performances, but I must say that the librettists ought to be hung without benefit of clergy.   The plot is just on a par with, and similar to, Wagner's "Fairies." The music is grand and lofty, spite of the heavy handicap, although the composer is obliged to repeat himself because of the absurd prolixity of his libretto. There was a fine tenor robusto in the cast, M. Gibert; the second and third acts are the best; and Miss Sanderson carried off the lion's share of the applause, with a sweet voice of remarkable compass. Almost every vein of composition, from rustic Villanelles to grand climaxes, is represented in the work.

After the third act I went back of the stage as agreed upon. Massenet was cordial and natural as ever, and soon introduced me to Miss Sanderson and her mother. Miss Sybil Sanderson has certainly achieved very much in Paris and seemed quite free from any disposition to vaunt her triumphs. She is remarkably attractive personally, and told me that she was then engaged in studying Manon with Massenet, and hoped to make a success of that role as well, (which she has since done). She had played " Esclarmonde" very many times, she told me, and longed to essay the other part, since the novelty had worn off.

The call boy's bell sent me off the stage, right into a green room filled with members of the *corps de ballet.* I had never had such a personal interview (or let us drop the "inter" and call it a "personal view") with a French ballet before. From close observation I am convinced that the French ballet girl is young, attractive, and makes a very little cloth go a very long way in the matter of dress. They all had on their summer clothes, and wore their war paint. There were angels with pretty wings and remarkable smiles; there were demons in very close-fitting tights; demons of the most attractive character; demons that would make most charming playmates. But when one of these demons came toward me with evident intent to speak, I remembered that I was a citizen of Boston and turned and fled.

I was with Massenet again two days later, and he was

kind enough to show me all that was then completed of the score of his new opera. He seems to be very exacting with his librettists, revising and changing even to the day of the performance, and his dress rehearsals are said to be terrific, the composer finding fault with everything, exactly as Meyerbeer used to do a half-century ago,—a result of nervousness. Massenet is progressive in his instrumentation and gains many new effects thereby. His use of sarussophone instead of contra-bassoon does away with the faulty intonation which is often the bane of the latter instrument. In a new score the master intended to introduce a new instrument altogether— a bass flute. "All the other wood wind instruments have their basses," said he, "the clarinet has the bass clarinet, the oboe has the bassoon; then why not try to extend the register of the flute as well?" For my own part, I think the idea is feasible, and I am convinced that both the ancient Greeks and Egyptians had deep flutes. The experiments were being made by a prominent instrument manufacturer, and if they were successful, Massenet was to use the new instrument in his ballet scenes.

On returning to my hotel I found that two fauteuils for the Grand Opera had been sent to me (I was getting the proverbial honors of a prophet out of his own country) and I went to hear the American prima donna, Miss Emma Eames, in "Faust." Naturally I need not dwell upon the opera, and the opera house is the best known in Europe, unrivalled for grandeur, although both the Vienna and Buda-Pesth opera houses may vie with it in beauty. The scenery and mounting were not astoundingly sumptuous, as the management were just then in an economical frame of mind. In the matter of chorus and orchestra the Paris Grand Opera takes the lead. The house was crowded with Americans, who had come to hear the triumph of their

JULES MASSENET,

countrywoman. This triumph was a very legitimate one; there has been no wire-pulling or artificial enthusiasm. Miss Eames made her way to the front by talent. She was first engaged at the Opera Comique, but the management repented them of their opening the door to an unknown singer and gave her no part whatever, and when she begged to annul the contract they very promptly let her go. Since that time I suppose they have been kicking themselves, secretly but unanimously. But the fair Bostonian came out so suddenly and with so little flourish of trumpets that even I, who am supposed to know the musicians of the Hub, and who attend about seven concerts a week as penance for my sins, at that time knew nothing of her. She had appeared in Professor Paine's excellent historical lectures before a vast audience of as many as fifteen people, and had been the " first spirit " when Mr. Gericke brought out " Manfred," but as I was not addicted to spirits, I had forgotten all about this. Miss Eames, in her first Parisian successes of 1889, had not the broad voice she has since developed, but her singing was already powerful and majestic. Her very first song, "The King of Thule," was a charming performance, unaffected and tender, while the " Jewel Song " aroused the whole audience to enthusiasm, but the grand success was in the trio of the last act, where she gave a marvelous volume of tone. The only fault that the professional fault-finder could discern was a degree of calmness in some of the more vehement scenes; it was a tranquil Marguerite, rather than a wretched and distracted one, but this may have been partially the fault of Faust himself, whose acting was remarkably conventional, and whose only mode of expressing intensity was by puffing like a disordered steam engine. Mephistopheles was excellent, even if he *did* sing his serenade to the gallery instead of to Martha. The opera was given without any cuts—except one alto solo—and with a splendid ballet in the Brocken scene, effective enough here, although I must say that these anatomical displays do not fit to England or America.

I was glad to hear most flattering comments on our Bostonian singer from the French portion of the audience. "*Marguerite chante bien*" seemed to be the universal verdict and was certainly a just one. The next day I called on Miss Eames, and found a most unaffected young lady, full of life and of fun, utterly unspoilt by her triumph, and remembering all her Boston friends and teachers. Mr. Gericke was among the first to recognize the future of her voice, she told me, and after her success in the small part in "Manfred" said that she had a gold mine in her throat, but when she asked for a chance to *debut* at the symphony concerts he said, "Not yet; you must study abroad and must appear abroad," and the advice was wise. Miss Eames spoke of Professor Paine with much regard and admiration. " You don't know how much good he has done me," said she, " for he kept me at work on old, old music, ancient masses and all that, until I could not help acquiring a correct taste." (Some time after this I asked Professor Paine what music he had given to Miss Eames in her student days. " Dufay, Des Pres, Di Lasso, and the old Flemish school," he replied, and this may be a hint to some of those who desire a solid musical foundation in vocal work). "And one of my other teachers I shall never forget: Miss Annie Payson Call; she gave me many valuable points in elocution and dramatic expression, and all the teachers here commended what she had done for me." Miss Eames told me many an anecdote of the difficulty of obtaining a hearing in Paris, of intrigue and of machination, and how, when she *did* appear, she was a " dark horse;" unknown to all of the critics, and as they expected little or nothing they were the more surprised.

Mrs. Eames, who looks far too young to be the mother of such a celebrity, came in at this point and the conversation became personal. One public point, however, was touched upon—the American voices abroad.

"Many of them are sweet, but light, so much so that 'une voix Americaine' has come to mean a fragile, delicate thing," said Miss Eames (whose voice is powerful enough to fill the vast room of the Grand Opera), and then she went on to tell of how bound up in traditions the stage at the Grand Opera was, and what difficulty she had in getting them to allow her to use her own ideas in certain scenes. In parting, she again spoke most enthusiastically of her friends and teachers in Boston, and sent them her kindest regards. Since that time Mrs. Eames-Story has carried her triumphs into America, yet this story of her beginnings in France may not be *de trop*.

The next day, at the exposition, I discovered another musical attraction, in an out-of-the-way theatre wherein were some beautiful gipsys, real Gitanas from Granada, decked in the gaudiest of colors.

A few days before a bull-fighter, in the neighboring show, tried to kidnap one of them, and got arrested for his pains. I should have done the same—if I were a bull-fighter. The troupe consisted of some dozen performers, three men, one very young girl, and the rest most attractive young women. Their music has that sad, wailing character (even in the midst of its frenzy) which is found in almost all the tunes of half-civilized nations and tribes, and, although built upon our scale, had many modulations that were by no means according to Richter, yet very effective. It was not as many-sided as the music of Hungary, where the true gipsy music of the world has its home. The singers and dancers became

wonderfully excited with their work, and their passionate
execution of tangos, fandangos and jotas was weirdly fasci-
nating.   They sang to their dances in a wild fashion, and
were accompanied by three very large guitar-like instruments, the bandurria, the true national instrument of Spain.
They flirted with the audience in a manner that indicated
that they were ready for further kidnapping.

In the Rue de Cairo, after the dance, I saw a row among
the fellaheen; tremendous chatter, great threats and no particular damage.   The crowd soon dispersed, presumably
singing—" He's a jolly good fellah."   Now a stroll in the
oyster pavilion, where the bivalves are exhibited in all stages
of growth, from molluskian infancy to full maturity.   I was
invited to devour some adults, which I did, but they tasted
as if they had died of old age.   It is very fitting that the
champagne gallery should be next door to the oyster section.

The next evening I went again to the opera, and heard
Shakespeare in a French dress.   The French must be under-
going a revival in this direction.   This time it began with
Henry VIII., but dressed up in an entirely new fashion to
suit Armand Sylvestre's views of what ought to have happened, and didn't.   Anne Boleyn is given a Spanish lover,
a mysterious letter is introduced, which Catherine of Arra-
gon magnaminously burns, and the latter queen dies very
suddenly (to slow music) in the presence of King Henry and
the fair Anne.   The music is not to the taste of the French.
A celebrated French editor recently said to me: "It is hard
work to listen to the St. Saëns' music."   In fact St. Saëns
stands to-day in France just as Berlioz did a half century
ago.   "Who then do you class as the greatest French composer?" I asked.   The answer was, "Undoubtedly Ambroise
Thomas."   The most delightful part of this opera is the
ballet—in the " Parc de Richmon," as the libretto says.
We have heard parts of this in the symphony concerts, and

I need not tell how prettily St. Saëns has caught up the
Scotch lilt. He can almost rival Bruch and Mendelssohn
in Scotch fantasie; but, like most foreign composers, he does
not seem thoroughly to know what is Scotch and what is
English, and after all, Richmond Park does not lie in Scotland. The end of the opera is quite tame, a veritable anti-
climax, and the managers have shortened the work with
merciless hand. It could not have been "cut" more freely
had it been edited by an Italian brigand.

Now followed Shakespeare turned into a ballet by Jules
Barbier, with music by Ambroise Thomas—"The Tempest!"
Fancy Miranda pirouetting in short skirts, and Ferdinand
capering all over the stage! Prospero didn't dance, and
they kindly left him out of the libretto altogether. Ariel
made up for this by dancing all the time, and so did Cali-
ban. An innovation is used in this work by employing an
invisible chorus in connection with some of the dances.
There are flying angels (who look as if they had much rather
be walking), gnomes, bees, and other choreographic impos-
sibilities. The music is pretty rather than deep, and there
is the usual tempest, of course, with lightning on the piccolo, and a final clearing up on the flute; there are some
melodious cornet solos, a brilliant flute solo at the beginning of the third act, an oboe solo, and a very sweet and
lulling finale. The best music is in the third act, but none
of it is strikingly original, while the honored play is made
nonsense of. I suppose the next subject will be "Macbeth"
in ballet form. How pretty it would be to have Duncan
killed in a *pas seul*, and then to have Lady Macbeth and her
spouse dance a remorseful duet; to have Banquo's ghost
come in with a polka step, and Lady Macbeth balance herself on one leg in the sleep-walking scene. How original it
would be to have Hamlet *dance* his soliloquy. There are
new possibilities in Shakespeare yet, and the French are
beginning to discover them.

There is a marvelous verse sung in the above described ballet which runs:

> Dans l'espace diaphane
> Et Bleu
> Plane
> Dieu.

If Jules Barbier wrote this he ought to be secured to write poems for some patent medicine. A Paris wit, evidently believing in this new variety of short metre, at once wrote the following charming poem:

> Tempete,
> M'embete,

Which expresses the matter in a nut-shell. The French composers had better let "the divine Williams," (as they have called Shakespeare), severely alone.

Through the kindness of Emile Devaux, I was invited the next day to a grand concert of the chief mixed choruses of France, in the Trocadéro. Nearly 2000 performers were present, M. Vianesi leading those in the choruses and M. Paulus, formerly musical director of the famous band of the Garde Republicaine, leading the military band. The Marseillaise began and ended the programme, and was given in a peculiar manner; first, it was sung by men, then a verse was given by women, then followed a verse sung by school children, and finally the entire forces united in the last verse. There were some harmonies given in the accompaniment which were new to me, and which certainly are not used in America, although very effective. The French rarely rise when their national anthem is being played, as the English do, but the majesty of the last verse caused the audience spontaneously to spring to their feet as a token of appreciation. There is no national hymn which bears such varied style of execution so well as the Marseillaise; it is effective all the way from a solo to the grandest chorus.

Speaking of national anthems leads me to add that in France, as in several other countries, the musicians have decided "Hail Columbia" to be the real national hymn of America. I heard it played at the Grand Opera in honor of Mr. Edison, and I spoke to some of the French band-masters about it afterward. They told me that they considered it the most dignified of our national tunes, and that is true enough, for "America" is borrowed from England, "Yankee Doodle" is English, and a trivial affair to boot, while "The Star Spangled Banner" was a drinking song originally—also English. But "Hail Columbia," although at first merely intended for a theatrical entertainment, is American, both in the words and in the tune, which was a popular march. In prowling around the London antiquarian resorts, I was fortunately able, a while ago, to find original editions of the drinking song which became "The Star Spangled Banner." It is entitled "To Anacreon in Heaven," and is one of those bombastic, inflated and metaphorical songs which were in vogue during the last century. That it was very popular in London is proved by the fact that Braham made it one of his repertory of songs, and I have also a copy (dated 1802) in which it is changed into a Masonic ode, beginning "To old Hiram in Heaven," and celebrating Hiram Abiff, architect of the Temple at Jerusalem. A Bacchanalian ditty, a Masonic ode, a national anthem—these were the successive promotions of "The Star Spangled Banner."

I was very glad when Edwin L. Weeks, the only American artist who took a salon medal that year, and a Boston boy, volunteered to go with me on my first visit to the section of American paintings in the Exposition; as he was on the hanging committee (this is not similar to a western vigilance committee) I was especially fortunate in this. In going to his house near the large gate of the Exposition, (the Trocadero), I had another encounter with the extortionate Parisian cabman. Bland was he and smooth of speech, he had a winning smile, and when he suavely told me that the Avenue de Wagram was far, far away, and that he knew I was a gentleman the moment I burst upon his vision, and that three and a half francs was almost tempting bankruptcy, it was difficult not to believe him, but I had been there often before, and knew that the distance was short, and the fare one and a half francs. The charioteer stood aghast when I got in his team and told him that I would engage him by the hour, at the regular price (two francs) and would show him the way. I stopped to make a purchase in the Rue de Provence, and when I came out of the store the smile was gone, and the cabman also. If I were disposed to write sensationally I should head this, "Mysterious Disappearance" or "Gone but not Forgotten," at any rate there was no reply to this repartee, and in a cab with an honest driver who was satisfied with both fare and pourboire, ("Do all these drivers have poor boys?" an American in Paris asked me recently) I found my friend and plunged into the whirl of the crowd at the Palais des Beaux Arts.

The American exhibit in general was so disgracefully poor that I am glad to state that our exhibit of paintings was excellent—probably the best exhibition of American art that has ever been made anywhere. The cream of the last ten Salons was there, and the average was higher than the Salon itself. As regards some of the awards, I believe that the cream aforesaid will turn rather sour. Social position does not count for as much in art in France, as it does with us, and some pet painters were very faintly recognized. Unquestionably some mistakes were made; judges are but human; for example, Kitson's remarkable statue of Mayor Doyle of Providence received only a third class medal, while his "Music of the Sea," a few years ago, took a gold medal at the Salon, I believe. If I know Mr. Kitson (and I think I do) the air around Paris must have been rather sulphureous when he arrived from America. George Fuller (we all loved him in the Paint and Clay Club) is not understood in Paris at all, and his "Quadroon" received no reward whatever, while the French artists even satirized it, and wondered what the dusky female was out so late for.

And now as I have devoted much of this chapter to music and art, let me continue in the same vein, and write up the opera that I heard next day. I went to the Annamite Theatre, and I still live! My sense of hearing has been impaired, and my musical ideas irretrievably mixed up by "Vo-hau," which is the name of the opera or music-play that I attended. It is noisier than the Wagnerian Marches, and considerably longer. It is in about fifty-six acts, and as each act is an hour long, and they make you pay a separate admission each time, it takes a Jay Gould and a Methuselah combined to see it all. Each act begins with an overture, which would be comfortable music at half-mile distance, but is rather vehement when taken at short range. The act with which I started began by a fierce-looking party with whiskers and streaks of whitewash on his face coming forward and emitting the most furious catcalls and howls. In this he was aided and abetted by two pages, who ought to turn over a new leaf. The oboe player in the orchestra, and the man who clashed the dish covers, grew excited and reached a point only to be represented in music by *ff f f f f f!* But they could not drown the speaker or singer. "Wow, Miaw! ! Wow! Wow! Wow! ! !"— (clash—bang) roared the Annamite—or dynamite—Salvini. I could not fully indorse such revolutionary sentiments and was pleased to see an army—of four men with flags—enter and chase him vigorously around the stage. Joseph Proctor as the "Jibbenainosay" never shouted as did this persecuted party at this point; it fairly made my throat ache to hear him. A tall man with a deep-red face and an extremely long moustache now came in and gave a soliloquy, full of the noblest sentiments (according to the programme), which he expressed by cries of terrific intensity. He stood on one leg frequently—probably to avoid wearing out the other—and each point he made was emphasized by the bass drummer with a single stroke of great power and expression. A mandarin now entered, and all began walking around the stage, varying this at intervals by twirling about on one leg. Now came a still greater mandarin with a soup tureen on his head, who also stood on one leg to show his dignity. The characters then executed a sort of "ladies' grand chain" intermingled with shrieks. The original party, with whiskers and whitewash (who I afterwards ascertained was a pirate) rather puzzled me by going off the stage and coming on again without any ostensible reason, and it was also annoying to watch the movements of two or three parties who came in among the preceding ones and then to discover that they were merely "supes" who were removing a chair or a table. At last one of the party was executed, and *his* yelling was stopped. Many of the audience had gone away before this happy consummation, for a little of Annamite drama goes a very long way. The music was sufficient to turn the milk of human kindness in any bosom into Limburger cheese.

I am thankful that my lot is not cast in Annam; to be a musical critic there would demand a stronger constitution than I possess. Nevertheless, I must say that the play was not altogether without interest, and it would make a very suitable work to produce before a deaf and dumb asylum, or the text might be slightly altered and it could be performed in New York under the title of "A Caucus in the Sixth Ward." I left the city in a dazed and helpless condition, and hereafter the most furious piano recital by the most energetic pounder will have no terrors for me. And soon after this I left Paris and the exposition.

Farewell, oh fair young Russian, who gave me my Bortzsch (cabbage, meat, gravy and buttermilk) daily, and smiled at me sweetly in Russian while I ate it; farewell, oh Viennese sausage shop, where I achieved so many a fit of indigestion; farewell, thou English restaurant, where my mother tongue was shattered, and where I was made to pay for its demolition; farewell, De Vaux, De Rillé, Massenet and the musical friends who made my stay so pleasant. But I need not say farewell to the Annamite-dynamite opera troupe, for if they remain in Paris, I have no doubt that I can hear them very comfortably in Brussels whither I am going.

CHAPTER XV.

Brussels—a female in a smoking car—amsterdam—
the jewish quarter on friday night—scheveningen
—a stormy passage across the channel—london—
quaritch's book store—aristocratic clubs and pov-
erty-stricken slums—a riot in trafalgar square—
life in the english metropolis.

After the events described in the last chapter, I started
for Belgium, and soon found myself in Brussels. I take
pleasure in anathematizing with bell, book, and candle,
the conductor who put seven smokers into one compartment
of the train on the road there, and then at the last moment
shoved a poor lady, for whom there seemed to be room nowhere else, in among us, to give us the refining influences of
female society. The conductor was not wholly to blame,
however; he had stood guard over the trumpeter (who had
rejoined me) and myself, and kept us in seclusion for a time,
against a host of invaders. At last, every other compartment being full, a couple of Englishmen, pipe in mouth,
stormed the breach and carried it. Then the conductor,
seeing that his chance of gaining the nimble shilling had
gone, filled our compartment entirely. The poor young
lady coughed once or twice, and I reluctantly put out my
cigar. The Germans, French, English, and Belgians gazed
at me with astonishment. Was it not a smoking compart-

ment?! Should they waive their sacred privileges because a woman had been thrust in?!! They all continued smoking, and the young lady got out at Brussels as thoroughly smoked up as any sugar-cured ham. I need not describe Brussels. It is simply a little Paris, and I have written up Paris so thoroughly that I am not going to imitate history and repeat myself. I will only mention that in a certain "English chops house" I ventured to ask for some Bass, Alsopps, Barclay & Perkins, or anything to drown the memory of the dust of travel. The gentle garçon said they had none of these, but I could have "pallal." Ever on the lookout for novelties I ordered this as a drink of the country. Frailty of human hopes (or hops) again—it was Bass's "pale ale," only translated into the Belgese tongue. In the further journey to Amsterdam I had opportunity afforded to study the habits of the French hog while traveling. Your American railway hog is an infant beside him; he comes in and brings a caravan of baggage with him, he distributes this all over the compartment, and then sprawls all over the remaining seating capacity; he is fat, he smells of garlic, he is nervous about travel, and questions you to death about every detail of the road. Never mind; one is certain to have revenge; for, once we get on the Channel he is sure to be deathly seasick, and then you can question him as to whether the French serve their pork with molasses or just swimming in gravy. He will probably not reply at great length; his reply will be rather in actions than in words.

Amsterdam is a delight from beginning to end. No wonder Thackeray wrote so enthusiastically about it. During the Spanish wars it remained on the side of the cruel Duke of Alva, and did not suffer as Antwerp and other cities of the Netherlands, which has preserved to it almost all of its old buildings and palaces. Every street, every alleyway, is a study, and when the modern bees begin to swarm about

this ancient hive the sight is of indescribable interest.   The
pavements are so clean that the people walk in the street
rather than on the sidewalks, and at night the city is replete
with life and activity.

Amsterdam shows evidence of the fact that it was a city
of refuge in an age of persecution, in its possession of a
Jewish population amounting to 70,000 souls, and the
quarter which they inhabit is one of the curiosities of the
world.   I could not have seen it at a better moment, for I
came there a few minutes before sunset on Friday, and the
various pedlars of second-hand wares were "rushing" things
to turn in just one more penny if possible before their Sabbath began.   I went into a rather cleanly looking barber's
shop to utilize the few moments which I knew must change
the scene, in being shaved.   The poor fellow was in haste
to get through before sundown lest he break the Sabbath,
and the only quick thing I had in Holland was that shave.
The razor was dull and so was the operator.   He asked me
if it hurt, and I told him it did, and he didn't understand
me, and pulled harder, and finally when he had cleared a
few patches on each cheek, he said he must close now, as it
was Saturday, and I went forth only three cents poorer, but
much wiser.   What a transformation!   The strident cries
of the hucksters had ceased; the hundreds of handcarts with
pickled cucumbers of enormous size, and kabbeljaw (codfish)
in brine, had vanished, and in their place was an endless
procession of pious Hebrews on their way to the synagogue.
In the doorways sat some earnest ex-pedlars, reading their
prayer-books.   All had made some change in their appearance; the women had some bit of clean white apron or
frock, which changed their *tout ensemble* immensely.   The
men had donned costumes in some instances quite worthy of
"Samuel of Posen."   The scene was well worthy of the pen
of a Zangwill.   But here, as everywhere in Holland,

everything seemed to go with deliberation and slowness. Even at the end of about an hour, when the procession was returning from its devotions, and when a very heavy thunder storm interrupted the calmness of the scene, nobody seemed to rush; perhaps they were acquainted with the Dutch style of weather, and felt that they could outstrip the rain in a square walking match. For myself I did not worry much even when the flashes grew remarkably vivid. I knew that the lightning in Holland could never catch up with a brisk American.

From Amsterdam a little side trip to Scheveningen was quite feasible, and it proved well worth the trouble, for this delightful suburb of La Hague has a beach as beautiful as any in all America, and on it swarms a cosmopolitan multitude well worthy of study. But there were few men among the summer boarders at the hotels, which caused a trifle of discontent which found expression once or twice in my hearing. The male summer boarder was as scarce as the dodo or the ornithorhyncus. The young ladies waited like Mariana in the Moated Grange:—

> She only said, "The day is dreary,
> He cometh not," she said;
> She sighed "I am aweary, aweary,
> I never *shall* be wed."

In this place I heard some music of a very quaint type; it was a Gammelong or Javanese orchestra, which had come to Holland to perform at a festival in Amsterdam.

The instruments were drums, bells, a flute or whistle, and a two-stringed fiddle. The bells resembled inverted basins set in frames, which held twelve each. Although I found that a diatonic scale could be played upon them, the native contented himself with three notes, thus:

forming the tonic chord, and never changing to any other.
Naturally this became a very monotonous organ point. To
this music there danced two native girls, both of whom were
very attractive and graceful. The dance consisted in waving scarfs and in moving the arms slowly in time with the
melody.

And now for Ostend and England. Matters looked rather
doubtful at the outset, for the wind was blowing in a very
fitful fashion, and an English sailor told me that it would
be choppy outside. I have forgotten the name of the boat.
Would that the voyage itself might also sink into oblivion.
Scarcely were we beyònd the pier when we began to appreciate the glories of a channel trip in a gale. The little craft
was wet from stem to stern; my hat blew off into the sea,
my overcoat was wet through, and I soon presented a picture of marine disconsolacy that would have touched the
stoniest heart. I sought the little cabin, but as numerous
temporary invalids, in a violent state of activity, were
spread all around, a few moments' reflection convinced me
that the ocean in its stormiest moods was preferable to man
in a state of seasickness, and I left the writhing company.

I had secured the upper berth of a tiny stateroom, but
there was a suspicious-looking tin basin attached to that
upper berth. This is done on most of the English channel
boats, and I have always found fault with the custom. Let
the gentleman in the lower berth open an umbrella, if circumstances seem to warrant it, but do not unduly excite
the gentleman above by presenting to his eyes so vivid a
suggestion. It is an excess of zeal, which reminds one of
the conscientious darkey who, on entering service at a hotel,
and finding the legend, " Gentlemen must spit in the cus-
pidores" on the wall, rigorously enforced it, whether the
gentlemen wanted to spit or not.

On deck I found a young lady enjòying her *mal de mer*

SYBIL SANDERSON.

in solitude. On my offering to escort her to the sheltered but unsavory cabin, she declined, wittily saying that seasickness was the one case where misery did not love company. My own troubles were soon alleviated by a sailor, who for a consideration (you have probably heard that sailors have a frank character; this man had a two-franc disposition) lent me his oilskin cape and sou'wester, and I was arrayed in a manner that would have satisfied any old salt.

I have crossed the channel by all the different routes, and can only commend the Calais-Dover one, and that only because of its brevity, for it takes but seventy minutes from shore to shore, under favorable circumstances, while Parkstone-quay to Rotterdam, Ostend to Dover, Harwich to Antwerp, Dover to Flushing, etc., etc., are all long and uncomfortable routes. In America they would be changed for the better at once, for the travel on them all is large and constant.

I will joke no more about seasickness; I just skimmed along the verge of it myself in that awful passage from Ostend to Dover. The sensation is not as pleasant as they describe it; the public has been misled in this matter. But the tempest was very high, and our little boat seemed to try to polka-mazurka all the way across, and the passengers all left the craft at Dover with pleasure—that is, as much pleasure as is consistent with total emptiness. What a painful thing it is to land at 2 A. M. on a rainy night! That is what I did at Dover. By the light of a dimly gleaming lantern a customs official gazed into my shirts, collars and cuffs. He found no dynamite. If I had had any I should have been tempted to kick it and explode it during the voyage. An hour's waiting in a desolate coffee room followed, the contrast between England and the continent as to railway refection being at once sharply marked. Lon-

don and the Cannon street Hotel came at 3:30 on Sunday
morning and I flung myself into the arms of Morpheus.

That metropolis on a Sunday is a poor man's purgatory.
The churches hold services half the day, and the bar-rooms
the other half.   Pray or drink is the choice held out to the
laborer, and unfortunately he generally chooses the latter.
Meanwhile in the near suburbs there is a perfect saturnalia
for the man with a few coins in his pocket. It is hard that the
poor laborer may not have, as with us, the full right of an
instructive museum or reading-room on the only day when
he can enjoy it.   His life is about as varied as the scenery
on the underground railway, But at Kew Gardens or at
Hampton Court, Sunday would not be recognized by any
outward signs.

There are tally-ho coaches, omnibuses, drays, dog-carts
and donkey carts all along the road.   The bar-rooms there
are open all day "for travelers," which keeps them within
the scope of the British laws, which do not deprive even
the most temporary tourist of his spiritual comfort.   Spite
of these accompaniments Kew Gardens is a sight worth
seeing on a Sunday afternoon, and is probably the vastest
botanical collection of the world.   But many of the visitors
do not come to botanize.   I saw, for example, one specimen of the British workman at Kew, whose wife remonstrated against further irrigation with gin, give her a friendly
kick as signal that the debate was closed.   He was a good
specimen of an arithmetical problem—a sort of Kew brute.

But at least the laborer who remains in London, has some
fine promenades left him, if the Sunday afternoon is fine,
for then one can go to Rotten Row in Hyde Park with
some degree of delight.   The English aristocracy have their
habits very much like lesser human beings.   On week days
one sees them in their carriages or on horseback, cantering
along the park, but on Sundays, at about four or five P. M..

they are all on foot, and one can jostle against an earl or a duke without great trouble, and I have felt seriously tempted to tread on the corns of some great nobleman to see what species of rhetoric he would use. But to see the nobility and gentry *sans géne*, one must go to the clubs, of which hereafter.

Who can write up London? I have visited the little village by the Thames time and again and each visit reveals it in a new light. The fact is that London is not a city, it is a nation; more than this, it is an epitome of all the nations! In such a gathering of races no American need fear to attract much attention because he is a foreigner, but, for the benefit of those Americans (?) who wish to abjure their country and become chromos of Englishmen, I will state that they must acquire a rising inflection at the end of each sentence, before they can deceive anything more than a deaf and dumb asylum. Your true Englishman ends every sentence with an interrogation point of alpine ascent. Perhaps the student could best begin by trying to say "thank you" after the manner of the London tradesman. It is the most unemotional expression of gratitude that mortal ever invented. It sounds as if the speaker desired to add, " but don't let it occur again!"

I once met an American in London who was going about hugging the fond delusion that by a long drawl and plenty of profanity he was causing the cockneys to believe him a Londoner to the manner born. Let no wise American ever make the attempt. It cannot be done. In a simple trade with a boot maker I asked for " gaiters " where I meant " boots," " Congress " where " Springside " was intended, and " rubbers " where the Londonese was " goloshes."

No! we must remain Americans; we were born so and cannot help it now.

May I give one more growl at an American habit? Why

does almost every male tourist in London steer at once for
Leicester Square, the Oxford Music Hall, *et id genus omne.*
and imagine that he is " seeing life?" Half of the scenes
are pathetic, the other half dull; but in the music halls, at
least, one can laugh a little at English " jingoism," which
casts American " spread-eagleism " entirely in the shade.
One young lady, whose economy in clothing must save her
a great deal of money, since she used as little cloth as possible in making her dresses, sang forth in strident tones—

> England in danger? I proudly answer—No!!
> Not while there's a Briton left in England!

I can imagine that lonely Briton defending his isle against
the combined forces of Russia, Germany, and France. He
certainly would take to the woods.

I always spend part of my time in London in the old
book stores, with which the city teems, and almost always
find something worth while to reward me for my search.
The most marvelous of all these is a store in Piccadilly,
around which I fluttered as a moth around a candle. This
is the greatest antique book store in the world—Quaritch's.
No museum could be as attractive to the book collector. I
made the acquaintance of its owner, who showed me around
the vast establishment with a pardonable pride, for he had
begun life in London almost penniless and now had a stock
amounting to millions in value.

For example, while I was with him there was offered for
purchase a whole autograph manuscript of Torquato Tasso,
a missal of the twelfth century, and some of the rarest black
letter books, and this seemed to be regarded as a slight trans-
action. He showed me into a room where the choicest ancient
bits were gathered, and took down book after book, each
one worth from $1,500 to $2,500, and then, being called
away, left me for fifteen minutes alone with the treasures

(like Lothair at the jeweler's), knowing that all journalists were strictly honest. He even was kind enough to offer to lend me a musical volume valued at £500, in which he saw that I was interested. His price list is now made the standard for the entire world. His own knowledge is something stupendous and naturally his store is the gathering place of the literati of the world. I met there, in one morning, the editor of the *London Times*, a celebrated botanical professor from a Nebraska university, and one of the most noted Spanish archæologists, and it wasn't a great morning for celebrities either.

Mr. Quaritch was just then engaged in preparing a history of book binding, and in the room where this was being prepared I found Byzantine, Florentine, Venetian, old French and many other specimens of the art. This branch of collecting has as yet been very little pursued by American bibliophiles.

I came back to London in the oyster season, with the memory of the French oysters still upon me. Seeing the sign "American Blue Point Oysters," I thought that I would tempt fate again. A rather ominous smell did not dismay me; I swallowed it (the oyster; not the smell, or rather both). "It's been laid in England, sir," said the host. I fear me it must have been laid in a sewer with a copper cent as a companion. I haven't got the taste of copper out of my mouth yet.

Instead of speaking of St. Paul's, Westminster and the Tower, let me speak of the rich and poor of the metropolis. The former may be seen at the clubs or at some very expensive rendezvous, like the "Ship and Turtle" in Leadenhall street. At this inn one may find the genuine aldermanic green turtle soup, and a lime punch that would make Delmonico green with envy. Here one may see the brokers and bankers from Threadneedle street, Bishopsgate, and other haunts of the bloated bond holders, allowing part ot their weath to get into circulation again. As for myself, it would be a toss up between a dyspeptic death and bankruptcy, to take many turtle dinners.

Let us begin with the dark side of London. We are to go with a detective, for there are one or two places where we might not be quite safe alone, and we provide ourselves with small coin in abundance to " tip " where such bribery is necessary, and let me add in parenthesis that it is always necessary in Europe. Never be afraid to tip any one because he looks majestic. I have seen porters who looked more lofty than a cardinal, pocket a shilling meekly. If I looked at the Prince of Wales I fear I should give him a half crown (more than he has, poor fellow), from mere force of habit. We go with our detective to the East End, and a walk from Aldgate brings us to St. George's-in-the-East.

At first it is only a revised and improved edition of American slums. Plenty of sailors, plenty of drink, and a coarse dissipation that is unfortunately common enough the world over. A dance was in progress, and the proprietor of the place asked me if there was any music I would like his band to play. I smothered the temptation to ask for a Berlioz or Wagner selection, and requested "Two lovely black eyes," which was accordingly massacred, and we proceeded further. There was a silver lining to the black cloud, for we found that charity (or rather beneficence) was becoming sensible in London, and clean lodging houses at 4d. a night, and excellent sailors' homes, strewed the way.

Our detective told us that the new school board had done wonders in civilizing the people and ameliorating the condition of the poor. Yet we found dark enough shadows on the picture, for turning from Ratcliffe Highway, along Cable street, we entered Angel Gardens, so called, I suppose, because there are no gardens there, and it seems to be inhabited by devils. Here we found an opium joint, kept by a wreck of a Chinaman called Ah Si, which has become anglicized into Dan Johnson. There are no laws against opium smoking in England, nor are any necessary. The English don't take to the habit. Dan seemed to be his own best customer, and in a den which may have been the original of Dickens' great description in "Edwin Drood," lay on a squalid couch smoking pipe after pipe. There is a rumor that years ago the Prince of Wales visited the place and smoked a pipe, and Dan still keeps the instrument he used, and allowed me to smoke an opium pill through it. It was the first time I had tasted the drug, but the terrible surroundings and the weird novelty prevented its affecting me, and but slightly stupefied I went on to the more criminal quarters at Florentine street

Here there were scenes at the memory of which my heart aches. There were those seeking shelter here who dreaded the police surveillance of the cleaner lodging houses of Ratcliffe Highway, and clustered together in dismal holes in gregarious but undisturbed misery. There were children too, in those terrible lodging houses where the police seldom came, and they looked at us with the air of frightened animals, while we stood there as if we belonged to a totally different race, and were examining a curious museum. Some women and a couple of children lay in wretched beds, forgetting hunger in sleep. There were vicious faces enough, but the prevalent type was rather suffering than vice. Our advent created a sensation, and a crowd of ragamuffins of all ages accompanied us on our tour until a friendly "bobby" espied the disturbance and with a "Move along!" dispersed the gathering.

And so, in spite of all the philanthropists, the wolf still exists in London, and one day I saw him show his teeth and growl ominously. A socialist meeting had been called in Trafalgar Square and had been forbidden by the police. Four o'clock in the afternoon found me on the field of action, before any battle had commenced. Crowds were walking to and fro, for the constitutional right of promenade seemed to be rigidly respected, and one thousand and forty policemen were also taking the air in the square. They were not in line, but circulating through the crowd, save at the Nelson Monument which was surrounded by a cordon of bluecoats to prevent any speaker from addressing the multitude from the pedestal. Just then a sound of cheering and groaning announced that a meeting was organizing on the steps of St. Martin's church. Calmly and firmly a lieutenant said "Fall in!" and a body of 100 of the police promenaders were in line and marching to clear the steps. Evidently the police had been warned not to aggravate matters; they rarely touched any one, but constantly repeated "Pass on, please! Move along, please!" not driving the public from the square, but keeping them in continual motion as if training them for a walking match. Even when one burly fellow pushed with tremendous emphasis against a policeman, that gentleman meekly ground out one more " Pass on, please!" I asked one of the guardians of the monument if it was likely to continue so through the afternoon; he replied that it might change any moment, and even while he was answering there came a tremendous cheering as one of the socialist leaders drove around the square on the roof of a 'bus, orating as he went. Result: A few grew more resistant, refused to " pass along, please " and got pummeled by the police for their pains.

I wish that our police were as slow to use their clubs as the London "bobbies" are. Even at this stage of the proceedings only blows with the fists were given. Another change in the kaleidoscope! On the Strand side the crowd suddenly made a rush, and then, presto! out came the

clubs, and a charge was made into the surging mass. Four
men went down just in front of me with as many police on
top of them; a misguided youth of about nineteen was
collared in the act of throwing a missile, and got a black
eye and was marched off in custody. Then matters began
to calm down. More police arrived, the chant of "Pass
along please!" was resumed in *recitativo secco*, and the
wolf retired to his lair, growling as he went. Yet the
throng did not impress me as altogether a dangerous one.
"You put them down with a stronger hand in America,"
said a policeman to whom I had slipped a cigar as a reward
for his not clubbing me during the "rush" in the Strand;
and so we do, and we have more dangerous elements to
contend with—the more the pity—and totally un-American
ones at that.

And now for the reverse of the medal,—the fashionable
clubs. London is far in advance of us in this matter, In
going from Hyde Park corner to Charing Cross (about ten
minutes) the stranger would imagine as many clubs in London as there are bar-rooms in Edinburgh. I have had the
pleasure of being introduced into some of them and am able
to speak of some of the most characteristic, merely premis-
ing that there are in addition all kinds of humbler clubs
for coachmen, cooks, footmen, and almost every other
menial condition.

The Whitehall Club is for civil engineers and scientific
men of all sorts. I had a good lunch there and a good deal
of polytechnical talk thrown in, which would scarcely interest general readers. The Savage Club is of a totally different order. Here meet, on a footing of seeming equality,
the *litterateurs* and artists, and professional men generally,
and take their ease in a truly Bohemian manner.

There is the Wellington (military), the Bachelors, the
junior Bachelors—for in England clubs beget offspring,

which afterward take the overflow from the senior organization; the Athenian (medical chiefly), Saville's (literary), the United Service, the St. James (diplomatists' club), the naval and military, the Turf (sporting), the Isthmian (members of great public schools, such as Eton or Harrow), the American, which is, I am glad to say one of the most aristocratic of its kind, containing not only almost all the prominent Americans in England on its list, but many very great English celebrities as well, White's and Boodle's (both very old and select clubs), the Meistersingers (musical and gives magnificent concerts with its members through the season), the Devonshire (liberal), the Beaconsfield (conservative), the Thatched house, the Cocoa Tree, the Pall Mall, the Marlboro—most exclusive this, although a small club in small quarters, and the stamping ground of the Prince of Wales and his set,—the Guards (military), the United Universities (Oxford and Cambridge), as well as two or three other clubs for college men, the Carlton, the junior Carlton, and dozens of others. The above very incomplete list will show that it is impossible to speak of all, even of those with whose interiors I became acquainted.

The most exclusive of them all is, I think, the Travelers' Club. Originally this club was formed of persons who had traveled over 1,500 miles from home, and in the old days of stage-coaches this meant a good deal. At present it is merely the gathering place of the highest aristocracy. I could mention a certain prince and a couple of dukes who were blackballed there a few years ago, and there are names on the waiting list which have been there for almost a generation. "Few die and none resign" in these very select clubs. The expenses are not nearly as heavy in a swell club in London as in New York.

The junior Carlton, which is one of the select clubs, charges but £50 initiation fee, and ten guineas a year dues.

The Constitutional (conservative), which is larger and more omnivorous, charges £15 initiation and five guineas annual dues. This latter club has some thousands of members all over England, and like most of the great clubs, affords board and lodging to such of its members as require it. Its quarters are the most perfect I have ever seen in club life. A noble staircase of marble in the centre of the great building is as impressive as the escalier of the Vienna Opera House.

The library is vast and well selected, so far as I could judge; the reading room is splendidly equipped and the smoking room a delicious place for a cosey chat or lazy lounge. The dining room is especially large, and like the others, is lighted with dozens of electric lamps fixed close to the high-studded ceiling, giving thus a soft and dispersed light. The cuisine is on a par with the rest of the equip-ment, and so are the wines. But I could not accustom myself to the large billiard room where my host initiated me into the mysteries of English billiards, after dinner. In the first place, the tables had so many legs that they gave the impression of being a set of huge centipedes.

Each had enough gas lamps to form a torchlight proces-sion. The English table has six pockets, and every time you pocket any ball you count; therefore it is best to hit hard and trust in providence. The cues are of the fishpole variety, and there is one about fifteen feet long to use when your ball lodges in some remote and inaccessible part of the vast meadow they call a billiard table. The balls are of the size of marbles, and one needs a telescope to make a long shot. Besides these afflictions there is a marker to keep the score for you, and he invariably keeps it wrong. He will suddenly be called away, and on returning, failing to recog-nize the fact that you have made half a dozen shots during his absence, will call out the score in a voice thick with

emotion and beer—"Mmmmty-mm, to mmmmty-mm!"—
which causes me to think that he is a relative of the American brakeman. Nevertheless, by a succession of "flukes"
I won the games and made an impression as an expert
player. Many of the shots I made in those memorable
games will lie heavy upon my conscience for years.

In connection with the English clubs, I may also speak of
London's celebrated taverns, or at least of a couple of the
most characteristic of them. Quaintest among these is the
"Olde Cheshire Chease," a tavern which has as large a
number of noted names upon its scroll as many a celebrated
abbey. It nestles in "Wine Office Court," just off Fleet
street, and you might pass it by a dozen times without
noticing its antique attractions; yet here Shakespeare took
his refreshment on the way home from the theatre, and in
this very room (for it was rebuilt after the great London
fire of 1666) sat Dr. Johnson and Boswell. I sat in his seat
but was not moved to vociferating "Sir!" and becoming
abusive and arbitrary as the old dictionary maker was. The
modern charms of the "Cheshire Cheese" are not less than
the old, and one can get there the best steaks and chops in
London, excellent beer, and as distinguished society as the
place boasted of old, while the landlord—Mr. Chas. Moore
—welcomes Americans with much heartiness, and still remembers a party of young ladies from our land who took
possession of the place a year ago and proved that English
appetites could exist in American frames.

But the Delmonico's of London is, as above said, "The
Ship and Turtle," in Leadenhall street, where one can eat
up a fortune as easily as Lucullus did. Turtle soup is the
specialty, five shillings per small plate the price, and aldermanic gout the consequence. Nowhere else in the world is
such soup obtainable. The turtle tanks are a sight in
themselves, some hundreds of these reptiles being kept alive

for epicurean purposes. We shudder at the ancient Roman refinements of epicurean cruelty, and read with wonder of pigs whipped to death to give their flesh a better flavor, yet these turtles are as scientifically treated as could be done by any ancient *chef*. They are kept four days out of water, then four days in the tank, and so on alternately until some fine day they are hung up, head downwards, for a few moments, and then decapitated. If you dare defy the doctor, and snap your fingers at apoplexy, do as I did, and wind up with a lime punch.

It is rather late in the day to declaim against "tips" in England, but I was astonished on emerging to the street, (N. B. This had no connection with the lime punch!) to have a policeman touch his hat and ask: "Looking for a cab, sir? I'll get you one sir," and the representative of the municipal force of London trotted off and came back with a hansom, for which he received a handsome gratuity. Fancy tipping the police!

CHAPTER XVI.

A DISCURSIVE TALK—MUSICAL EUROPE—A DESCRIPTION OF
THE MUSICAL ADVANTAGES AND DISADVANTAGES OF DIF-
FERENT EUROPEAN CAPITALS—WHERE THE AMERICAN STU-
DENT OUGHT TO GO—IMPORTANT MUSICAL LETTERS BY
ROBERT FRANZ.

I am often asked by young musical students, "Where
ought I to go to study in Europe?" The question is so
vast and demands such detail in its answer that I have determined to leave, for a while, the paths of travel, and speak
of musical Europe in its relations to the student. America
at present offers as thorough a curriculum, to the musician,
as Europe. There are, in the conservatories of our own
land at present, many musicians who have been members
of the faculties of foreign conservatories, and it is not to be
imagined that their teaching is inferior in America, to what
it was in trans-atlantic countries. The fault is to be sought
elsewhere; many a musical student, when studying in his
native land, takes matters altogether too easily; the same
party, when placed in a foreign land, separated from friends
and kindred, studies as if life itself depended on his efforts.
It is not an extravagant statement to say, that if musical
students would give the same ardor to their work in America that they do in Europe, they would achieve the same
results.

"But," says the apologetic student, "there is a musical

ROBERT FRANZ.

(TAKEN IN 1870.)

atmosphere in Europe, which is not attainable in America!'' This idea is so firmly rooted in the American mind, that it seems almost impossible to tear it out; yet I can truthfully say that I have heard music in Munich that would have been hissed in New York, and some operas given in La Scala do not begin to compare with the same works as presented in the Metropolitan Opera House in New York.

It is undoubtedly true that Europe, as a whole, stands higher than America in art, but the slavish acceptance of everything European, as excellent, or even as better than our own, is nonsensical. There are very few orchestras in the world, for example, which can equal the playing of the Boston Symphony Orchestra, and Thomas' Orchestra in its best days would have excelled the performance of many a European band. As regards opera, the performances in the large cities of the United States do not suffer by comparison with the representations given in Frankfort, or London, or many of the other great European capitals. We have made gigantic strides in music; we can say this without being at all vain-glorious. It is very much the same thing as it was with literature; a half century ago the English contemptuously inquired, '' Who reads an American book?'' but now there are some of our authors quite as popular on the other side of the great dampness, as at home. I must confess, however, that many of the European musical celebrities with whom I conversed, knew very little about the work done among us, but, on the other hand, when they did see the compositions of our best musicians, they gave unstinted praise, and exhibited their astonishment in the most lavish manner.

Europe must stand to America, in the domain of music, exactly as foreign countries do to France in the matter of its advanced musical students. When, for example, a student has won the great prize for composition, the Prix de Rome, at the Paris Conservatoire, he is sent into other countries for a while, to study other schools, in order that his work may not be one-sided. In exactly the same manner, after the student has attained the best that our country can afford him, he should go to other countries for the finishing touches, that he may not become wedded exclusively to the style of his teachers. When a student, male or female, has become master of his art in his own country, then let him seek Europe with a firm conviction that it will broaden his views and help his work.

There are many teachers who can only spare the summer months for European pilgrimages; to these there are only two musical Meccas open. London is musically active until about the middle of July, and Bayreuth, when the season is on, begins its representations about a week later, and continues until the middle of August.

London is a musical city, in spite of all that Rubinstein has said about the unmusical character of the English. The opera there is quite as good, although not as cheap, as that of Milan, or of any other Italian city. But the musician who seeks the peculiar benefits of each country abroad will endeavor to attend one of the great choir festivals in England. These do not take place in London, but in Birmingham, Manchester, (a very musical city), Hereford, etc. In such a festival there will always be one or two of Handel's oratorios given, for the Englishman would consider the omission of these as the giving of "Hamlet" with the part of the royal Dane left out, and there is no country on the globe in which the musician can so well study the art of oratorio singing as in England. Should you go to one of these festivals, oh musical reader, notice how well your native tongue is sung there. America is the land where the English language is worst mangled in vocal work, and in England it is treated the best. I have heard a singer, (yes, and more than one), sing an invocation to the God of Battles, and in the course of the work the warlike Deity became "the god of *bottles*," yet not a soul of that American audience felt that the change was ludicrous. But in Great Britain they have a wholesome respect for the poetry they are singing, and spite of the difficulties with which our language is strewn, you can lean back in your seat, without buying a libretto, and can follow every word which the English singer is warbling. If, therefore, you desire to study clear pronunciation, or true Handelian phrasing, (for they do not cut the phrases of the grand old master into mincemeat there), or the correction of a vicious tremolo, go no further, but settle down in London to conscientious work, which will be lightened by the fact that you need not study a new language to take your lessons in, and your teacher will be scrupulously honest, and will probably not attempt to get up a flirtation with you, if you are of the feminine gender. Besides this, you will have the advantage of hearing good music constantly. London draws to itself the cream of the whole musical world, and at the Crystal Palace concerts, and at Albert Hall, not to speak of the dozens of other entertainments, you will hear about as good music as you could in Germany or Italy. Only in one field London is rather poor; it has little really great orchestral music. Richter comes there almost every season, and is an oasis in the desert, but it may be doubted if even his concerts, with a picked-up band, can compare with the music we have, in this field, in America.

What teachers? Ah, my dear inquirer, I dare not whisper that, lest my enemies, (every man who writes a book has enemies, according to the Scriptures), should say that I am writing a paid circular for certain musicians, and cast me out into the ranks of "puffers;" but there are some world-famous professors to be found in London always.

Paris! Yes, Paris is rich where London is poor, for in Paris you can hear as good an orchestra as exists in the world,—the band of the Conservatoire. In the domain of opera Paris is good, but not very great. The management of the Grand Opera generally pays more attention to mise-en-scene than to the engagement of great singers. Yet at this opera house you will hear an excellently balanced orchestra and a chorus which will obliterate the memory of the warbling antiquities you have heard. The house itself is worth seeing, for it is the grandest legacy that Napoleon III has left to Paris. It is at the end of a noble avenue, and if you should stray out on the balcony during the entr'actes, as you undoubtedly would, you would see the finest part of brilliant Paris stretching out at your feet. The *escalier* is a marvel of beauty, and the *foyer* is as bright as lamps and mirrors can make it. But you must go in a dress suit or you will be forbidden to enter even the choice seats you have paid for. And if you should sit in the parquette you will be obliged to separate from your wife or sister, for the parquette is like the Walhalla of the Vikings— no females are allowed within its hallowed precincts. Once I met the full dress rule and half overcame it. I had come to Paris from Nancy (let every reader understand that Nancy is a town and not a female), and had no time to change into the solemn habiliments which constitute "full dress" in our civilized world, (and which we share with waiters, butlers, etc.), and presented myself in a suit of tweed at the entrance, with my *fauteuil* ticket. The look of horror and disdain which overspread the face of the guardian of the portal was in itself sufficient rebuke, but when I showed him a personal note from the prima donna of the evening, he allowed me to pass, but with a supplicatory remark that he supposed that I would not take my seat "like that!" Heedless of his feelings, I did take the seat I had paid for, and enjoyed the performance almost as well as if I had been clothed in a swallowtail; but when, at the end of the second act, I presented a pass to the back of the stage to another official, he refused to corrupt the morals of the Parisian stage by allowing me to enter the green-room in a traveling suit. That shook my confidence somewhat, and when I found that even the programme seller, and the pew-opener, (or at least the ancient dame who was to conduct me to my seat—for a consideration), and all the other underlings, attempted to show me their outraged feelings, I gave up the unequal contest, and ever after basked in a dress-coat and their smiles

France is tied up in tradition as regards its theatrical usages, and the most annoying of all is the ticket speculation, which is not only not prohibited, but is countenanced, by every theatre and opera house. At some theatres it is impossible to buy a seat a day or two ahead of the performance, save through speculators, and although you can nominally purchase a seat at the opera a few days ahead, yet to do this you must mingle with a rough and ill-smelling crowd, must stand an hour or so in line, and must take the chance of finding all the good seats gone when you come to the fat lady (she is always fat), who sells the tickets. If, however, you give it up in disgust, and turn away, you will be accosted by some five or ten individuals, each of whom will promise you a glorious seat for an equally glorious price, while just under the eaves of the grand opera house are three offices, where they are ready to do the same kind of a Good Samaritan act. If you yield to the solicitations of one of the street peddlers, he will walk you around to some dingy café, where you can see a plan of the theatre, but there is just a chance that you will find some pillar or other obstruction when you attend the performance, which was forgotten in the plan you examined. Of the common

sense mode of selling tickets to theatrical or musical performances in America, the Parisian knows nothing, and as
regards serving the public, he seems imbued with the spirit
of the celebrated, but profane, remark attributed to our
own Mr. Vanderbilt.

There is one point in which the French have an admirable
system; it is in the classification of their operas, and the ap-
portioning of them to the opera company, which is especially trained to produce them.   The government grants a
subvention to more than one theatre and opera house, and
aims at giving the best possible performance.   As a consequence one always finds a great, and generally tragic, mas-
terpiece, at the grand opera, and a bright, or at least
melodious work, at the Opera Comique.   It is like the gentleman in the western restaurant, who desired the waiter to
bring him the hairs and the butter on two separate plates.
The mere fact of an opera having a tragic termination would
make no difference; if it has any comic touches it is *opera
comique*.   Thus "Carmen" falls in the latter classification
in spite of its tragic libretto.

I have heard some very fine bass-singers at the Grand
Opera in Paris, but German Opera, on the whole, seems to
possess the best of the deep toned soloists.

Is there any reason why the possession of a bass voice
should indicate depravity and general wickedness?   At the
first glance the reader might readily answer—"No!"—but
if he will look over all the various opera plots and librettos
he will see that bass singers have been metamorphosed into
villains, by musical authors, with surprising unanimity, so
much so indeed, that the phrase, "a villain of the deepest
dye" might readily be changed into a "villain of the deepest voice."

Verdi has set the fashion for the modern school in his
Count di Luna, (a title which might be freely translated

into the Count of Lunatics) who is as bad as bad can be, and the more wicked he becomes the deeper he sings. He has a strange predilection for roast gypsy, and 12-8 rhythms. He is not successful in love,—very few basses are,—but he is in accord with all his tribe of deep vocalists in being rich and powerful. The basso (in opera) is so generally obnoxious that he almost always drives the soprano to insanity or death, but this has one mitigating feature, for the crazier she gets the better she sings, and her death is always preceded by a grand aria full of trills and chromatic runs.

Mozart seems to have felt some pity for the non-success in amatory matters, of the vocalist of low compass, and he allowed his baritone to succeed in a couple of thousand love affairs, but the depraved character of the low-pitched singer was not elevated by him, and Don Juan is finally escorted to a warm realm, which, according to the operatic librettists, must be crowded with basses and baritones.

Meanwhile the tenor pursues the even tenor of his way, in paths of purity and propriety. He is always beloved by the soprano, he is also always hated by the basso. In the realms of the Italian opera there are no villains who can reach high C. The higher the voice the higher the character.

It may have escaped the notice of many, but Wagner has broken the fetters which forever bound the tenor to virtue and the basso to vice; he has also given the basso a chance in his love affairs. The Flying Dutchman is a bass-baritone who wins his lady, to the exclusion of a gentleman with a voice of higher range who has previously courted her, and this is one of the very rare instances in which the bass cut out the tenor. We know that occasionally a very high minded basso profundo appears upon the stage, but you will notice that he is always a priest, and therefore condemned to celibacy.

In real life we have sometimes met people with deep voices who were not bloodthirsty, and who were not priests, and some of them have even been looked on favorably by the fair sex. Cannot we have something of the same sort on the operatic stage? Give us a hero or two with a deep voice. Let us plead with the librettists of this end of the century to give the basses a chance!

While I am on musical subjects I feel impelled to say a few words about the practical character of the French laws relating to art; they might well be copied by our own country. In the first place, there are the subventions mentioned above. These are given to opera and theatre. It may be stated emphatically, that opera, properly given, can never pay its own expenses, and never has since the popes, the de Medicis, and Henry IV., paid the expenses of the works of Peri, Caccini, and Monteverde, in the sixteenth and seventeenth centuries, at the beginning of this school of composition. If we are ever to have grand opera in this country, outside of New York, where the merchant princes foot the bills in return for the privilege of chattering through the performance, the government must assist. Again, in France there is a uniform and sensible musical pitch (435 vibrations for one-lined A) established by law, while in America the vocalist is at the mercy of every piano manufacturer who seeks brilliancy at the expense of mellowness, and of the singer's voice. But best of all, in France there is a degree of protection for the composer, for he obtains a legal royalty every time his opera is produced. This prevents a popular opera composer from dying a pauper because of the grasping character of publishers or managers, a trait which my readers can find fully enough exemplified in the biographies of Schubert or Mozart. Had Mozart, or Schubert, or Lortzing, had the benefit of the law of the *tantieme*, they would not have died so wretchedly. May the United

States, some day in the near future, take example of France and protect our native composer from theatrical sharks, and from himself.

My barber in Paris, not the one whose fleecings I have described, was one of the host of ticket sellers spoken of above. Many a ticket to the Theatre Francaise have I obtained through his friendly agency (paid for, of course) but, as it happened, I never bought any opera tickets through him. This led one day to a very humiliating result. We were conversing about the exposition, and he found fault with the sparsity of fireworks and the plenitude of concerts; he wanted more pyrotechnics, and less tone. " What the deuce do you and I care for their concerts!!" said he, and I yielded a sad assent, but somehow I felt wounded at the remark, and the conversation lagged for a while thereafter; but after all, the phrenologists say that Beethoven's head shows no musical bumps, and I can therefore bear it if my physiognomy is similarly untonal.

The literary reader in Paris, will surely go often to the *Comedie Francaise* where Moliere is given in pristine purity. The French language can be studied here with the least possible exertion and the greatest possible delight. The first point, however, which will jar on the American auditor is the singsong tone with which all the rhymes are delivered. But he must not protest—it is traditional. But he may protest, and so will I, at turning good Anglo Saxon blank verse into the chief poetry known to Frenchmen—rhymed couplets. Fancy Hamlet singsonging

> "To be or not to be, that is the question,
> Whether 'tis nobler, at the mind's suggestion
> To bear the arrows which our fate doth send,
> Or by opposing, make to them an end." !!

The military music of France deserves a word or two. The band of the *Garde Republicaine* is one of the finest military bands I have ever heard, and all the bands have a chance for frequent hearings, for the public squares are alive with their melody, in the summer months. If our Marine Band could only hear the music of these organizations, they would repent of their manifold sins.

But Paris is not all of France, although the Parisian thinks that it is; if the traveler has time for the lesser cities, Rouen, Nancy, Lyons, etc., he will find a different race of Frenchmen, strong, burly, and a trifle brusque withal. And if he goes to the smaller villages, he will possibly find some types of folk music that will be worth his while. The folk dances are a constant delight to the musical traveler if he can find them. A country fair is one thing in America, but another thing altogether in any part of Europe. With us, there is a horse trot, a few prizes for crazy quilts, bread-baking, etc., but abroad, from Norway to Spain, the village *fête* is devoted to other sports. The peasant is there in his very best costume, and let me tell you that all those gold and silver ornaments that you see on the women, are real and solid, for almost all of the peasantry deny themselves jewelry until they can have something beyond plated ware.

There is plenty of dancing, some drinking, and if it is a *kirmesse*, some right enjoyable fighting, for many of the peasants would not think that they had had a really good time unless they had a few black and blue spots to show for it. But the folk-dancing in the provincial part of France, as in Holland and other parts of Central Europe, is especially rhythmic because of the *sabots* or wooden shoes, which are worn by men and women alike. Fancy a clog dance participated in by some hundred dancers at one time. The "click-clack," if the dance takes place in a barn, is wonderfully effective, and I think that some dances, the *Bourrée* for example, which had its origin in Auvergne, had their inception in the rhythmic thump of the wooden shoes. The composers are beginning to draw classical inspiration from the folk dance, and they will find it a mine of musical wealth. For example, in Norway there is the Halling, used by Grieg and Svendsen; in Russia there is the male dance, the Kamarinskaia, used by Rubinstein and by Tschaikowsky; in Poland the Polonaise and Mazurka, both idealized by Chopin; in Bohemia there is the Pulka and the Furiant, used by Dvorak; in Hungary there exists the Czardas, of which Liszt has made royal use; but of the folk dances of South France and of Spain, no composer has as yet made classical employment, and yet there is even more beauty in some of the Tangos, Jotas, and Basque dances than in some of those mentioned above.

But about musical study in Paris; there are few Americans who pursue the French course of musical study, because most of our countrymen believe that the Germans have a first mortgage on music, and no other nation has anything to do with tuition. This is a mistake; while giving every homage to the excellence of Teutonic pedagogy, I must say that the course at the Paris Conservatoire is remarkably thorough and effective. The harmony course, for example, extends over years, instead of, as with us, being merely a series of dry exercises, or, as is the case in some of the new music schools, leaving the pupil stranded on a dreary waste of secondary seventh chords. They make composers there, and the Grand Prix de Rome, the largest musical prize awarded in the world, (for which they allow only Frenchmen to compete), is the keystone of an arch which such men as Massenet and Ambroise Thomas have assisted in building. Especially commendable is the inflexibility with which the authorities add solfeggio to the musical studies; I believe that if a person were to apply to them as a student of the bass drum, they would force him to supplement his course with a few terms in solfeggio. The result is that all the advanced pupils are splendid sight-readers. We are, however, beginning to appreciate the need of this in America, and the larger music schools are following the French lead in this important matter.

Competition, public competition, keeps the standard of the Paris Conservatoire at a high level, but it is not always an edifying affair to the audience. Berlioz has humorously told of a public piano competition wherein, after twenty pupils had played a certain piece, on a single piano, the tortured instrument began playing it of itself! Back of such competitions, and back of all the debuts, particularly in the vocal branches, there is an incredible amount of wire-pulling. I should betray confidences if I were to mention names, but during the race for a position at the grand opera recently, a great composer alluded to one singer who has since become world-famous, as a "voice like the hinge of a gate, that needs oiling," and I am afraid that in France, as in Italy, the critics are venal, (there are noble exceptions), and a pretty face often carries more weight with a teacher than solid musical attainments.

And this leads to a very important statement; no young lady should ever dare to study in France or Italy without a parent, or a brother, as protector or adviser. Americans often think those who raise this cry prudish, but the cold, calm truth had better be insisted on; it is not safe! In more phlegmatic Germany the unprotected musical female may sometimes venture, in the more fiery Latin furnace, never.

Of course the vocalist will steer straight for Italy, and Milan will probably be the city of his choice. Milan is the most American of all Italian cities, and the musical student will probably feel at home there from the very first. He will, however, be astonished at the small amount of "special

method" the great Italian teachers manage to get along
with; there will be very little said about "inter-costal mus-
cles," or "the crico-thyroid," and even the highly honored
"diaphragmatic action" which some of our voice builders
manage to orate about every few seconds, will be taught, but
never once mentioned; in fact, many of the Milanese teachers
get through a vocal lesson without having used a single word
of more than four syllables, which would cause them to be
treated with proper contempt in America. But somehow
or other they manage to teach thoroughly, and if you
possess a good voice they will "finish it" in a different
sense from that of the "patent method" voice-architects.

But the dark side of the picture is that the young lady
student is exposed to the dangers alluded to above, and that
some of the Italian teachers will take a poor voice, out of
which nothing musical can ever be made, and feed the
victim on promises until her money is all gone. The hopes of
a *debut* in opera are held out in glittering fashion, even to
the most unpromising pupils, but when the *debut* comes it
is nothing to be especially proud of; the pupil is made to
pay roundly, and an engagement for a single night is obtained in some little town, for the smallest Italian towns
have some sort of opera house. The critics (?) of one or
two weekly papers are taken from Milan or Florence to re-
port the matter. These critics are openly bought, and
shower down "egregissimos" and "stupendissimos" upon
the debutante according to cash received, and a few weeks
thereafter the leading journal of the young lady's native
city in America has an item running, "our gifted towns-
woman has won great distinction in Italy. Her recent *debut*
in opera there was a wonderful triumph. The Italian critics
are wild in her praise, and predict a glorious career for so
distinguished an artist," and meanwhile nobody in Italy,
outside of the dependent coterie above mentioned, knows

anything of Miss Hitone, but the teacher is able to milk his pecuniary cow a little longer. The picture is not over-drawn; most of these *debuts* of American vocal students in Italy amount to nothing at all; it is merely "trying it on the dogs" as the theatrical expression runs.

Yet the true artist must receive some instruction in Italy before his vocal training is entirely complete. One may declaim against Italian music in the ultra-Wagnerian fashion of to-day, as much as one pleases, yet it should not be for-gotten that Italy is the mother of music, and even while granting superiority to other schools of modern composi-tion, we may still insist that one must study in Italy in order to sing the songs of Germany. Madame Albani once told me that she felt that her success in Wagnerian roles was chiefly due to her Italian vocal training.

In the matter of piano playing and composition the American student generally turns to Germany, and wisely, for although the French course in composition is very thorough, Munich or Leipsic present no such temptations to turn aside from work to pleasure and dissipation as Paris does. The models, too, are somewhat higher in Germany, for Mozart is generally made the foundation and Bach the apex there. Counterpoint can be studied either in Munich or Leipsic to advantage, for Rheinberger in the former city, is one of the greatest of modern contrapuntists, and Jadas-sohn in the latter, is one of the most fluent writers in canon and other intricate forms, that the world possesses to-day, and he has besides the faculty of making his pupils enthu-siastic in their work; as the eminent American composer Chadwick once said to me, "after each lesson I wanted to run all the way home, to get at work on the points of the lesson at once!" While I consider Wagner's operas the highest point reached in this great school of music, I still deem it a very good thing for the students of Germany that such men as Reinecke and Rheinberger, at the head of great schools, have not yielded to the Wagnerian influence, for Wagner wrote a language which no other composer can speak; he can never have followers in the creation of art works, and Liszt, Bruckner, and all the others who have tried to imitate, have found the path too thorny for success. Wagner swam in a "sea of tone"—his disciples only drown themselves in it, and the conservative music schools mentioned above do a good work in forming themselves into a species of musical life-saving stations. Stuttgart, Dresden, Frankfort, and Berlin, also draw their quota of American music students, but as I personally know nothing about the musical life in these cities, I can say nothing about them. The conservatory at Vienna, however, deserves mention; very few American students ever go there, yet the course is admirable, and especially in the branches of composition.

There is one great influence in Germany which I have not yet mentioned; it is that of the most conservative of modern composers, a man who can be ranked in the domain of vocal music only with Schubert and Schumann, a man who has only recently passed away, but whose works are built for countless generations of posterity—Robert Franz. He stands as a grand bulwark against the modern effusion and formlessness in music; he is the great conservator of the heritage which the world has in the works of the old masters. It is a singular instance of the meeting of extremes, that Wagner should have highly esteemed Franz and his works. His self-abnegation in retouching the works of Bach and Handel has never received the acknowledgment that it deserves; and his songs, I venture to predict, will attain their greatest appreciation in the twentieth century.

I cannot better end a chapter in which I have momentarily departed from the paths of travel and spoken of European musical influences, than by imparting to my readers

a few extracts from letters written to me in the three years
preceding his death, (October 24, 1892), by this most
classical song-composer. These letters contain so much
that is of the utmost value to the young composer that
I feel that no confidence is violated in their publication,
particularly as I have suppressed all personal matters
which have been touched upon in them. In order that
I may do no injustice to the composer's meaning, I have
deemed it best to give the original German, followed
by an English translation. In speaking of a review of the
character of his songs (Feb. 12, 1889) he says:

" Was ich aus Ihrer Kritik meiner künstlerischen Leist-
ungen zu errathen vermag, ist mir der Passus über die Be-
arbeitung ganz besonders werthvoll; er trifft den Nagel auf
den Kopf und stellt die verschrobenen Ansichten, denen
man hier zu Lande heute noch in Betreff dieser Angelegen-
heit begegnet, in den tiefsten Schatten. Aber auch die Be-
sprechung meiner Lieder hat ihre grossen Verdienste und
steht im directen Gegensatz mit der vielverbreiteten Mein-
ung, dass sie alle über einen Leisten geschlagen wären; es
bedarf freilich eines feineren Verständnisses als den Leuten
gewöhnlich zueigen ist, um die Unterschiede meines musi-
kalischen Ausdrucks herauszufinden. Einer der character-
istischesten Züge derselben dürfte darin bestehen, dass ich
keine Musik zu den Textvorlagen *mache*, sondern jene aus
diesen *entwickle*. Die beiden ersten Verse eines Heine'schen
Gedichtes lauten:

> 'Wenn du gute Augen hast,
> Und du schaust in meine Lieder,
> Siehst du eine junge Schöne
> Drinnen wandeln auf und nieder.

> 'Wenn du gute Ohren hast,
> Kannst du gar die Stimme hören,
> Und ihr Seufzen, Lachen, Singen
> Wird dein armes Herz bethören.'

Instinctiv leistete ich dieser Weisung Heine's Folge, und ging dabei nur von der Ueberzeugung aus, dass mehr geheimnissvolle Beziehungen zwischen Poesie und Musik walten als der nüchterne Verstand begreift; 'jedes echt Lyrische Gedicht enthällt latent seine Melodie in sich!'

Lediglich auf Grund dieser Thatsache ist es mir nicht ganz misslungen unter Benutzung guter Uebersetzungen aus dem Russichen, Schwedischen, Schottischen, etc., meiner Musik nationale Färbungen, ohne von diesen Kenntniss zu haben, einzuführen. Daraus erklärt sich's denn auch, dass ich die Dichter bestimmt zu individualisiren im Stande war.

Kurzum, ich bestrebte mich stets mein persönliches Empfinden mit dem Allgemeinen in Einklang zu bringen und gelegentliche Ausschreitungen des ersteren zu Gunsten des letzteren rücksichtslos zu beseitigen. Die Studien welche ich an den Meisterwerken aller Zeiten machte, gaben mir dazu eine sichere Directive.''

(Translation.)

'' So far as I venture to understand your criticism of my artistic endeavors, the review seems to me of especial value; it hits the nail on the head, and throws the distorted views which one even now meets with, on this subject, in this country, in the deepest shade. But the analysis of my songs has also its merit, and stands in direct opposition to the widespread idea that they are all struck upon the same last; it naturally requires a finer perception than people are generally gifted with, to understand the differences of my musical expression. One of the most characteristic traits of this may lie in the fact that I do not *make* the music to the text, but rather *derive* it from the subject. The two first verses of one of Heine's poems run:

'If you gaze with earnest eye,
And upon my verses ponder,
You will see a beauteous maid
Through their mazes gently wander.

'If you list with careful ears,
E'en her voice to you is calling,
And her sighing, laughing, singing,
Soon shall be your heart enthralling.'

"Instinctively I gave my adhesion to this direction of Heine, aud worked only from the conviction that there were closer hidden connections between Poetry and Music than the barren intellects comprehended; *every true lyric poem holds latent within itself its own melody!*

"Solely from this cause I have not entirely failed, through the use of good translations from the Russian, Swedish, Scotch, etc., to give to my music a national coloring, without having actual knowledge of it. This also explains how I was able with surety to individualize the different poets. In short I constantly strove to bring my personal feeling into unity with the universal (Allgemeinen), and to put aside all excesses of the former for the benefit of the latter, relentlessly. The studies which I had made, of the master works of all ages, gave me a sure impulse towards this."

It is singular, in reading the above letter, to see how closely the theory of this master comes to that of Wagner, in the connection of word and tone, only Franz here expresses himself more tersely. Every word of the advice embodied in the above is of direct value to the music student, but it must be remembered that the quiet musician of Halle (Franz is one of the most modest of men) did not write these utterances as an essay, as Wagner's pamphlets were written, and may himself be surprised at their becoming public.

In a later letter, speaking of the influence of the song on music in general, Franz says:

"Hier zu Lande sieht man auf dergleichen Dinge sehr von Oben herab, von dem albernen Vorurtheile ausgehend, es handle sich hier nur um Formen, die so ganz beiläufig entstehen. Und doch ist gerade das Lied eins der Haupt-fundamente unserer Kunst; eine Ueberzeugung die Sie offenbar theilen.''

Which may be rendered:

"Hereabouts men look very condescendingly on such things, (song-forms), starting with the silly conception that one has to do here with forms that arise only incidentally; and yet the Song is actually one of the *chief foundations of our art;* an opinion which I see you openly share with me.''

In another letter, dated March 23, 1889, Franz expresses himself still more emphatically as to the true position of the *Lied*.

"Bisher sah man diese Form nicht ohne mitleidiges Achselzücken an, und doch ruht auf ihr, einer der wesent-lichsten Factoren der Musik. Was mich betrifft, bereue ich es keinen Augenblick, dies Gebiet ausschliesslich cultivirt, und es mit meinen Vorgängern zu Ehren gebracht zu haben.''

"Sie bedauern es dass von mir keine Werke im grossen styl existiren; meines Erachtens war aber *nach* Beethoven nur noch Terrain für den specifish lyrischen Ausdruck vor-handen, und wurden auch lediglich auf diesem Gebiete namhafte Resultate erzielt. Das sage ich nicht etwa zur Rechtfertigung meines Standpunktes, sodern berufe mich dabei auf den thatsächlichen Verlauf unserer Kunst; die Music begann mit der Lyrik und schliesst mit ihr ab—ein Entwicklungsprocess den die Poesie ebenfalls genommen hat.''

(Translation.)

" Until now men never looked upon this form [the song

form] without a compassionate shrug of the shoulders, and yet upon it rests one of the most substantial factors of music. As regards myself, I do not regret for an instant that I have cultivated this school exclusively, and with my predecessors, brought it into honor.

You write that you are sorry that there exists no work of mine in the large forms; my opinion was, however, that after Beethoven there was only room for specifically lyrical expression in music'' [Here again we have a resemblance to a theory which belongs also to the school of the future.] `` and solely in this territory have especial results been achieved. I do not say this in any wise as a justification of my standpoint, but rest upon the actual facts in the progress of our art. Music began with the lyric and will end with it—a process of development that poetry has also undergone.''

I am sure that my readers will need no apology for disgressing from the path of travel when the results are as precious as the truths enunciated in these letters, and if all do not give their entire adhesion to the last theory, at least every thinking musician will coincide with the splendidly expressed views regarding the worth of the lyrical form, and the intertwining of poetry and music.

In ending this rather serious chapter, I must reiterate what I said at the beginning;—don't go to Europe for musical study until you have entirely exhausted what resources are offered you in your own fair country, and study just as vehemently and persistently in Boston, New York, Cincinnati, Chicago, or any other American musical centre, as if you were in Milan, or Paris, or Leipsic, or London, and you may become an adept in your art before having seen Europe at all.

CHAPTER XVII.

THE ROUTINE OF EUROPEAN TRAVEL—USEFUL HINTS AS TO
COSTUME—PREVENTIVES OF SEASICKNESS—P A S S P O RT S—
STRASSBURG REGULATIONS—LANGUAGES—CUSTOMS OFFICERS
—TIPS.

Having given several pages of admonition to the musical
traveler, I may as well swing for a sheep as for a lamb, and
proceed to lecture the general tourist. In doing this, however, I shall still endeavor to keep the resolution of my first
chapter and avoid stating those things which are intermin-
ably insisted upon in the regular handbooks of travel.

The chief vice of American tourists is the desire to see
everything, by which they generally succeed in seeing
nothing. It is a fallacy of these lightning voyagers, to
think that the trip itself is bound to be uncomfortable anyway, and that the only enjoyment of trans-Atlantic travel
is in the ability to talk of it afterwards. Never was there
a greater mistake! If one will only adapt himself to circumstances, and *never hurry*, he can get both rest and education out of a European tour.

It is wise, however, to cut the coat according to the cloth,
both in the matter of time and money, at the very beginning. If it is to be a four weeks tour, go to Scotland,
through the Trossachs, the land of Rob Roy. Read up
Scott, and take four or five days in Edinburgh, go down to
Melrose Abbey, see Abbotsford, then take in Stratford and

·Kenilworth, and take a week or more in London, but don't imagine that you are seeing a hundredth part of what the latter city has to offer. After this, to Liverpool and home. If you have two weeks more at your disposal, go to Antwerp and Rotterdam, then take a few days in Amsterdam, then to Cologne, up the Rhine, strike back to Brussels, Flushing, and go home again. It is a great pity that with some tourists, seeing European life means only tasting the lower kinds of dissipation in London or Paris; I have known very stately Americans take up this meretricious style of "seeing life" from the moment they arrived on foreign shores.

Of course all the handbooks give instructions as regards costume on shipboard, but not one of them dwells upon the fact that it is not necessary to make oneself a scare-crow just because one has temporarily left *terra firma*. I suppose that there is scarcely any phase in traveling, in which a well-dressed lady looks better than when reclining in somebody-else's steamer chair, in an interesting, languid state of convalescence from seasickness, and she has the additional satisfaction of knowing that most of her unwise sisters are waddling around the deck in old clothes and frightfully unbecoming bonnets or other head gear. Of course the dressy extreme is more absurd still; I shall never forget a lady of uncertain date, who crossed on the " City of Rome " once with a personally conducted party. She had an extensive wardrobe and she determined to show it at all hazards; she sat in the music room every day, and every twenty-four hours brought forth a new and gorgeous costume. I wish that I were a fashion reporter that I might give some idea of her paraphernalia; she did not feel very comfortable, but she sat through the ordeal of the voyage with the persistency of a martyr, and altogether was the greatest example of traveling vulgarity that it has ever been my fortune to run across.

It is singular that newly wedded couples should brave the qualms of the sea so frequently. Nothing can so quickly eclipse the honeymoon as the perception of a once fair female, now white-nosed and limp. If, as is often the case, the young husband is too absorbed in his own troubles to see anything, all is well; but if the husband is wilted and the wife is entirely well, the marital balance is disturbed for ever after.

Let remedies severely alone on your sea trip; there is no cure for seasickness! I have noted many come on board almost stupefied with bromide of sodium, and these have frequently been the worst of all the sufferers.

As regards passports, it is just as well to have one, even if you only use it for purposes of identification. At Strass-burg they used to demand them, but this is about the only place outside of Russia, where they have recently been called into actual requisition, and that only on the German side of the fence. How rigidly they enforced passport regulations may be judged by the following incident which occurred but a year ago: A young mother from Australia had traveled all the way to Paris with her boy, a pale and pitiable lad of seven years, who was a sufferer from some spinal complaint. Finding no relief for the invalid in Paris, she set forth to one of the German water-cures in anxious haste. Naturally she knew nothing of passports, and had provided none; arrived at German Avricourt, the frontier, an officer boarded the train to examine these documents. It had been an exhausting all-night ride, and the child was nearly dead, but that made no difference to that officer; I assured him that the little cripple did not intend to overthrow the German empire, but received no reply. The boy was turned back with his mother; whether he ever reached Paris alive is just a trifle doubtful to me. Of course the officer was not to blame, for the German discipline is so strict that he probably would have been court-martialed had he let the invalid pass through. Going from Strassburg to Paris no passport is needed, for the French fear the effect of such a scrutiny on the trade of Paris (the merchants of Strassburg complained bitterly that their business was almost ruined by the restriction), but they try in some occult fashion to make it uncomfortable for the Germans who get over the frontier. I experienced this once at French Avricourt (for the town is divided in two sections of opposing nationality), where the lieutenant mistook me for a ferocious Teuton. "Vous etes Allemande?" he angrily said, only half inquiringly. "Mais non!" I replied, "je suis Americain!" and the smiles and apologies which ensued led me to inquire what would have been done to me if I had been German, and I was told that I would have been watched, but I am convinced that I should have been led to the deepest dungeon beneath the castle moat, just as happens in G. P. R. James' novels. The contrast between the dapper, undersized French soldier and the heavy-built German, is a very marked one, but it may be safely stated that there will never again be such a walk-over as occurred in France in 1871.

Of course, if you speak only English, you will miss a great deal of possible pleasure on your European tour, yet it is possible to get along without knowledge of any foreign tongue, for in the hotels every porter is proud of his English and the larger shopkeepers have studied the language, with designs upon your purse. In France there is quite an English fever at present, and every one who knows a few words of our tongue will trot them out to astonish you on every available opportunity. Even the railway officials are attacked with this fever. On the railway, near Rheims, shortly after the Strassburg episode noted above, I gave the conductor some good Chicago French, desiring to know when I could change into the dining wagon; he returned me

my change in Rheims English by saying " Ha! Five-teen
minutes is arrest!" which caused me some tribulation as I
could only interpret it to mean that I was to be arrested in
fifteen minutes, possibly on account of my breaking into,
and mangling, the French language; what it actually did
mean, I found out at the next station, where we stopped
fifteen minutes. And *apropos* of the crossing of frontiers,
do not trust to the word of any official whatever, as regards
your baggage; look after it yourself. In Strassburg every
railway official, from the station master down to the porter,
told me that the trunk which I had registered to Paris would
be examined there and nowhere else, yet just as the train
was starting away from the frontier, I thought that I would
take a look at the unfortunates who were obliged to go
through the ordeal of examination at the station of Avricourt; and there, in solitary grandeur, stood my trunk, and
would have stood there to eternity, if I had entirely relied
upon the German railway officials.

Customs examinations are a necessary evil, and vary
greatly, according to the humor of the party who is to probe
into your dirty linen. Sometimes he will just glance at
your face, size you up as an inoffending tourist, who will
only endeavor to cheat the customs at New York, open the
lid of your box, smile, take a cigar, and chalk you through.
At other times you will meet a governmental party who will
take an interest in every detail of your wardrobe, who will
muse over your tooth brush as if he thought that you might
have hidden something between the bristles, and will explore
your socks down to the very toes. Once, at least, I was
able to overcome such an official; it was on the Italian frontier, and I had just had a charming example of what *octroi*
meant, by a custom house officer at Trieste wanting to charge
me two dollars on one dollar's worth of candy which I was
taking to a friend at Adelsberg; I gave the official the candy

as a souvenir and swore at him a little in English which he did not comprehend. When, therefore, at the Italian custom house I found another suspicious-looking party ready to unpack my washing for me, I determined to presume on his ignorance of my native tongue. He asked me in Italian for my keys; I gazed out into space; he repeated the question in French, but I still was absorbed in the beauties of the landscape; he then tapped me on the shoulder, and repeated the whole story; I asked him in English, " What do you want?" He grew excited and took refuge in pantomime; he pointed to the trunk and then to me; I nodded vehemently and pointed to myself, intimating that the trunk belonged to me, and then paused, as if that was all that there was to it; he now danced around with more frenzy than grace, and finally, struck with an idea, pointed at my pocket; I gave a nod of comprehension, and drew from my pocket —my railroad ticket! At last the now thoroughly aroused officer exhibited a gleam of almost human intelligence, and made a pantomime of unlocking the trunk! It was impossible to misunderstand that, and with a very bland smile I handed him my key, but everyone else had been examined, and the train conductor was getting impatient, and he thought that an idiot of my caliber wouldn't have the brains to smuggle much anyway, and therefore he made a hurried chalk mark on the trunk and I went on my way, avenged.

Much more serious than this is quarantine, which sometimes falls to the lot of the unfortunate tourist, in cholera times. This means passing from one to three weeks on an island, or on shipboard, without a book, a paper, or any communication with the outside world whatever. I have seen the harbor of Trieste black with ships that were in quarantine, and the wretches on board could do nothing but gaze at the water, or the wharves in the distance, until their term of imprisonment was over. If a person has only a six week's vacation, I should not advise spending three weeks of it in quarantine. Fumigation is better, only because the ordeal is shorter. They put you in a room and then burn things that make an odor beside which all the hundred smells of Cologne, and all the Danish cheese factories, sink into insignificance. Once in a while a person faints at the perfume. The odor lingers in your memory forever, and in your clothes nearly as long. A story is told of a New Yorker who went into the country and fainted because of the fresh air; they tried every means to revive him, but all in vain; at last a person who had been in the metropolis and knew the atmosphere, held a very dead fish under the Gothamite's nose, when he murmured, "That smells like home!" and recovered. Well, that New Yorker would feel at home in the fumigating chamber, but less-seasoned mortals had better avoid it. It is a very rich smell! A sort of Vanderbilt smell!

If you speak no language but English, pray avoid falling into two errors while abroad; firstly, do not imagine that people will understand you more readily if you shout, and, secondly, never forget that almost every person of culture, in central and northern Europe, speaks English. As regards the first of these faults, almost every American shouts his way through Europe, and American ladies can be recognized quite a distance off, by their thin, shrill, acidulous tones. Every person who listens will be struck with the difference between the strident quality of the conversational tone of the American and the full, mellow, agreeable voice of the Englishwoman. I hope that none of my readers will think me unpatriotic in holding up the vulgarisms of the American snob abroad, to scorn. There are hosts of gentle travelers from America, in Europe, every season, but there are others who set one's teeth on edge by their flaunting, flaring manners, and the worst of it all is that these attract attention while the better bred travelers do not, so that the reputation of the American tourist is lowered. Once, at the railway station in Stratford-on-Avon, while waiting for the London train, I had an illustration of both the rapacity of the Briton and the vulgarity of the American tourist. In a sweltering hot day, after a walk of half an hour or so, every one came to the station in a state of thirst and collapse. Not a drop of water was to be found in any of the waiting-rooms. The canny guardian of the refreshment room improved her opportunity and sold a rather warm sort of brackish water at a penny a glass! Thus ended the first lesson. Then there entered a party of American tourists (a New York party, I believe), and took possession of the restaurant altogether. They came in like an invading army, and they treated the occupants as natural enemies. They abused the waiter, the food, the drink; they cast their money about in wild and reckless profusion, and after spending a small fortune one of them asked the proprietor how she liked Americans. "I don't like 'em," was the candid answer of the water pedlar. When pressed for details, this aqueous speculator launched forth against the manners of American tourists. With the examples standing before her, the lecture became a sort of animated object lesson, and the money-grubbing Englishwoman, and the loud-voiced, vituperative, but generous Americans stood in very vivid contrast there. Thus ended the second lesson.

Another trait which the tourist cannot well avoid seeing if he is only moderately observant, but one which is by no means exclusively American, is the selfishness which is developed by travel. The best seat in the railway compartment, the best berth in the steamer, the upper perch in the diligence, is always struggled for, and sometimes in a most

annoying manner. About all of the flying tourists that I
have seen making a dash at Europe, have this fault, but I
remember one rather over-religious dame, unmarried but
still a trifle mouldy, who adopted the opposite course, and
would ostentatiously take the poorest of steamboat, railroad, or stage-coach hospitality; and she was a little worse
than the other kind, and decidedly more unnatural.

As regards tips in Europe, the traveler who does not give
a *pourboire* to the waiter, coachman, or whatever else his
occupation may be, is really robbing the man of part of his
salary. I once had a conversation with some waiters who
were on a strike, in Paris; and then the whole system of
tipping was laid open to me; in some of the cafés on the
boulevards, the waiters not only receive no salary but
actually pay for their situations! In other places the waiter
is under pledge to turn in half of his tips to the proprietor,
and if these amount to an insufficient sum, he is obliged to
pay a certain fine over and above this depletion of his purse.
Of course it is greatly to be desired that the proprietor
should add a trifle to the price of his wares and pay a higher
salary to his help, but any effort at a reform here would
only make matters harder for a class who are overworked
and underpaid as it is; therefore it is as well to go on paying the slight tribute, and remembering that it is only paying to Cæsar the things which ought to be Cæsar's. And
furthermore, that traveler is a very unwise one who stops to
combat every extortion; one must learn to be cheated occasionally, with equanimity. I once had for a traveling
companion one of those uncomfortable fellows who stand
up at every slight imposition, ''just for the principle of the
thing.'' In Cologne he found a waiter who overcharged
him two pfennige (a half-cent) when he settled his reckon-
ing at one of the cafés. He made such a riot about the
matter that the proprietor discharged the culprit. The

next day the waiter met the man who had made such unexpected resistence to his prices, and there was a disgrace-
ful fisticuff fight in the street.   The party who had been
overcharged stayed two days extra in Cologne for the small
satisfaction of seeing the waiter sent to prison.   It may
have been perfectly just, I don't doubt but that it was, but
I left that companion at once, and I always felt a little
sorry for the waiter whose reputation was irretrievably
ruined for a half cent.   For myself, I always regarded myself as the legitimate prey of the garçons up to two or three
cents, and I allowed that amount of extortion calmly, for I
did not come abroad to reform Europe, but if the squeez-
ing went beyond that I resisted, and always effectually,
since even the barrelhoop, when trodden on, will turn;
therefore I hope that no strict puritan will hold me guilty
of compounding felonies or encouraging crime.

There is one subject of which no guidebook speaks, yet
which will impress the American most forcibly of all his
European experiences.   It is rather a medical subject, and
possibly a false delicacy leads to its being passed over in
silence.   It is that four out of every five Americans will
feel the change of climate in the shape of a very itchy rash
which will invariably be ascribed to the maligned and
long-suffering flea.   As this rash breaks out almost simultaneously with the arrival in Europe, this insect which goes
on its career, as Gilbert and Sullivan describe it

> "Gaily tripping,
>   Lightly skipping,"

may be acquitted of the " rash " deed; the flea is enterpris-
ing, but not so much as that.   The annoyance probably
comes from the change of air and of diet, and if wines and
ale are abstained from, and a cooling diet used, together
with much bathing, the trouble soon disappears.

Shopping on the continent is a never-ending delight to ladies, and there are some elements of surprise in it. I could never fathom the implicit trust which shopkeepers repose in their American customers. Go to any of the large stores in Switzerland or Italy, for example, and buy until your purse is empty, and the salesman will show you yet one more desirable purchase; "but," you say, "my money has given out;" it will not matter in the slightest degree; the shopkeeper, who has never seen you before, will urge you to take it along, and send him the money "any time." This has happened to me again and again, yet I have never found out the cause of such a child-like faith. It may be that my countenance inspires confidence, but why do not the shopkeepers of New York or Boston come under its influence?

I think that, upon the whole, in calm blood, after his traveling is over, the American will conclude that our system of railway and steamboat journeying is superior to that of Europe. There are no steamers, for example, which can compare with the large passenger boats of Long Island Sound, in any part of Europe, and the foreign system of baggage transportation is simply abominable. In Great Britain you simply put your trunk on the van, and claim it at the station. What surety there is for you if anybody else gets there and claims it first, I do not know. Once, in Glasgow, I came very near to getting away with another person's luggage, through the incorrect description given to me of my companion's trunk.

If time hangs heavy on the male tourist's hand, he will find never-ending surprises in devoting himself to the game of billiards. I feel that I should not be doing my duty to my male readers if I did not add a short disquisition on the European methods of this game. In England, where the tables are of tremendous size, the balls as small as homœopathic pills, and the cues as long and pointed as trout poles, the chief interest in the game is to denounce the "scratches" (now called "flukes") of your opponent and to trust to winning the long siege by outliving him. In France, the tables are as small as a summer hotel bedstead, and the balls as large as cannon balls, and there the only interest centers in getting a blind man to play with you; and even then he generally wins the game. But in Hamburg I found the acme of primitive billiards. The tables were evidently fossils of the palæozoic period, and the cushions were primeval flint. When the ball lodged under the cushion, it was a pleasing athletic diversion to wedge it out again. There were no means of counting, but the players were expected to carry the score "in their heads." As for a long time neither counted anything, this was an easy burden. After an hour or two, we concluded to leave the Hamburg championship undecided.

CHAPTER XVIII.

DEPARTURE FROM LONDON—A FUNEREAL CABBY—SCOTLAND
—EDINBURGH AND GLASGOW—ABBOTSFORD—LIVERPOOL—
HOMEWARD BOUND—A TYPICAL STEAMER CONCERT—THE
HUMORS OF AN OCEAN VOYAGE—STEERAGE LIFE—HOME
AGAIN.

London can never pall upon the true cosmopolitan; the
cockney, too, loves London with an ardor second only to
that of the Frenchman for Paris. The traveler who sees
London only for a week or a month, may imagine it dull,
but he who pitches his tents there for a good length of time,
comes gradually to understand why Dickens could not be
permanently happy away from it. One can study human
kind better there than anywhere else in the world. It was
not, therefore, that I was tired of London, that I was obliged
to leave it suddenly; it was simply that I could, by immediate departure, have a glimpse of some Scotch friends and
scenery before the sailing of the steamer that was to carry
me home from Liverpool. Every moment counted, and
therefore I packed hastily, and calling a hansom, was soon
on my way to the Euston Station. I had, however, calculated without my host, or at least without my cabman, who
went at a most leisurely pace, and ingeniously got entangled
in two blockades. We thereupon had two or three passages
of repartee through the hole in the roof, which made the
horse go slower than before, as he evidently desired to stop

and listen to the lively conversation, and then stop again and think it over. Total result, train missed by two minutes, and no other train for six hours. And now ensued a very animated parliamentary debate, which necessitated a policeman, who kindly consented to act as chairman, to call us to order. I moved a series of resolutions, that, in view of the tardiness of the entire operations, the financial question should be indefinitely postponed; and also passed a vote of lack of confidence. The house divided on the former point, after a stirring address from the cabby, in which he eloquently touched upon the fact that I wanted a race horse for a shilling. I rose to a personal explanation here, and begged to inquire if, when desirous of reaching an evening train at Euston Station, one should start the day previous. The cabman here moved the previous question—financial budget. I then made the "greatest effort of my life," and extended a formal invitation (R. S. V. P.) for the cabby to come down and get it if he could, also promising that he would find a warm and hearty reception. The chairman declared this point out of order and suggested a compromise. The debate now became less spirited and a reduced appropriation bill was finally passed.

After all, the cabman had the best of it in our little passage-at-arms, for his final repartee was to drive off with my umbrella and overcoat (which I forgot in the heat of debate), and I am left to sing *a la* Tosti—

> "I feel that they are lost to me
> Forever and forever."

But the average London cabby only obeys the scriptural injunction as regards the stranger; he "takes him in"—awfully. The moral of my experience is—never hire a London hansom by the hour. The original of Rip van Winkle is said to have thus hired one to go from Brixton to Cam-

den (both in London); when he arrived his friends were
dead, the old house was pulled down, no one remembered
him, and everything else happened *a la* Joe Jefferson and
Washington Irving.

But if you can once get the hansomite to appear ridiculous the battle is won. I knew a lady once to overcome
one thus: As he received his proper fare he held it forth
contemptuously in his palm and asked "Wot's this?" The
fair fare merely gave a glance and said, " A very dirty
hand." Exit hansom.

They sell drinking water in English railway stations!
Fancy taxing a freeborn American a penny for a glass of
very inferior *aqua pura*. That is why the Britons seldom
touch the article, I suppose. Even that scriptural drink,
mineral water (" Though Paul may plant, and Apollinaris
water," I think is the biblical quotation), is not readily
forthcoming.

I went through to Glasgow, intending to begin Scotland
at the further end, and work back to Liverpool. Of Glasgow itself I will say but little. It is a purely commercial
city and of no greater interest to the *litterateur* than, say
Chicago. But I had a glorious combination of Chicago and
Glasgow with me in the shape of a native Glasgonian, who
had lived in Chicago for fifteen years—Mr. William Bunten, an extensive grain dealer. When Scotch and American (Western) hospitality unite in one host, the result is a
headache to the guest. I can prove this mathematically.
After Mr. Bunten had introduced me to everybody in Glasgow (including Mr. Lambeth, the city organist, somewhat
in his dotage, but an excellent musician), we wound up
with a real Scotch dinner at Forrester's, the Delmonico's
of Scotland. To me the foreign dinners possess an interest
not exceeded by the foreign ruins, and they are seen with
less personal inconvenience. We began with a " hotch-

potch,'' which is a soup in which all possible and impossible vegetables are thrown. This did not inspire me greatly, for I had already tasted all the herb soups of that soup-herb country, France. But now followed the real dish—a Scotch '' haggis.'' I doubt not but that all of my readers are familiar with this dish in the abstract, from the verses of Robert Burns, and by the way, Mr. Bunten recited the whole poem most fervently before we attacked the dish, and especially the stanzas running—

> "Fair fa' your honest, sonsie face,
>   Great chieftain o' the puddin' race,
>   Aboon them a' ye tak your place,
>   Painch, tripe or thairm;
>   Weel are ye wordy of a grace
>   As lang's my arm.
>   * * * * * *
>   Ye powers wha mak mankind your care
>   And dish them out their bill o' fare,
>   Auld Scotland wants nae skinking ware
>   That jaups in luggies;
>   But if ye wish her gratefu' pray'r,
>   Gie her a *haggis*!"

But of the constituent parts of a haggis, ask me not. I only know that it is of meat, oatmeal, suet and a thousand other things, and is boiled in a sheep's stomach. A zealous Scot told me that the dish is mentioned (not by name but by implication) in the scriptures, in the Book of Kings. That night I dreamt I dwelt in marble halls, with haggises by my side, for the mess is as indigestible as it is seductive.

But the succeeding trip through the Trossachs to Edinburg is likely to chase away every trace of indigestion, for the air is as invigorating as a tonic, and even the showers have a softness and beauty that prevents a " Scotch mist " from becoming doleful or depressing. One should do a good deal of walking on this part of the tour if one desires to enter heartily into the spirit of the countryside made immortal by Scott.

Loch Katrine, Stronachlacher, Loch Lomond, and a whole family of "bens," greet the eye in never-ending panorama. It is indeed—

"Yon bonnie banks and yon bonnie braes,
    Where the sun shines bright on Loch Lomond,
    Where me and my true love were ever wont to gae
    On the bonnie, bonnie banks o' Loch Lomond."

One regrets when Callender is reached and the train is to be taken for Edinburgh, but to the traveler who desires to study man rather than scenery, antiquity rather than beautiful views, Edinburgh will make ample amends.

Edinburgh always retains its charm for me. Immediately on arriving there I strolled over to the old town and went down the Canongate. This is the true Edinburgh, the city with which all readers of Scott's works are familiar. But the city is, in fact, a double one, the two parts being in most striking contrast. In the old town one is transplanted into the middle ages at once, for every building dates back to times immemorial, and in the new town one has not only a most elegant, modern city, but in many places (public buildings, etc.,) a perfect imitation of ancient Athens. The topography of the city was excellently suited to this reproduction, and the architects have used their opportunity admirably. Walking down High street, by an odd coincidence, right under the window of John Knox's house, whence he used to harangue the people 300 years ago, I found a street preacher holding forth on the cheerful doctrine of eternal damnation. "You are all condemned," he shouted, "you are all lost," and he was not so far out, for when I left him, I had considerable difficulty in finding my way back to the Royal Hotel. I was well fleeced by the tradesmen that I met in Edinburgh.

"Scots wha hae wi' Wallace bled"

now do the bleeding themselves, and the innocent tourist is the victim.

After Edinburgh, a short run by rail took me to Melrose. The abbey here is the most magnificent ruin in Great Britain.

"Ye have no ruins like that abbey in America," said the guide. I thought of our great Henry E. and his first year of operatic management, and told the Scotchman that he was mistaken. This same guide took me to Abbotsford, and when I quoted some passages from Scott relative to the scenery, he was ready to fall upon my neck and weep. He mastered his emotions sufficiently to put an extra shilling or two into the bill, as a penalty for my mangling the poet, perhaps.

Sir Walter must have been the Barnum of his period. He had no white elephant, to be sure, unless Abbotsford itself might be called one, but he had the "Greatest Collection of Napoleonic Relics" and a "Gigantic Aggregation of Scotch Antiquities." He charged no admission to see his museum, but his descendants have got bravely over that failing. But really the collection breathes taste and refinement, and the beautiful town of Melrose breathes peace and tranquility.

Of Liverpool there is nothing to tell, save that it is the most uncomfortable city in the world for the traveler, just before "sailing day." There were some 3,000 Americans taking their departure on the morrow, and the hotels were full to the window sills. I obtained rooms at "The Waterloo," however, and slept oblivious of cares, while the landlady must have sat up all night making out my bill, judging by the length and amount; but then the charges at Waterloo are a matter of history, and I ought to have expected it. The account gave my flattened pocketbook one last affectionate squeeze, and then I was upon the vessel, Before the steamer sets sail for home, however, let me give a few final European remarks. I have not endeavored in these pages, most ferocious reader, to speak of places in England which must be familiar to you if you are not oblivious to the influence of all the poets; thus I have not spoken of Stratford-on-Avon, nor Kenilworth, nor Chester, nor of the beautiful Lake Country in England; yet I must not give the impression that these places are not worthy of your attention; on the contrary, a walking tour, or, best of all, a bicycle tour through England will give you the greatest pleasure that you have ever experienced in travel. And also at the close of our European travel together, oh, fierce and justly aroused one! let me mollify your resentment at the familiar tone I have taken throughout. If I have turned aside too frequently to speak of food, of drink, of barbers, of billiards, of cabbies, and of baths, remember that I have not been writing history, but only a series of vacation tours, and that in traveling all the worst and most selfish qualities of the human animal come to the surface. If you are a rich young man, and are contemplating marriage, just take your intended and her mother on an extended European tour, and you will save the expense of a wedding-suit (probably), although I can't guarantee as to the breach-of-promise suit, and although I have here spoken of a trip via Liverpool, let me assure you that the voyage to Glasgow gives one of the most beautiful approaches to Europe; therefore try and make at least one trip that way; and now let us shake the dust of Europe from our feet and hie aboard.

Of course the voyage began with the usual turmoil and bustle of preparation, in the midst of which I met my long-lost organist and pianist, who had been wandering 'neath Italian skies since my Bayreuth chapter and who had now returned to share the discomforts and perils of the passage with me.

One man's joy, alas, is always another s sorrow. As we, light-hearted, were going to all that was dear to us, we saw others standing upon the pier, weeping.   Some sturdy bread-winner was going to seek fortune in a far-off land. The home over there was to seem empty and sorrowful for a long, long time.   The cold rain mingled with the tears of parting, and the desolate picture touched our own hopes with melancholy.

Now followed all the delights and discomforts of the beginning of an ocean voyage.   The general scramble for baggage, the machinations for special seats at table, the donning of quaint, old-fashioned or seedy garments which are to be "worn out" on shipboard, and the great screw begins its revolutions, and off we are.   It was blowing a summer gale as we left Liverpool, and many paid tribute to Neptune before we reached Queenstown.   At this place the vessel made an unusually long stop.

There was ample time to go on shore and take a run up to the town, but alas! no boatman seemed hardy enough to tempt the waves.   At last a large sailboat came alongside. But the hardy mariner would close only half a bargain with me; that is, he agreed to take me ashore, but would not promise to bring me back.   "There's no trusting a wind like this," said he.   I am a Vanderdecken as regards storms at sea, and was ready to contract to come back in a cyclone if necessary, but the "party of the second part" (as lawyers say) would not take any return contract, so I stood on deck gazing at the shore, like the Israelites at the promised land, knowing—which the Israelites didn't—that a superb whisky was doled out by a certain red-headed maiden there, and that blackthorn shillalaghs and bog-oak jewelry were purchasable for a mere song.   Then I shook my fist at the unattainable shore "across the stormy water," and bowed to the inevitable.   The emigrants soon came up in a tug, and had a very lively time in getting on board. As one poor fellow came over the side, the boat lurched and he struck his bundle heavily against the rail, a crash followed, and a liquid began to flow down over his shoulders, a balmy aroma filled the air around him, and I knew then that he had visited the red-headed girl above mentioned. Again the vessel forged ahead, and soon we were out upon a stormy ocean. The vikings in the "Frithjof Saga" sing

"It is glorious on turbulent sea,"

but the passengers did not seem to agree with this idea. Possibly none of them had ever been in the viking business. The decks were soon deserted save by a fond but sea-sick couple, who were regurgitating a duet in C minor. I suggested a change of key, but they told me to go to the d—ominant. The ship was so lightly laden that she rolled fearfully. It recalled the Bacchanalian song, "As we go rolling home." In a very short time the passengers, with few exceptions, were ready to shoot the man who wrote "A Life on the Ocean Wave," if they could have found him.

How marked is the approach of the illness of the sea! The patient suddenly ceases conversation, and becomes deeply meditative. The nose grows pale; the face assumes a greenish tint; the patient makes a faint attempt to rise; and then—, let us draw the curtain. Some of the invalids bravely endeavored to keep up their regular attendance at meals, but this was attended with inconveniences. I saw one gentleman totter to the breakfast table, and sit sadly waiting for the waiter, who came not. Finally he wildly wailed forth, "Steward, a plate of fish, *quick!*" But it was too late, and as the waiter rushed for the fish the guest rushed for the door.

Higher and higher grew the wind and waves. To sit at

the leeward side of the table was not unattended with trouble. Occasionally the pickle jar would become affectionately intimate, and unexpectedly sit in one's lap. The butter would frequently come unasked, and there was a lively race between three stewards and a soup tureen, in which the latter won by going the entire length of the saloon before it was captured. Finally the weather culminated in a gale which made things very lively for two days. Some of the timorous ones thought that the end was nigh, and even the calmer ones, in the height of the storm, expected each moment would be their—next.

The chief trouble was the screw. When that rose out of water it shook the ship from stem to stern, and caused a wail of anguish to ascend. I sought out the chief steward, and besought him to explain how, under such circumstances, the quantity of food to be cooked could be regulated. "How can you tell, for example, what these people will eat to-morrow, or whether they will eat at all?" "Very easy thing," quoth he. "You know we started out in a storm. Everybody tries to come to the first dinner, but not one in five could stay the meal through; so I went it heavy on soup and light on pudding. To-morrow it will be light all round." And so it was; all the next day only seven passengers were visible at meals. It was a case of

> "None but the brave deserve the fare."

and for those two days the vessel behaved like a good singer, that is, she never lost her pitch.

As our stateroom was near the bow of the boat we had the full benefit of this in a constant succession of rises and falls of about fifty feet. At night this became rather noticeable to my companions, who, having seen Vesuvius, gave me practical examples of its workings. For myself I did not mind the rise, but when the vessel fell my berth seemed to keep about two inches ahead of my person in the downward race, and my stomach seemed to remain, like Mahomet's coffin, in space. But I was not seasick—I remained with the veteran band of seven who took their meals with triumphant regularity. One or two of even these made a hurried skip from the soup to the coffee during a specially boisterous dinner.

Seasickness certainly brings out all that there is in a man. One of my companions, who is the sweetest-mannered gentleman imaginable on shore, under the influence of the malady, brought forth orations that were both terse and curse.

Poets have pictured every human sorrow in verse, and under the stirring influences of the scene I sought for immortality by singing of a woe that the muse has too long neglected.

ODE TO SEASICKNESS.

Let poets inspiration borrow
  From hearts bowed down by weight of grief;
I sing a deeper, truer sorrow,
  And one without relief.

Where food and comfort are rejected,
  Where life is filled with black despair;
Limp, hopeless, woe-begone, dejected;
  That is the *mal de mer!*

Hark to yon note of sad bereaval,
  In dismal, baleful monotones;
Upheaval follows on upheaval,
  Each intermixed with groans.

The victim with a manner frantic
  Doth hasten to the vessel's side,
Sends articles to the "Atlantic,"
  Yet feels no thrill of pride.

He thinks on Scriptural epistles,
  And full of anguish is his cup,
As loud the gale around him whistles
  The text "Cast ye then up!"

One wish within his heart is burning,
  Others of many things have dearth,
He only has a single yearning,
  He only wants—the earth!

There was a more serious side to the storm, however, for one afternoon a heavy wave swept the forward deck and flung half a dozen sailors in a bleeding heap among the iron stanchions. The next day one of the poor fellows was delirious and in a very dangerous condition.

It was a trial even to those who were not injured to be shaken about in such an unseemly manner. I went into my berth, for example, in full confidence that I was lying near the side of my stateroom, but on awakening an hour later I found that I was trying to sleep on the ceiling. Before I could quite recover from my surprise, I found that it was an optical illusion; I was lying upon the floor. That night Boreas murdered sleep. If by any chance I dozed off for a moment, I dreamt that I was alternately ascending the Alps and falling down the crevasses. Meanwhile the ship was gaily pirouetting, and on Monday the tables, erst so crowded, were still vacant. Sick transit Gloria Monday.

"Music hath charms," but I never expected it to charm a person into playing piano at an angle of forty-five degrees. Yet a young pianist, with an undying affection for Scharwenka's " Polish Dance " and Mendelssohn's " Wedding March," alternated these pieces, even in defiance of the elements. At last, one day, a friendly lurch, of more than usual vehemence, sent him from the piano wildly clawing into space.

One day it was whispered that a death had occurred on board. It was a mysterious affair altogether. At first the officers would say nothing at all about it, but finally it came out that a fireman or "trimmer" had succumbed to the heat of the furnaces and died out of hand. Then there came other details, told me by some of the deck hands, that deceased had been a "stowaway" on the ship, and upon being discovered (possibly weak enough, and wretched), had been put to work in the fire-room, the hardest labor that the mind can imagine. This was his sentence to death.

Can you imagine what the fire-room is in a large steamer burning 300 tons of coal daily? It is worse than Dante's Inferno. "Leave hope behind all ye who enter here," might well be written over the portals for all those who have not gradually accustomed themselves to labor in its stifling atmosphere. I know of the case of a poor German schoolmaster, homesick in America, desperate to reach his fatherland, taking the position of trimmer on an outward bound steamer, and after two days of unspeakable torture, running to the deck, taking a breath or two of heaven's pure air, and then leaping over the rail into the ocean. When will some new Plimsoll arise and force legislation regarding the temperature and ventilation of these fire-rooms? The matter can be easily remedied, at slight expense, but then, of course, it is cheaper still to bury a fireman occasionally at sea.

Was Charles Johnston a stowaway? I cannot say with certainty, for against the statements given above, are those of the purser and doctor, who asserted that he was a regular member of the crew. At any rate there was noticeable reticence on the part of many whenever the subject was broached. But the next day there was a large wooden box, covered with the British flag, standing on the grating at the side rail, and the purser stood at one end of it and a few of the officers beside him. We were to have a burial at sea. The Church of England funeral service was read by the purser and its allusions to "our brother" seemed rather sardonic to me. At the words "we commit this body to the deep," the sailors pulled at a tackle, the grating with its heavily leaded burden was lowered to the water level (the ship going nearly twenty miles an hour), the waves almost instantly swept it off; it floated a few yards, then turned on end and went down, and the mystery was on the bottom of the Atlantic until the day of judgment, while our world on board ship went on, just as the waves went on above it. I am not going to moralize, even upon such a solemn event; the poor have few rights which anybody is bound to respect, and the respect in this case ended with the funeral, for immediately afterward it seemed all forgotten in the excitement attending the declaration of the daily run, on which some £20 or £30 depended.

At last came peace. The gale passed away, calmness settled upon the waters, and new faces began to appear on deck and at table. Some of the young ladies, in their pallid, semi-invalid condition, looking as beautiful as divinities, were soon surrounded by sympathetic young men, possibly divinity-students. And this reminds me that we had nine divines on board. It was embarrassing how to arrange the service, for one could not ask the reverends to toss up as to who should lead the services; but this was neatly overcome by giving each a short portion of the work.

I determined on this trip to study steerage life thoroughly, and therefore asked Dr. Love—the surgeon has closer relations with these passengers than any other high officer—to help me in my scheme. He kindly cross-examined me as to my medical knowledge, and finding that I knew enough to hold the quills during the operation of vaccination, appointed me, with the consent of the captain, medical assistant. The United States laws on vaccination are very strict. Every emigrant must be examined before entering a United States port and receive a certificate of vaccination, or, if there are no vaccination marks, he must be vaccinated by the ship's doctor. Cabin passengers are not subjected to this search, because the small-pox caught from a cabin passenger would be of a more enjoyable order than that caught from an emigrant.

The doctor and I, therefore, went hunting for marks. The steerage passengers were marshaled in long rows and defiled before us. Each showed the vaccination marks in turn, but they were not all in one place. Some were vaccinated on the arm, some on the shoulder, some on the leg, and two, strange as it may seem, on the forehead! It was a strange levee that we held — Irish, Scotch, English, Americans, Belgians, Danes, Swedes, Norwegians, Russians, Italians, Germans, Austrians, Greeks, etc., made up the motley procession. I found out that of all countries Russia is the most careless as to vaccination; also that the Irish generally have two small vaccination marks, while the Scotch have one broad one. It was a task of some difficulty to deal justly with each case, and Dr. Love's conscientious inspection took nearly two days. Occasionally the wily emigrant would try to pass a burn or an old scar as the result of vaccination; but this was always useless, and the subject was vaccinated. The hardest task of all was searching out those who were too sick to come in line. These generally lay in unapproachable positions, and had reached that stage when laws on vaccination or any other subject were uninteresting to them. But I must say that the emigrants were really treated in a proper and careful manner. Once or twice a day the doctor and his assistant (myself) would start out to taste the food, which was to be served out for meals. We invariably found it pure and well cooked. The very

seasick ones received special food and often a daily glass of
porter or Seidlitz powder gratis.   It was amusing to see the
tricks resorted to in order to obtain some of these agreeable
remedies.   I fear that the doctor's assistant closed his eyes
to more than one imposture of this kind.   The arrangements
for lodging the emigrants were excellent.   The unmarried
men had one steerage forward; fifty feet away, with no direct communication, was that for married couples; far back
of this again was that for young women.   Care was taken
to keep the different nationalities together during the trip,
so that they could help each other and not feel lonely.   An
interpreter was on board who spoke all their languages also.
The officers told me that there was no money in carrying
steerage passengers now.   In former times, when each paid
six guineas at least, the service yielded a profit, but I heard
horrible tales of the treatment in vogue at that time—of
wretches battened down under hatches and fed like beasts,
by throwing food among them and allowing them to
scramble for it.

What does one do on such a voyage to pass the time?
Everything that *ennui* and ingenuity combined can suggest.
The appearance of a sail is a signal for at least a half-hour's
comment.   Charades and music alternate, and no voyage
is considered quite complete without a breach-of-promise
trial.   Pools on the daily run of the ship are sold, and this
kind of gambling attracts many of the vicious ones who
began in life by playing marbles "for keeps," and have
ascended the ladder of crime until they even arrived at the
infamy of staking a shilling on the number of the pilot
boat that would come to meet us.   I am glad to say, however, that these reprobates shared their winnings fairly with
the Sailors' Orphan's Home, whose contribution box was
kept well filled by these heterodox proceedings.

But saints and sinners alike seem to unite in charitable

deeds at sea; Neptune seems to be a superb purse opener. If only one could hold church fairs at sea,—after the invalids have recovered, they would be very remunerative.

Do I need to say much regarding the concert given on the last night of the voyage? I think not. Every steamer has a charitable concert on every voyage in summer. Our programme is a decidedly mixed one. Managing a concert is a work which is always a penitential task fit for the training of saints, but when this is combined with the making up of a programme for charitable purposes, on shipboard, it becomes a labor which only angels should undertake. On every European steamer in summer time there are concerts given for the benefit of the seamen's orphans in Liverpool. Judging by the regularity and number of these concerts, and the pecuniary results obtained, the Liverpool orphans must be incipient Goulds and Vanderbilts. Each of these concerts, however, leaves the manager a shattered wreck, with his ideas of music in a hopeless state of confusion. At the first everything is *couleur de rose;* life is bright and volunteers plenty. Alas, he does not know that the anxious volunteers have 90 per cent. of assurance to 10 per cent. of ability, and that the real artists, if there are any on board, are hiding their lights under three or four bushels, and keep in the background. The programme is made, and the concert begins; so do the managerial woes! The piano, from long association with the sea, has a tone of sepulchral solemnity, when you can get at it, for often when the keys are forced down they stay there, so that it really takes two artists to play a solo, one to put down the keys and the other to wedge them up. The organ, however, makes up for this deficiency by giving a great many more notes than are wanted; it gives an unexpected accompaniment of half a dozen notes which sound all through the performance without touching the keys,—a very startling kind of pedal point. A couple of amateurs begin with a piano duet marked "selected." It proves to be a French quadrille with one hundred and fifty "repeats," each one of which is conscientiously made by the faithful performers. The audience feel old age coming on, and the manager's hair turns gray during the performance of this work, which ought never to be undertaken by any one but Methuselah. Finally it is done, and the next piece makes some amends by being fairly artistic. Where is the lady who is to sing number three? An anxious search reveals her on deck; she has become seasick by waiting her turn in the close and tossing cabin, and is bringing up everything except notes. How can one ask a person to toss off a ballad when she is diligently engaged in tossing off a salad instead.

Now a young miss sits at the piano and prepares for an encounter with "Gottschalk's Last Hope," which becomes a forlorn hope instead. The next is an infant prodigy about three years old, pushed into the manager's scheme by sheer force, and a pair of doting parents. The child has decided not to warble that evening, however—for which the manager is devoutly grateful—and ten minutes of fruitless, parental coaxing fill the time instead. Now comes another song—"selected"—which proves to be a cheap Music-Hall style of affair with a dance attached, and which makes every one ashamed of having participated in the programme. Such was a specimen concert on our ship, and such is often the style of music on the briny deep. The audience pay out their money nobly (they would have done so without any musical inflictions whatever), and the cause of charity is helped along—even if the cause of art is not. To those who feel tempted to begin a managerial career on shipboard, I can only give Punch's celebrated advice to those about to marry—"*don't!*"

At last the pilot boat arrived. It found us some five-hundred miles from New York. There seems to be as sharp a competition among pilots as among cabmen, for they go a long way after their customers, and often have an exciting race for a steamboat. With the arrival of the pilot our voyage seemed to come to an end. There was of course, a scramble after fresh news, and newspapers three days old were devoured with avidity.

And now we began to approach the Long Island shore and to brace ourselves for our encounter with the customs officials.

Light after light appeared (it was early evening), and at midnight the great screw, which had been revolving and pulsating for seven days without intermission, stopped, and we were in New York harbor. And, after all, home was the pleasantest sight of all the long, long tour. The musician's vacation was ended, and I now prepared for the final chords of my short, allegro movement. These came in the shape of a health officer, who seemed satisfied with the fact that I was not ailing, and custom-house officials, who soon became satisfied that I was not a wild smuggler of the type found in the third act of "Carmen." A grateful smell of garbage and a more persistent solicitation on the part of the hackmen told me that I had indeed arrived in the "possible metropolis of the world." The conductor gives the signal for the final cadence, the instruments slow up, the allegro is finished. With a strange, indescribable pleasure, but not without a sigh that the vacation was over, I stepped across the gang-plank—

"And now, all in my own countree.
I stood on the firm land."

[THE END.]